Research Like A Pro

A GENEALOGIST'S GUIDE

Research Like A Pro

A GENEALOGIST'S GUIDE

DIANA ELDER, AG *with Nicole Dyer*

FAMILY
LOCKET
BOOKS

PUBLISHED BY
Family Locket Books, an imprint of
Family Locket Genealogists LLC
Highland, Utah

The views expressed in this book are those of the author and do not necessarily represent those of the International Commission for the Accreditation of Professional Genealogists (ICAPGen).

The International Commission for the Accreditation of Professional Genealogists, internationally recognized by its proprietary service mark, ICAPGen℠, owns the registered certification marks AG® and Accredited Genealogist. Genealogists who meet the competency standards established by ICAPGen are given a limited license to use the certification marks in connection with the providing of genealogical and historical research services.

ISBN 978-1-7321881-0-5
Made in the United States of America

To every genealogist who knows there's a better way.

Contents

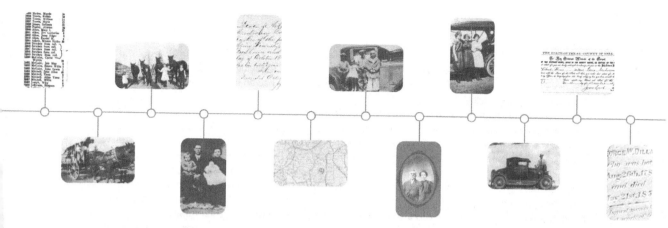

Foreword

What's the Secret?

Like every researcher, I have brick walls in my family tree. I have often considered hiring a professional researcher to solve them. Then I would think to myself, "maybe I can learn the secret of the professional genealogy research and do this myself!" Little did I know that the secret to researching like a pro would soon be within my reach.

My genealogy journey began when I was 16 years old and my mother, Diana, started investigating her roots. She invited me to help and I began researching alongside her. At first, we explored records available online. Later, we went to the Family History Library together, packing granola bars and long lists of call numbers. We attended family history classes, conferences, and workshops to become more educated in the ways of genealogists.

After several years, my research skills became more and more advanced. I began teaching others about genealogy research. One day I looked up the requirements for earning a genealogy credential. With three children under age seven, I knew that it would take me a while to finish the process. But I mentioned the idea to Diana, thinking the timing might be right for her. It was!

She set a goal to become an Accredited Genealogist and began working furiously to develop her genealogy skills. She watched webinars, listened to podcasts, read books and articles, and practiced non-stop. We talked every week and I picked her brain about the methods she was learning.

After two years, Diana completed her accreditation and began taking client work. Along the way, she developed a system for working on research projects. I finally had an insider who could reveal the formula for solving brick walls!

I was surprised to learn that the secret of professional genealogy research is a straightforward, step-by-step process. Diana uses the "Research Like a Pro" process for each client project she undertakes. I use it for tackling my brick wall questions. The process has helped me stay organized, plan my research, document what I find, and prepare for the next research session. I have learned that researching like a pro will always put me closer to the discovery I want to make, even if I don't find what I'm looking for the first time. The wonderful thing about the "Research Like a Pro" method is that it can be repeated over and over. With new records becoming available and more information coming to light, you may never feel that you are completely done researching a particular family.

However, you *can* complete a finite research project. When you have completed all the steps and written suggestions for future research, it's easy to come back to the project months or years later. Based on your findings, you may change your objective or come up with a new hypothesis.

Diana gave me the opportunity to try her genealogy research process when she organized the first Research Like a Pro Study Group. I joined the group hoping the peer reviewed assignments would help me advance my skills. I began with a research objective to discover the actions of three brothers in the Isenhour family during the Civil War. I learned that studying three people at once is a difficult task. Next time I will focus on a narrower objective. I learned how to create a citation the first time I looked at a source. This was a laborious task, but an essential one. Before learning how to cite genealogical sources properly, I didn't truly understand the source and the information it provided. Learning to create citations was a huge step forward for me.

I learned that the "Research Like a Pro" process can be applied to research projects of any size, from a 3-hour research session to a 30-hour project. The flexibility of the process helps me research efficiently no matter what kind of project I'm doing. I made many discoveries about the Isenhour Brothers and their Civil War service as I completed the study group assignments. At one point, I found records for two men of the same name, Moses Isenhour, and had to find additional records to differentiate my relative from the other Moses. You can read my assignments from the study group in Appendix B, "Work Samples."

A few months later, I used the "Research Like a Pro" process to revisit my Lucinda Keaton brick wall. I have been trying to find her parents for several years. Using the timeline analysis template, I was able to see the clues more clearly and put together a hypothesis for her parents! I'm now working to prove the hypothesis and summarize my findings.

I am excited to be partnering with Diana to share the "Research Like a Pro" process with you. The more genealogists who research like a pro, the better off the entire genealogy community will be. Learning the process has been eye-opening for me! I hope it will be for you, too.

Nicole Dyer

Am I Up to It? A Novice's Questions about Joining the Research Like a Pro Study Group

Although I'd not done much actual research beyond exploring the tools of *Ancestry* and *FamilySearch*, I had a desire to expand my knowledge. I had often referred to helpful articles on the Family Locket Blog related to various family history projects.

In spring 2016, I decided to take the challenge to do 30 minutes of family history daily for 30 days. I'd felt too many other commitments kept me from spending as much time on genealogy as I would have liked. The 30-Day Challenge was a remarkable eye opener. I saw what progress could be made, with just that minimal time, although I confess I looked for ways to up those minutes whenever I could. I learned how to record my searches and progress so I'd know where to pick up the next day. I was able to explore several family lines and see so many possibilities for further research. This was a surprise to me as most of my direct family lines have had many active family historians collaborating for many years.

One family line posed a conundrum, trying to identify whether an ancestor, William Atkins Gheen, truly did appear in two different 1880 Census records in neighboring states, or if these were two different individuals. Answering this question seemed important as a wife and child appear in one record. I couldn't ignore those individuals. So when the study group was offered, it seemed a perfect chance to move my skills beyond just dabbling and see what help I could get in resolving this question.

I had been referring to Diana's multi-part blog series "Research Like a Pro" and "Back to the Basics" to help me, which had been very beneficial. However, I'm so glad I became accountable to prepare and show up every two weeks as part of the study group. The pace of the class was perfect, allowing time to complete assignments but still keep focus and energy. Diana's lessons were well organized. She is a master at covering learning material but still engaging group participants and allowing time for questions. Although packed with valuable information and tools, lessons never felt overwhelming.

Having access to the week's study materials was so helpful in actually applying what I'd learned. We asked each other questions during our preparation time via chat. Opportunity to both give and receive feedback provided more growth. It was great to see the varied purposes, geographical locations, time periods and ways of organizing information that members brought to the group. Several of the research objectives of group members and the work they shared could be helpful for me in work on other family lines. Having these materials available for reference and ongoing study will keep me moving ahead.

A significant benefit of participating was in learning the orderly process, the foundation laid step by step that makes for successful genealogical research. The course is aptly titled "Research Like a Pro," as it is the process that Diana uses when researching for her clients. We worked through analyzing evidence to clearly identify a research question all the way to concluding with a readable research report and then some suggestions for organizing all these family records.

Seeing the "big picture" was eye opening and provided the most overall benefit for me. It was liberating to be able to define a discrete and manageable objective, see it through to its conclusion, then begin the process again. Although the work of family history is never "done," we can finish a specific project, set it aside and select another focused objective. This may be an outgrowth of that just completed project or we can apply these tools to a totally different family line. The productivity tools and organization ideas shared by the group have answered so many questions and given me a way to pursue this interest, even when life is full of many other duties right now.

I've kept you in suspense. Did I figure out the identity of my two Williams? I've learned so much about the location, its geography and local history that informs my family history. I've found valuable records that add to my understanding of the lives of these families. But the research question remains unanswered. I have other ideas to pursue suggested by group members. I will search, record and interpret findings and write a report. At that point, I can say that I have done due diligence to support whatever conclusion emerges. That is a satisfying perspective. So although I have much more to do, I'm far more confident about how to proceed.

Nancy Brown

My Research Like A Pro Study Group Experience

I have been researching my family history since 1997 and have tried to apply high standards to my research process from the beginning. However, there really were not many educational opportunities back then other than genealogy conferences that required expensive travel. So I pretty much went on gut instincts and what I could glean from email lists and the odd conversations with others in the same boat I was in. Consequently, my research would not hold up under scrutiny as well as I would have liked it.

When I retired from the corporate world, I decided to become more educated in genealogy standards and to bring my research up to those standards. I began watching as many webinars as I could, went to a few national conferences, and to every seminar within driving distance. My grand "finale" was to earn a certificate from the Boston University Genealogical Research Program this past summer.

When I heard about Diana's Research Like a Pro Study Group, I thought it would be an excellent opportunity for me to practice the skills I had learned and receive feedback from a professional genealogist and a group of genealogists with a wide variety of experience, skills, and knowledge on my own family research rather than an assigned project. I got that, and much more.

The research process Diana took us through was very structured and made a lot of sense. It was important to do each assignment in the order it was given and we saw the benefit as we went along. We learned to formulate a focused research objective, which is my biggest weakness. Although I knew theoretically that I had to start with that, my objectives have always been too broad or too narrow and my working hypotheses were non-existent or made absolutely no sense. Diana's examples caused those light bulbs to shine! My research objective was a simple one—find the parents of Elizabeth (Betsy) Thompson, born March 1791 at St. Mary's County, Maryland, and married Joseph Masterson on 7 September 1814 in New Hope, Nelson County, Kentucky.

One of the most helpful tasks for me, also an assignment set in the beginning of the process, was to develop a timeline and analyze the evidence supporting it. The analysis part was something I had never done before. That analysis spotlighted many areas in the research on my Masterson-Thompson family that I hadn't realized was so weak. Those weak areas generated a lot of questions for me, which were all written into my research plan (an assignment for another week).

Another step we were taught that I had never done before was to create a locality guide for the area(s) in which we were researching. I have to admit that this step surprised me and I didn't understand at first why we needed to do that. After all, I had been researching in Kentucky for many years and surely I knew what records were available by now and I wanted to spend some time doing research. But as I worked through the assignment I saw the incredible value it had for me now and for my future research. It was in many ways the most helpful assignment I was given, not to mention how much fun it was! I was sorry to have to stop and start work on the next assignment. I plan to create guides for all the areas of my research in the future before diving into researching that locality again.

The course ended with writing a research report. While people generally think of writing a research report as something you would only do for a client, it is necessary to write one for your own research problems as well. Writing the report allows you to organize your findings and record your thoughts so that you fully understand the evidence, or lack thereof, that you have found and to record your next steps as you think of them. That way, you can put it aside for a few weeks or months and be able to return right where you were without wasting time going through all the evidence again.

The ability to see how a professional genealogist tackles the research for her clients as well as some of the work she did to earn her accreditation was valuable. It has encouraged me to pursue certification or accreditation myself.

Foreword

    I did not find Elizabeth (Betsy) Thompson's parents, but I made some progress and I know what steps I need to take next. I will revise my research plan and be sure my timeline and locality guide is updated and start the process over again. I will no longer feel the frustration of disorganized research and resolve to take the time to perform my research like a pro. The satisfaction I feel on a job well done, even though it is not really done yet, is unparalleled.

Sherri Hessick

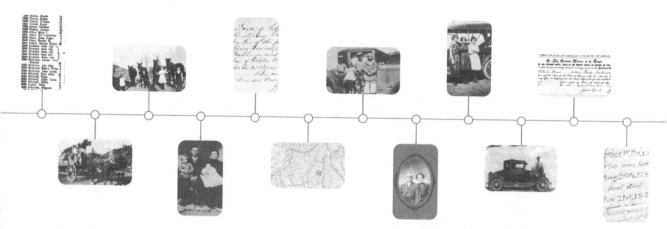

Introduction

Are you feeling stuck in your genealogy efforts? You've learned the basics of using *FamilySearch* and *Ancestry*. You've created an online tree with loads of attached records, although you're not sure if all of them apply to your ancestors. You may have accumulated bulging files of records from years of research, yet you're spinning your wheels, not making progress on your brick wall problems. You know there's more you could be doing to find your family, but you're not sure how to make the jump to the next level.

I felt the same way the summer of 2015, sitting in a class at the Brigham Young University Conference on Family History and Genealogy. The session track was learning about Accreditation through ICAPGen, The International Commission for the Accreditation of Professional Genealogists. As I listened to the lectures, I realized that I had developed experience and many of the skills necessary to be a professional genealogist. I just needed to figure out what was different between my way of researching and that of a pro.

In January 2016, I decided to seriously work towards the accreditation credential and published a blog post on *Family Locket* announcing my goal. I hoped that public accountability would keep me motivated and moving forward. I wrote about the process for the next 18 months and in July of 2017 became an official Accredited Genealogist®. Doing the necessary steps for accreditation taught me the skills that a professional genealogist uses every day. These weren't secret skills; I just hadn't realized the importance of putting them together in the correct order.

I decided to write a series of articles titled "Research Like a Pro" to help the readers of *Family Locket* have more success in their genealogical research. The idea of starting a study group to go through each of the steps kept swirling in my head. I resolved to give it a try and in September of 2017, started the first Research Like a Pro Study Group. We met online twice a month for a total of six sessions. I presented the topic, and then each member completed the assignment, working on their own family research problem.

Study group members had varying degrees of expertise and researched in different localities. Giving feedback to each other helped them see new ways of solving their brick walls. Some had great success in finding new information and others discovered where not to look, but they all learned the process that a professional genealogist uses.

Watching the growth in my new friends, I knew I needed to share this process with more genealogists. Combining the "Research Like a Pro" blog posts with the course presentations I developed, this book took shape. In it you will discover the skills and methods I learned as I made the leap from researcher to professional genealogist. Researchers of all skill levels can use the ideas and assignments to learn to research like a pro!

This book would not have happened without the assistance and encouragement of my daughter, Nicole. It was her suggestion that I look into earning a credential and her invitation to write articles for *Family Locket* that set me on the path to sharing my love of family history and genealogy through the written word. This book reflects a perfect pairing of our skills. The design of the book is entirely her creation. She always makes my work look its best! My husband, Mark, encouraged me through each step of my accreditation and the launching of my genealogy career. He has proofread and offered valuable suggestions for content. Many thanks to the Research Like a Pro Study Group members for taking a chance on me and my ideas. To the readers of *Family Locket*, thanks for reading and commenting as we learn and grow together in our love of family history and genealogy.

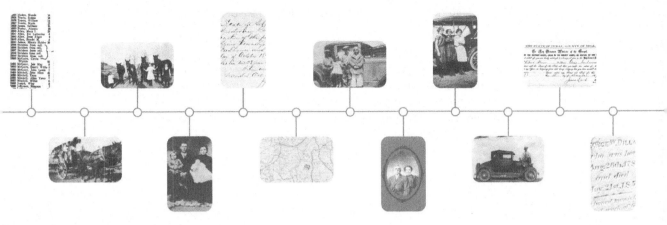

How to Use This Book

This book is designed to take you from the beginning of a research project to the end. I've provided real life examples throughout to help you understand the concepts. You'll reap the most benefit if you follow the steps in order, working through your own research project. Because this is an organized method, if you need to take a break, you'll be able to pick up right where you left off.

Appendix A contains links to templates for your use and Appendix B holds work samples because viewing another's work can help you better understand important concepts. Since genealogists must always be learning, Appendix C lists books we recommend for further study. Appendix D contains bonus articles on organization, productivity, and education to give you an extra boost in your research.

With the purchase of this book, you are eligible join the exclusive Research Like a Pro Facebook group. Simply email a copy of your receipt to info@familylocket.com with the email address associated with your Facebook account and Nicole will send you an invitation to join. You'll be able to share the progress of your research project, ask questions from group members, and get exclusive research tips from me.

We recommend working through the assignments in a study group. This allows you to give and receive feedback and learn from others. Sign up for our newsletter at FamilyLocket.com to receive updates about future study groups and webinars. Host your own study group and work through the assignments together. Let's get started!

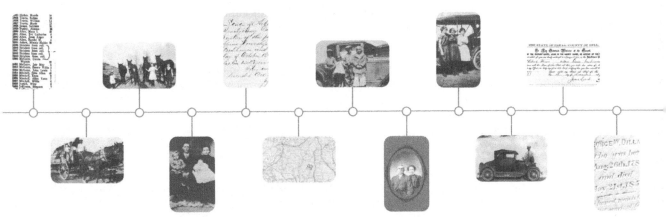

Research Objectives

1

All research begins with a question. Looking at your family tree, you notice there is no death date for an ancestor. A great grandfather has a questionable second marriage. No parents are listed for your 2nd great grandmother. You may have so many questions you feel paralyzed and don't do anything.

As you begin to randomly surf the web looking for an answer to your question you get side tracked and after a few hours you may have more questions than when you started. How do you focus your questions into research that is productive and relevant?

Formulating a research objective is the key to your success and the first step a professional takes in working with a client. Consider yourself your own client. You want to get the most out of your limited research time and see results, so you need to turn your questions into a working research objective. Working from an objective will keep your research focused. No longer will you surf the internet for two hours and come up not knowing what you've found or where you've been. You'll discipline yourself to stay on track with your research and turn each hour of research into a productive session.

Your genealogical questions will generally fit one of the following three categories: identify an individual, prove a family relationship, or discover ancestor actions. Let's look at each category in more depth.

Research Objective Types

1. Identify an Individual

What does it mean to identify an individual? Think of some of the specific facts that make up his unique identity: name, parents, birth date and place, spouse, marriage date and place, children, death date and place, residence, military service, and occupation. These are details that uniquely identify your ancestor.

Your research question could involve differentiating men of the same name, separating bad merges on the *FamilySearch* Family Tree or identifying the correct "John Smith" on a document.

> EXAMPLE: Which of the three John Smiths in Greene County, Georgia, is my ancestor?

2. Prove a Family Relationship

If you're working on the *FamilySearch* Family Tree or viewing other online trees, you will soon discover many unproven relationships: children added to marriages that don't fit, multiple spouses listed for an individual, or two sets of parents. These are all common scenarios in today's world of online genealogy where incorrect information is copied from tree to tree. Sometimes you need to prove a relationship that has been in place for years, perhaps written in a family history book.

Questions of relationship could include discovering the parents of a brick wall ancestor, finding the spouse of an individual, or locating all of the children of an ancestral couple.

> EXAMPLE: Who are the parents of John Smith?

3. Discover Ancestor Actions

You might want to discover how your ancestor lived. Was he involved in a war? Did she serve in the community? How did the family worship? When did your third great grandparents marry? Where did your great uncle die? Researching the actions of your ancestor's life can often provide clues that will also help you prove his identity and family relationships.

> EXAMPLE: Did John Smith serve in the military?

Now that you've considered the three different types of genealogical questions, three steps will aid you in creating a research objective that will focus your research: analyze your pedigree and choose a question, formulate a research objective, and lastly record your objective in your Research Project Document.

Steps for Creating a Research Objective

Step 1. Analyze your pedigree and choose a question
Step 2. Formulate a research objective
Step 3. Write down your objective

Step 1. Analyze your pedigree and choose a question

Your first step in researching like a pro is to analyze your pedigree. Look through your family tree on *FamilySearch* or *Ancestry*. Is there a nagging question? Do you have a feeling that something isn't right? Are important relationships missing? You might have several questions, but you need to choose one.

For example, I have five glaring holes in my family tree. Five of my 32 ggg grandparents have no parents. I am currently focusing on proving the parents of just one of the five, Cynthia Dillard, shown in the screenshot below. My research question is simple: Who are the parents of Cynthia Dillard?

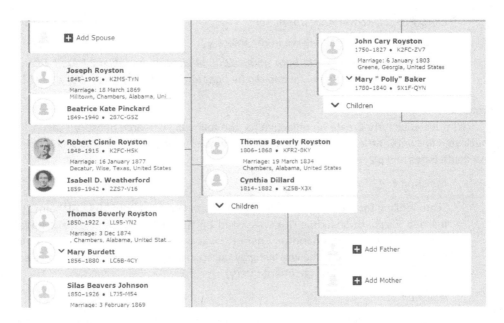

Figure 1-1: FamilySearch.org Family Tree screenshot showing Cynthia Dillard with unknown parents

Step 2. Formulate a research objective

Once you've chosen a research question, turn that question into a research objective that will ground your research for the entire project. Use specific key identifiers to create the research objective. Think of what you know about your ancestor and include full names, dates, and places of events such as birth, marriage, and death.

Looking again at the three examples of research questions for the fictional John Smith, let's now create focused research objectives by adding in the key identifiers.

EXAMPLE 1: Identify an Individual

Question: Which of the three John Smiths in Greene County, Georgia, is my ancestor?

Objective: *The objective of this research project is to determine which of the three John Smiths listed on the 1820 census in Greene County, Georgia, is my ancestor. He was born about 1800 in Georgia and died 23 April 1854 in Chambers County, Alabama.*

EXAMPLE 2: Prove a Family Relationship

Question: Who are the parents of John Smith?   •

Objective: *The objective of this research project is to find the parents of John Smith, born about 1800 in Georgia and died 23 April 1854 in Chambers County, Alabama.*

EXAMPLE 3: Discover Ancestor Actions

Question: Did John Smith serve in the military?

Objective: *Was John Smith, born about 1800 in Georgia and died 23 April 1854, a member of the Georgia militia and did he fight in the Indian Wars or War of 1812?*

Practice

Now it's your turn. Create an objective for the following research questions, and then check your answers at the end of this chapter. Remember to use key identifiers such as birth and death dates and places.

Question 1:

"I am looking for the father of Walter Robertson who was born 1832 Alabama. He married Elizabeth Shaudoin. He was listed on the 1850 Louisiana Census Caddo Parish with his mother Charlotte. Charlotte was born 1793 North Carolina. I do not know her last name, but she was living by the Spann and Brown Families in Louisiana in 1850." (*Ancestry* message board query)

Question 2:

"Right now I'm searching for information on my 2x-great-grandmother, Bashaba Adeline Underwood. Bashaba could be Bathsheba, Barsheba or some variation. I know she was born in Elbert County about 1834, lived in Habersham, and Cherokee. She married Abraham Perry Latham (or Lathem) also known as Abram or Ped Latham in 1857 in Cherokee County. They had 8 children. This is where I need help. I'm reasonably certain she died around 1871 (maybe in childbirth?) but I cannot find any record of her death or burial. Any help would be most appreciated." (*Ancestry* message board query)

Question 3:

"I'm researching Paul Lee, born about 1835 in Florida. Married first to Annie Keeney, then married Ludora Colvin. Seeking to know the names of Paul's parents and where they were born. Paul was a steamboat captain who later moved to Geneva, AL. Any information will be greatly appreciated." (*Ancestry* message board query)

How did you do? If this was your first time creating a research objective, know that it gets easier. Remember to include the key identifiers such as birth, marriage, and death information. Your objective should be simple and to the point. Save extra information for the background
section of your project.

Step 3. Write down your objective

The final step in setting your research objective is to write it down. Your objective will guide you through each step of the Research Like a Pro process. Appendix A includes a link to a Research Project Document template that you can download and use to record your objective. You'll add to this document in subsequent chapters.

YOUR TASK

Analyze your pedigree and choose a question. Formulate a research objective using key identifiers, and then begin your Research Project Document. Place your objective at the beginning of your document. That's it! You're on your way to researching like a pro.

Answers

Question 1:

"I am looking for the father of Walter Robertson who was born 1832 Alabama. He married Elizabeth Shaudoin. He was listed on the 1850 Louisiana Census Caddo Parish with his mother Charlotte. Charlotte was born 1793 North Carolina. I do not know her last name, but she was living by the Spann and Brown Families in Louisiana in 1850." *(Message Query on Ancestry.com)*

> **Incomplete objectives**: What was Charlotte's maiden name? Who was the father of Walter Robertson?
>
> Because this query contains two separate questions, two different objectives could be written: one for identity and one for relationship. It's important to be clear about the objective because the research plan would be different for each scenario.
>
> **Complete objective for relationship**: The objective of this research project is to identify the father of Walter Robertson, born about 1832 in Alabama and listed on the 1850 census of Caddo Parish, Louisiana. Walter married Elizabeth Shaudoin.
>
> **Complete objective for identity:** The objective of this research project is to identify Charlotte, born about 1793 in North Carolina and listed on the 1850 census of Caddo Parish, Louisiana in the household of Walter Robertson.

Question 2:

"Right now I'm searching for information on my 2x-great-grandmother, Bashaba Adeline Underwood. Bashaba could be Bathsheba, Barsheba or some variation. I know she was born in Elbert County about 1834, lived in Habersham, and Cherokee. She married Abraham Perry Latham (or Lathem) also known as Abram or Ped Latham in 1857 in Cherokee County. They had 8 children. This is where I need help. I'm reasonably certain she died around 1871 (maybe in childbirth?) but I cannot find any record of her death or burial. Any help would be most appreciated." *(Message Query, Ancestry.com)*

> **Incomplete Objective**: Find out when and where Bashaba Adeline Underwood died.

Complete Objective: The objective of this research session is to discover the place and date where Bashaba Adeline Underwood died. She was born in Elbert County about 1834 and married Abraham Perry Latham in 1857 in Cherokee County.

Question 3:

"I'm researching Paul Lee, born about 1835 in Florida. Married first to Annie Keeney, then married Ludora Colvin. Seeking to know the names of Paul's parents and where they were born. Paul was a steamboat captain who later moved to Geneva, AL. Any information will be greatly appreciated." (Ancestry message board query)

Incomplete Objective: Who were the parents of Paul Lee?

Complete Objective: The objective for this research project is to discover the parents of Paul Lee of Geneva, Alabama, born about 1835 in Florida. Paul first married Annie Keeney, then Ludora Colvin.

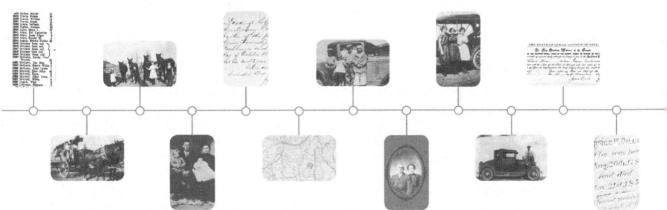

Analyze Your Sources

2

Once you've created and recorded your research objective, what's the next step? It's time to revisit the records that have already been found. Often the key to your research problem is found within those sources. A professional researcher doesn't waste time looking for new information until he first analyzes the client's existing records. Consider yourself your own client and do the same.

Dig out your papers and locate the sources on the *FamilySearch* Family Tree or other online trees that pertain to your ancestor. When you've gathered all the source documents, a thorough analysis of each and the information found within can clarify what you know and point you to your next avenue of research. Several types of analysis will help you view your records with new eyes. Before you start the analysis process, putting your records into a timeline will help to order your research.

Create a Timeline

One of the best ways to look at your ancestor's records is to make a timeline of their life. Record each family event, the date and place, and your source of the information. As you work, look for inconsistencies. Was your ancestor in two places at once? Is the mother too old to have children? Keep a list of questions to research in your Research Project Document. Even if they don't apply to your current objective, you can return to them in a subsequent research project.

I discovered the value of using a timeline while writing my four-generation report for accreditation. I had finished writing the first generation, but I lacked any mention of church records, important for researching in the southern United States. My family moved around so much in Indian Territory/Oklahoma, that I didn't know where to start. To find church records, I needed to know my family's religion and locations between 1890 and 1920 where they might have attended church.

Two personal histories gave me clues to both church attendance and the movements of my great grandparents Dora and William Huston Shults: one by my grandfather, Charles Leslie Shults, and one by his sister, Loraine Shults Bassett. Written many years after the events, the histories agreed for the most part on names, dates, and happenings; but it was confusing going back and forth between the two accounts. I also had historical records that needed to be inserted into the appropriate time frame. It was time to track this family with a timeline.

I created my timeline in Google Sheets. For some time now, I've been using only Google Docs and Sheets for my family history endeavors because they are accessible on all of my devices. If I'm researching at the Family History Library and I need to view my timeline, I can pull it up on my smart phone or sign in to my Google account on one of the many computers.

As I started entering my information I decided to add an analysis feature to my timeline. Writing my accreditation report, I needed to show that I understood the types of sources: authored, original, and derivative; the types of information in those sources: primary, secondary, or undetermined; and the kind of evidence provided by that information: direct, indirect, or negative. I had studied *Genealogy Standards* and the works of Elizabeth Shown Mills and Tom Jones to learn these terms.[1] Filling in those blanks on my timeline helped me boost my analysis skills and better evaluate the evidence.

Because I am a visual learner, I color coded the types of events so I could see at a glance the movements of the family. Moves to a new location were colored gold, births of children, blue, residences, green, etc. This helped get the information straight. I also noted discrepancies between the two histories, such as the birthplaces of the oldest children.

Objective:	Determine the location of the Shults family from 1890-1920.						
Event	**Date**	**Place**	**Source**	**Source**	**Info**	**Evidence**
Birth of Dora Algie Royston	25 Jan 1882	Texas	Texas State Board of Health, death certificate, Dora Algia Shults, Reg. Dis. No 3184, Registered No. 476. Lubbock,1925; "Texas, Death Certificates, 1903–1982," Lubbock, 1925, Jan-Mar, image 11, Ancestry (http://search.ancestry.com: accessed 20 February 2016).	original	secondary	direct
Marriage to William Huston Shults	11 Dec 1898	Chickasaw Nation, Indian Territory	Carter County, Oklahoma, photocopy of marriage license and certificate, Shults-Rayston,11 Dec 1898, Indian Territory Southern District, recorded 1943, County Court Clerk, Ardmore, Oklahoma.	derivative	primary	direct
Residence	1898	Elmore, Indian Territory	Effie Lorain Shults Bassett, "Memories," personal history p. 1, between 1971 and 2000, photocopy of typescript from Bobby Gene Shults, Burley, Idaho , files of author.	authored	secondary	direct
Residence	1900	Township 1S, Ranges 5-6 W Indian Territory	1900 U.S. Census, Chickasaw Nation, Indian Territory, population schedule, township 2S range 5W, enumeration district (ED) 166, sheet 24B (penned), dwelling 378, family 396, W.H. Shults; digital image, Ancestry, (http://www.ancestry.com accessed 17 February 2016); citing NARA microfilm publication T623, roll 1849.	original	primary	direct
Move	1900	Maxwell, Indian Territory	Effie Lorain Shults Bassett, "Memories," personal history p. 1.	authored	secondary	direct
Birth of Robert Cisnie Shults	12 Jul 1900	Indian Territory	Mrs. Jack Lambert (Stratford, Oklahoma) to Mr. Shults [Bobby Gene Shults], letter, 18 August 1966; privately held by author, [ADDRESS FOR PRIVATE USE], 2016.	derivative	primary	direct
Birth of William Linard Shults	8 Dec 1901	Indian Territory	Mrs. Jack Lambert (Stratford, Oklahoma) to Mr. Shults [Bobby Gene Shults], letter, 18 August 1966.	derivative	primary	direct
Birth of Charles Leslie Shults	11 May 1904	Ada, Pontotoc County, Oklahoma	State of Oklahoma - Department of Health, Delayed Certificate of Birth: Charles Leslie Shults birth,11 May 1904, Document number 1449-186, Oklahoma City, Oklahoma.	original	secondary	direct

Figure 2-1: Page 1 of Dora Algie Royston Timeline

My timeline pointed out one glaring inconsistency. The family is enumerated on the 1910 census in Jefferson County, Oklahoma, but neither history mentions this location. Instead, both accounts had the family living in Pontotoc County at this time, about 100 miles northwest. To corroborate the family's residence in Pontotoc County I researched the FAN club (friends, associates, and neighbors).[2] Both Charles and Loraine mentioned individuals that I could locate on the 1910 census.

"Dr. Sam Therekill" who Loraine described as delivering several of the Shults children was actually Sam Threlkeld, his occupation listed as a farmer on the 1910 census. "Mack" McGuire who Charles spoke of owning a dairy was named Reuben McGuire on the same census. His sons, named in the history, helped me pin down the right McGuire family. Locating these neighbors in Pontotoc County gave further evidence that the Shults family did indeed live in that location. My timeline clearly pointed out that the Jefferson County residence from the 1910 census must have been short lived, so no need to look for church records there.

My timeline showed William Huston Shults purchasing Indian land at a government sale in 1912. How had I missed that? I also had forgotten that the family took a wagon train trip to Melrose, New Mexico, in 1907 where they stayed with Grandpa Royston in his hotel giving me another place and set of records to research. I added these questions and notes to my Research Project Document.

Loraine's history gave me clues about the family's church attendance.[3]

> On Sunday afternoon, we went to the river for baptising [sic] services for our community church (no denomination.)

> On Sunday we would go to church and Sunday school.

> We [Loraine and spouse] were married by Rev. Clements.

Now that I knew the Shults family attended church I could contact local historical societies in Pontotoc and Pushmataha Counties to find more information about the community churches during the early 1900s. Without my timeline, I might have searched Jefferson County as well.

What did I learn from analyzing the family's movements on the timeline? That I had more work to do! My ideas for future research:

- *Contact the Pontotoc and Pushmataha Historical Society for information on churches from 1905-1920*

- *Look for records from 1912 sale of Indian lands*

- *Search for homesteading records in New Mexico in 1907*

- *Contact the county courthouse in Roswell, New Mexico, for information on the hotel*

Check the Dates

Once you've organized your ancestor's information into a timeline, take a look at the dates. Are the ages of the couple compatible to their marriage date? Are the children all born within their mother's childbearing years? Was your ancestor old enough to be taxed, own land, serve in the military? Examine the life events for feasibility. Take notes of inconsistencies and records to search as you go, recording them in your Research Project Document.

Analyze the Evidence

As you're evaluating the source, the information it contains, and the evidence it provides, take time to do a complete analysis. Elizabeth Shown Mills describes the basic principle.[4]

"**SOURCES** provide **INFORMATION**
from which we identify **EVIDENCE** for **ANALYSIS**."

Confused by those terms? Let's examine each and look at some examples to help your understanding grow. As you work with your own records you'll start to see the value of evidence analysis. For additional learning see recommended books and articles in Appendix C.

Sources

Sources are defined as any material or person that contains genealogical information. A source can be an artifact like a sampler or photograph; or a document such as a certificate. Censuses, books, deeds, DNA, newspapers, and church records are some of the sources commonly used for genealogy. A source can also be an individual's memory of past events, recorded in an interview or written as a personal history.

Sources are divided into three categories.[5] Understanding the true nature of a source will help you evaluate the information it holds.

- **Original source** – the actual document or image of it such as a census, certificate, or ship's passenger list.

- **Derivative source** – indexed or abstracted information created from an original record: an indexed marriage collection on *FamilySearch*, a book listing all the gravesites in a cemetery, an abstract of a will on an online family tree.

- **Authored narrative** – an online family tree, a family history, a biographical sketch, a research report, basically anything that involves someone compiling facts and information into a new form.

Why does understanding the source matter? When I was a beginner, taking my first steps in this fascinating new world, I found a marriage listing of an ancestor in a book of marriage abstracts. I happily added the information to my database, researched the couple and their children and went merrily on my way.

A few years later I discovered that I had connected the wrong marriage record to my ancestor. Essentially, I married her to the wrong man. How did I completely miss the boat? It all has to do with original versus derivative sources.

An original source is what it says, original: a handwritten marriage record in the county marriage book, a death certificate filled out at the time of the death, a birth entry of a child in a family bible at the time of birth. On the other hand, a derivative record is created from the original: a book listing all the county marriage records, a birth registration index, or a will book abstracting pertinent information.

With the digitizing and indexing of records in the modern genealogy world, you've experienced or will eventually experience errors in the process of looking at an original record and trying to decipher the handwriting. It is no wonder that names or dates may be incorrectly reproduced in a book, online index, or other derivative record. The burden of genealogical proof is not with the indexer, it is with you, the researcher.

Do you always take the time to locate the original record? Do you look at the image provided by *FamilySearch*? Or do you quickly attach the record and move on? You can make major errors if not careful to evaluate the sources used.

In my case, I was researching my 2nd great aunt, Texana Isenhour. I found a marriage record for a Texana in a Bell County, Texas, marriage book. Her maiden name wasn't Isenhour, but since the family lived in Bell County, Texas, I thought it was probably her and linked her to the groom, J.W. Drake. I thought perhaps she had married previously and was using that name at the time of the marriage. How many Texana's could there be in Bell County anyway?

A few months ago, I returned to that family and warning bells went off in my head. Something didn't seem right and I decided to revisit my research. I headed to the Family History Library and looked up the marriage record in the book abstracting the marriages of Bell County, Texas.

I found the record of Texana married to J.W. Drake. Then another Texana caught my eye at the bottom of the page, "Texana Gochouner." This marriage showed Texana married to a Richard Blevins. My Texana had a stepbrother named Richard Blevins, could this be the same family? Only one way to tell – I needed to look at the original marriage record on microfilm. When I located the image, seen in Figure 2-2, my heart started racing. This was my Texana!

If you were indexing or abstracting this record, how would you have spelled Texana's last name? I've used this example in several classes and not once has anyone come up with the correct name. But, because I knew what I was looking for, I clearly could read "Isenhowner" or "Isenhowuer." I've seen this name spelled multiple ways, so this wasn't a problem. I had my Texana and she wasn't married to J.W. Drake. She married her stepbrother, Richard Blevins.

Turns out Richard Blevins married again about 1872, so Texana almost certainly died soon after their marriage in 1870. I haven't been able to find any record of her after the marriage or mention of any children they had together. Locating the original marriage record made all the difference in getting Texana's story right.

Recognize that derivative sources such as indexes, abstracts, and transcriptions can all introduce human error. The only way to verify the information in a source is to view the original. Now let's learn about the second piece of evidence analysis.

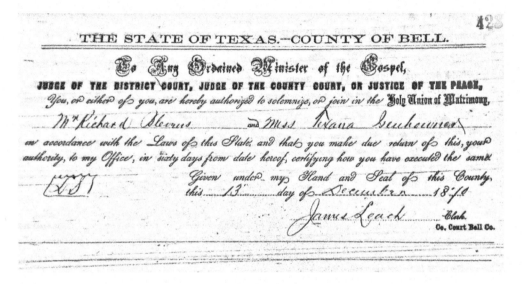

Figure 2-2: County Court, Bell County, Texas, "Marriages, 1850-1935," v. D-E, Blevins – Isenhour marriage, 1870, FHL Film 981034, Family History Library, Salt Lake City, Utah.

Information

Pieces of information are facts found in the source. These can be dates, places, names, occupations, religions, land description, and much more. When examining the data, try to determine who gave that information. This person is called the informant and can be reliable or unreliable depending upon the circumstance. Information comes in three types:[6]

- **Primary information:** Given by a person who witnessed the event firsthand. A mother reporting the birth of her child in a family bible would be considered primary information.

- **Secondary information:** Given by a person who first obtained the information somewhere else, then reported it. That same child recording his birth on his draft registration would be secondary information. Although he was present at his birth, his mother told him his birthday.

- **Undetermined information:** Sometimes it's unclear who the informant is, such as in a census record. You can make a guess, but it's impossible to know who gave the names, ages, and birthplaces contained in a census record (except for 1940 where an ⊗ marks the informant).

One source can have both primary and secondary information. A death certificate, for example, contains primary information – the date and place of death, generally filled out by the attending doctor who attested to the death. That same death certificate can also include secondary information- the birth date and parents of the individual – given by the informant who is often the next of kin. If they were not present at the birth, this information is based on hearsay and is secondary information.

Evidence

The third piece of evidence analysis is evidence. Evidence is taken from information in the source and answers the research question. It also comes in three forms.[7]

- Direct evidence: The information clearly states the answer to a research question, such as the date on a marriage certificate, answering when a couple married.

- Indirect evidence: The answer to the research question must be deduced by combining two or more facts. A woman listed as the mother-in-law of the head of household in a census record could be deduced to be his wife's mother.

- Negative evidence occurs when the ancestor is not found in the expected time and place. If he had paid taxes on a piece of property for ten years and suddenly disappeared, that would signify either his death or his move to another location.

Why does this matter? You can miss important clues and even come to the wrong conclusion about your ancestor if you don't clearly analyze the records.

Practice

For example, let's look at the birth certificate for Dora Christine Shults, Figure 2-3. Answer these questions to test your understanding of sources, information, and evidence:

Is this birth certificate an original, derivative, or authored source?

Is the information primary, secondary, or indeterminable?

Is the evidence direct, indirect, or negative for the question of Dora Christine's birth date?

Are there any inconsistencies that should be noted?

Answers

Is this birth certificate an original or derivative source? Original, although an image, it appears to be complete without any tampering.

Is the information primary, secondary, or indeterminable? The attending physician, Dr. Castleberry may have filled out the certificate. His signature matches the handwriting for the certificate information, but the initials "G.G." seem to have been written later. He certifies that he attended the birth of Dora so the birth date of 11 February 1925 is primary information, as is the name of the mother. However, other information reported is secondary, such as: Dora Christine's birth order of 6, the age and birthplaces of the father and mother, and the number of children born to the mother and now living.

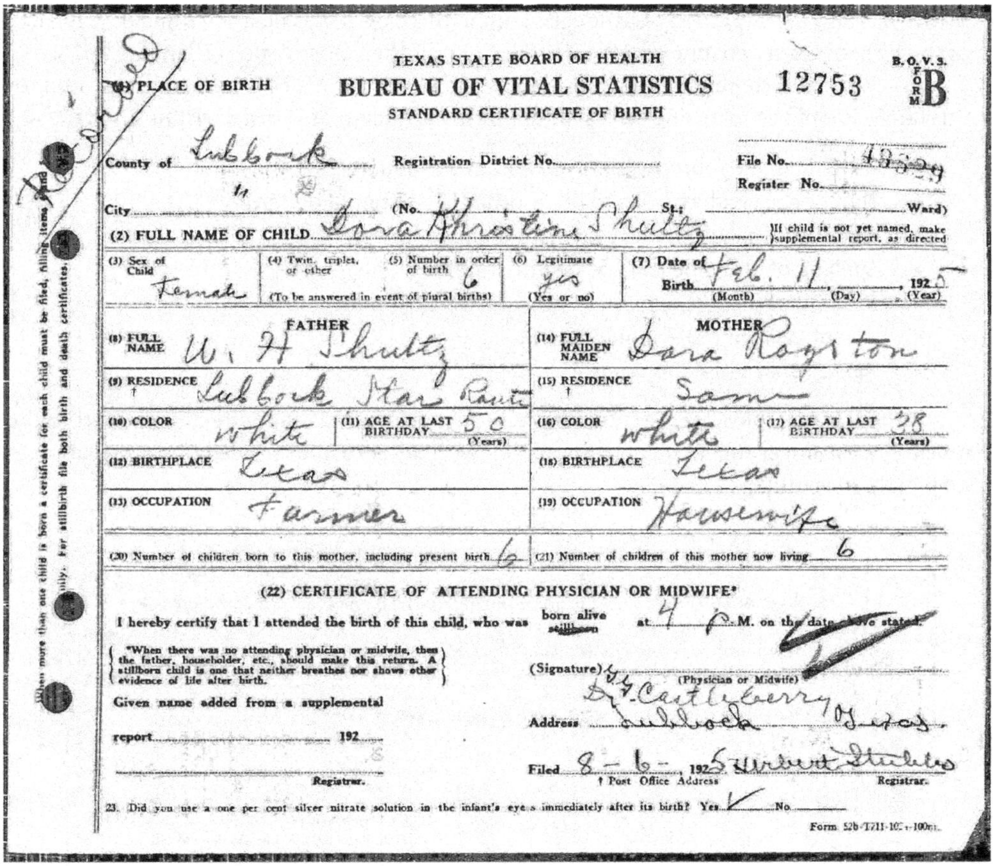

TEXAS STATE BOARD OF HEALTH

(1) PLACE OF BIRTH **BUREAU OF VITAL STATISTICS** 12753 B.O.V.S. FORM B

STANDARD CERTIFICATE OF BIRTH

County of Lubbock Registration District No. File No.

Register No.

City " (No. St.; Ward)

(2) FULL NAME OF CHILD Dora Khristine Shultz (If child is not yet named, make supplemental report, as directed)

(3) Sex of Child Female | (4) Twin, triplet, or other | (5) Number in order of birth 6 | (6) Legitimate yes (Yes or no) | (7) Date of Birth Feb. 11 (Month) (Day), 1925 (Year)

(To be answered in event of plural births)

FATHER		MOTHER	
(8) FULL NAME	W. H. Shultz	(14) FULL MAIDEN NAME	Dora Royston
(9) RESIDENCE	Lubbock Star Route	(15) RESIDENCE	Same
(10) COLOR	white	(16) COLOR	white
(11) AGE AT LAST BIRTHDAY	50 (Years)	(17) AGE AT LAST BIRTHDAY	38 (Years)
(12) BIRTHPLACE	Texas	(18) BIRTHPLACE	Texas
(13) OCCUPATION	Farmer	(19) OCCUPATION	Housewife

(20) Number of children born to this mother, including present birth 6 (21) Number of children of this mother now living 6

(22) CERTIFICATE OF ATTENDING PHYSICIAN OR MIDWIFE*

I hereby certify that I attended the birth of this child, who was born alive ~~stillborn~~ at 4 P.M. on the date above stated.

*When there was no attending physician or midwife, then the father, householder, etc., should make this return. A stillborn child is one that neither breathes nor shows other evidence of life after birth.

(Signature) (Physician or Midwife)

Given name added from a supplemental report ..... 192...

Address Lubbock, Texas.

Registrar.

Filed 8-6-1925 Registrar.

† Post Office Address

23. Did you use a one per cent silver nitrate solution in the infant's eyes immediately after its birth? Yes ✓ No

Form 52b

When more than one child is born a certificate for each child must be filed, filling items ... only. For stillbirth file both birth and death certificates.

Recorded

Figure 2-3: Texas, "Birth Certificates, 1903-1932," database with images, Ancestry (http.ancestry.com: accessed 14 March 2016), certificate image, Dora Khristine Shults, 11 Feb 1925, no. 12753; citing Texas Department of State Health Services.

Is the evidence direct or indirect? The certificate contains direct evidence of Dora Christine's birth date. We don't have to infer anything.

Are there any inconsistencies that should be noted? The certificate was filed 8-6-1925, probably August 6, 1925, the usual writing of dates in the United States. Dora's reported birth took place on 11 February 1925. How reliable was this physician's information? Given that he apparently filed it several months after that fact, it is understandable that almost all the information on the certificate is incorrect.

Her certificate does correctly state her parents as W.H. Shultz and Dora Royston, but her date of birth is incorrectly listed as 11 February 1925 instead of 11 January 1925. How do I know this is incorrect? Other sources give information that contradicts the birth month of February. Dora died giving birth to her baby, Dora Christine. The death certificate shown below was also filled out by Dr Castleberry; but in this case it was filed the same day, the day of the birth of Dora Christine and the death of her mother, Dora Algie: 11 January 1925.

Analyzing and comparing the information I gathered from all of the sources located for this family I note the following errors on the birth certificate of "Dora Khristine Shultz."

- Birth date (11 February 1925 instead of 11 January 1925)
- Number of children born to the mother (six – should be ten)
- Number of children now living (six – should be eight)
- Spelling of Khristine (should be Christine)
- Spelling of the last names as Shultz instead of Shults
- Age of William (50 – should be 47)
- Age of Dora (38 – should be 42)

Although the birth certificate was an original source and directly answered the questions, careful examination and correlation with other records proved the information to be mostly inaccurate.

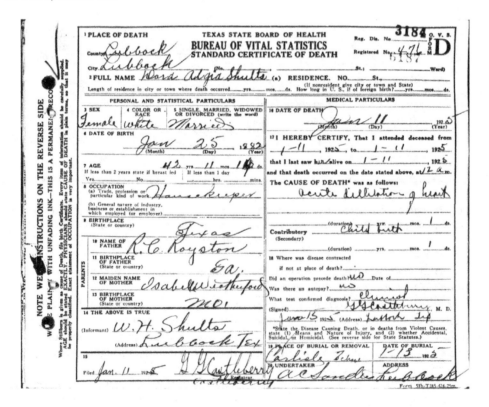

Figure 2-4: Texas State Board of Health, death certificate, Dora Algia Shults, Reg. Dis. No 3184, Registered No. 476. Lubbock, 1925; "Texas, Death Certificates, 1903-1982," Lubbock, 1925, Jan-Mar, image 11, Ancestry (http://search.ancestry.com : accessed 20 February 2016).

Now try answering the same questions for the death certificate of Dora Christine's mother, Dora Algie Shults, Figure 2-4. Check your answers at the end of this chapter.

Is this death certificate an original, derivative, or authored source?

Is the information primary, secondary, or undetermined?

Is the evidence direct, indirect, or negative for the question of Dora Algie's death date?

Are there any inconsistencies that should be noted?

As you analyze the records for your ancestor, take the time to understand the source and the information it holds. That will prepare you to extract the evidence items you'll need to answer your research question.

YOUR TASK

Revisit everything you have found about your ancestor. Look at the sources on the FamilySearch Family Tree. See what others have found on Ancestry public trees. Create a timeline using the Timeline Analysis Template in Appendix A. You may prefer to create a written chronology in a document. View the samples in Appendix B. Analyze the source, information, and evidence. Write all your questions, hypotheses, and ideas for future research in your Research Project Document.

5 Tips for Using A Timeline to Improve Your Research

- Create a spreadsheet in Google sheets or Excel using appropriate headings
- Assemble your sources: histories, records, personal knowledge, etc.
- Enter information and color code events
- Analyze events looking for new research opportunities
- Make a list of questions in your Research Project Document

Answers

Is this death certificate an original or derivative source? The image of the death certificate is considered an original source. It is complete and doesn't appear to have been tampered with in any way.

Is the information primary, secondary, or undetermined? The listing of the date of death and Dora's name is primary information, given by G.G. Castleberry, the attending physician. W.H. Shults, Dora's husband, was the informant for her personal information. Because he was not present at her birth, her birth date and place is secondary information. His listing of her parents could be primary or secondary, depending on if he knew them personally. His naming of their birthplaces would be secondary, as he was not present at their births.

Is the evidence direct or indirect? The death certificate clearly answers the questions of Dora's birth, death, and parentage, and is direct evidence.

Are there any inconsistencies that should be noted? There is some crossing out on the report of Dora's age, suggesting a possible error. Further research on the Royston family discovered that Dora's father, R.C. Royston, was actually born in Alabama, not Georgia. Dora's name was always spelled by the family "Dora Algie," not "Dora Algia."

Notes for Chapter 2

1   Board for Certification of Genealogists, *Genealogy Standards,* (Tennessee and New York: Turner Publishing, 2014), 63-79. See Appendix C in this book for recommended works by Elizabeth Shown Mills and Thomas W. Jones.

2   Elizabeth Shown Mills, "QuickLesson 11: Identity Problems & the FAN Principle, *Evidence Explained: Historical Analysis, Citation & Source Usage,* (https://www.evidenceexplained.com/content/quicklesson-11-identity-problems-fan-principle : viewed 19 February 2018).

3   Effie Lorain Shults Bassett, "Memories," (Sanger, California, between 1971 and 2000), p.1; photocopy of typescript was supplied to author by Bobby Gene Shults, Burley, Idaho, 2003.

4   Elizabeth Shown Mills, *Evidence Explained: Citing History Sources from Artifacts to Cyberspace,* Third Edition (Baltimore, Maryland: Genealogical Publishing Company, 2015), front endpaper. Used with permission.

5   Defined by the Board for Certification of Genealogists, "*Genealogy Standards,* 63-79.

6   Ibid., 72, 77-78.

7   Ibid., 66, 70-71.

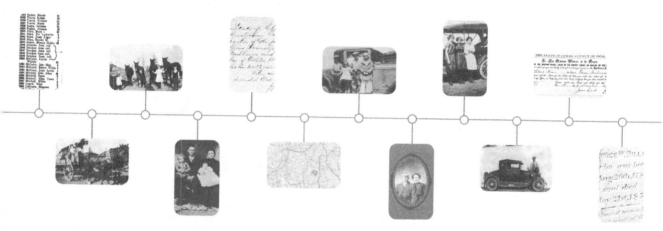

Locality Research

3

W hen faced with a tough research problem, have you considered digging into the location? Often clues or even the answer to your question can be found with an in-depth look at the places your ancestor lived, worked, and died. Professional genealogists thoroughly research a new locality as part of their planning and so can you!

In Chapter One you learned to form a research objective with key identifiers that would guide you in creating a focused research plan. Your task from Chapter Two was to revisit everything you or others had already found, create a timeline, then write questions and ideas for future research in your Research Project Document. This chapter will teach you the importance of location in researching your family.

When I first started researching my family, I didn't understand the importance of learning about the location. Twelve of my fifteen paternal ancestors shown in Figure 3-1 lived in the Chickasaw Nation, Indian Territory, between 1880 and Oklahoma statehood in 1907. You would think that I might have studied this important location in my family history, but I didn't.

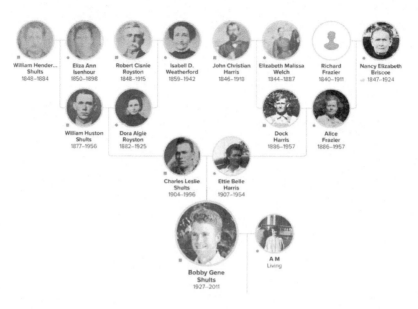

Figure 3-1: FamilySearch Family Tree printed portrait pedigree showing the paternal ancestors of Diana Elder. Of the 15 pictured here, 12 lived in Chickasaw nation, Indian Territory.

My four-generation report for accreditation began with Dora Algie Royston, my great grandmother. She and my great grandfather, William Huston Shults lived in Indian Territory. To thoroughly research their lives I needed to understand the what, where, and why of this location. I asked myself three questions and you can do the same.

- What happened?
- Where did it happen?
- Why did it happen?

Ask "What Happened?"

Review the timeline you created from the records of your ancestor. What types of questions could you ask to fill in the blanks? Did he marry a second time? How many children did he have with each wife? What is the name and birth information of each child? What was his state of origin? Did he serve in the military? Do church, land, court, military, or probate records exist to help you achieve your research objective?

Look for clues in each record that you might have previously missed such as witnesses, neighbors, the minister, emigration, or military service. You might have done this as you worked on your timeline analysis and made notes of your questions on your research project document. If not, go back through your sources and check for clues, especially locations.

After making my timeline for the family of William and Dora Shults and thoroughly analyzing the records, I had several questions about locations, particularly with their marriage record. I had a copy of the marriage license and certificate and the listing of "Indian Territory, Southern District" was puzzling to me. Also, Lorain, daughter of William and Dora, wrote in her personal history that they were married in Pauls Valley, Oklahoma, in 1898. How did this fit with the record that lists their residence as Elmore, Indian Territory?

I definitely needed to learn about the location to make sense of these seemingly conflicting places. Once you have a sense of what happened in the life of your ancestor, you can ask the next question.

Ask "Where did it Happen?"

The timeline analysis of your ancestor revealed different locations that could be researched. Choose one place that might hold the answer to your research question. Once you've settled on the location, several avenues of research will get you started.

- Look at a map of the area
- Use a gazetteer to track down historical place names
- Discover the migration routes leading to the area
- Examine the jurisdictions where records were kept
- Learn about the boundary changes that might affect the records
- Research the history of the location

Let's take a look at each of these suggestions in depth.

Look at a Map of the Area

Several internet resources can help you map the location, view it topographically, or even pinpoint a specific landform. Bookmarking favorite map websites can streamline your research. Some excellent websites to start mapping your ancestor's location:

- *Search – Places: FamilySearch*
  https://www.familysearch.org/research/places/
  Enter any place name in the world, and then view that location on the map. Get research links, alternate names for the location, and places with the same jurisdiction. This is definitely a good place to start.

- *Atlas of the Historical Geography of the United States*
  http://dsl.richmond.edu/historicalatlas/
  Historical, cultural, and geographic information from 1492-1931.

- *Cyndi's List*
  https://www.cyndislist.com/us/
  A website of genealogical links. Use the search box to locate links to maps for your location or browse the "Maps & Geography" category.

- *David Rumsey Map Collection*
  https://www.davidrumsey.com/
  Thousands of maps for numerous time periods and locations worldwide, all available to view from the website.

- *Google Maps*
  https://www.google.com/maps
  Shows streets, schools, lakes, rivers, cemeteries, and more in a traditional map format.

- *Google Earth*
  https://www.google.com/earth/
  Google Earth allows you to view any area topographically as it looks today. Discover the mountains, valleys, and rivers that influenced your ancestor's movements.

- *Library of Congress Maps*
  https://www.loc.gov/maps/
  This database has thousands of United States historical maps, many of which are online. Some are only available to view on-site.

- *Maps.familysearch.org*
  http://maps.familysearch.org/
  Shows counties of England with parish and civil jurisdictions.

- *Vision of Britain through Time*
  http://www.visionofbritain.org.uk/
  Contains topographic, boundary, historical maps and more for the British Isles.

Using several of these map resources I discovered the exact location of the Chickasaw Nation, Indian Territory, and was able to view the area using Google Maps, shown in Figure 3-2. The locations of Pauls Valley and Elmore from the marriage of William and Dora Shults now made sense. They lived in Elmore, as noted on the marriage record, and traveled the 15 miles to Pauls Valley for the actual marriage ceremony.

Use Gazetteers to Find Historical Place-names

Have you used gazetteers in your research? A gazetteer contains historical place names such as a town, creek, or valley mentioned in a deed or family history.

The *FamilySearch Wiki* (https://www.familysearch.org/wiki) is an excellent place to begin a search for gazetteers for any country or U.S. state. Enter "gazetteer" and location into the search box. Many of these have been digitized and are available to view from your home. Also check the websites *Google Books* (https://books.google.com) and *Internet Archive* (https://archive.org) for digitized gazetteers.

The *Geographic Names Information System* (GNIS – https://geonames.usgs.gov) is an online gazetteer that allows you to search names of current locations such as trails, reservoirs, post offices, lakes and much more. You can use it to get the exact latitude and longitude of a place that would help in locating it on Google Earth.

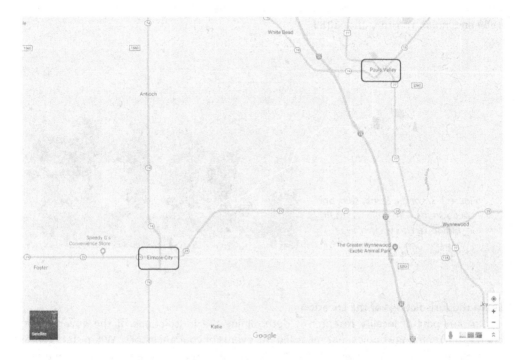

Figure 3-2: View of Chickasaw Nation, Indian Territory, currently Oklahoma, proximity of Elmore city to Pauls Valley, Google Maps (https://www.google.com/maps/ : accessed 24 February 2018).

Discover the Migration Routes Leading to the Area

The *FamilySearch Wiki* (https://www.familysearch.org/wiki/en/Main_Page) contains excellent links and information on migration routes worldwide. Enter "migration" and your location into the search box to see what you can discover. Some questions to consider when thinking about your ancestor's migration:

- How did the settlement grow?
- Where did the settlers originate?
- Why did your ancestor leave his previous home?

I learned from the *FamilySearch Wiki* on Oklahoma Emigration and Immigration that "only a few thousand non-Indians lived in the Territory before 1889. After the Civil War, a few people from the South moved into the Indian Territory. Anyone wishing to live in this area needed permission from the Indians, but some white settlers tried to move into the Territory without permission."[1]

This information from the *FamilySearch Wiki* told me that my ancestors probably didn't move into Indian Territory until after 1889. With the 1890 census mostly destroyed, I have a twenty year span from 1880 - 1900 between census records. Knowing the migration pattern for the settlers gave me a better understanding of where the records might be - Texas until 1889 and Indian Territory after 1889.

Figure 3-3: Lorain, Scrub, Lola, and Della Shults with mule teams in Indian Territory, circa 1917

Learn the Jurisdictions of the Location

A key part of locality research is determining the jurisdictions of the government, church, or community bodies that recorded the events of your ancestors. When states were created, county boundaries were large. As the population grew, the counties divided and boundaries changed. Your ancestor's records might be in the parent county as well as the newly created county.

When researching, you'll need to consider looking at each jurisdictional level for records. A breakdown of possible jurisdictions and types of records in each will help you plan your research. Consider looking for records at each level.

- National records: federal census, federal land, military, pension
- State records: state census, tax list, land record, pension, vital, military
- County Records: court, land, probate, vital
- City / township records: directory, vital
- Church records: vital, membership

The marriage record for William and Dora Shults in Figure 3-4 shows "United States, Indian Territory, Southern District" as the jurisdiction. Was this a national record? A state record? A county record?

No. _____

MARRIAGE LICENSE

UNITED STATES OF AMERICA,)
Indian Territory,   ) SS.
Southern District.   )

TO ANY PERSON AUTHORIZED BY LAW TO SOLEMNIZE MARRIAGE-GREETING-

You are hereby commanded to solemnize the Rite and publish the Bans of Matrimony between Mr. __W. H. Shults_____ of __Elmore_____, in the Indian Territory, aged __20___ years, and M__A. D. Rayston_____ of __Elmore___ in the Indian Territory, aged __16_____ years, according to law, and do you officially sign and return this License to the parties herein named.

Witness my hand and official seal, this __7th___ day of ___December___ A. D. __1898_____.

C. M. CAMPBELL,
Clerk of the United States Court.

By _____ Deputy

CERTIFICATE OF MARRIAGE

UNITED STATES OF AMERICA,)
Indian Territory,   ) SS.
Southern District.   )

I, __A. B. Hughes_____ a __M. of G._____ do hereby certify that on the __11th___ day of __December___ A. D. __1898__ I did duly and according to law, as commanded in the foregoing License, solemnize the Rite and publish the Bans of Matrimony between the parties therein named.

Witness my hand, this __11th___ day of __December___ A.D. __1898__

A. B. Hughes_____

a __M. of G._____

My Credentials are recorded in the office of the Clerk of the United States Court in the Indian Territory, _____ Judicial Division, Book __A.____ Page __108___ .

Filed and duly recorded, this__10th__ day of __January_____ 1898

- - - - - -

Certificate of True Copy

STATE OF OKLAHOMA)
) ss.
CARTER COUNTY   )

I, Willie Maddox, do certify that I have compared the foregoing copy of a Marriage License with the original now remaining on file in this office, and that the same is a full, true and exact copy thereof.

In witness whereof I have hereunto set my hand and affixed my official seal this __6th___ day of __March_____ 1943

Willie Maddox Court Clerk

By _____
                     Deputy

Figure 3-4: Carter County, Oklahoma, marriage license and certificate, Shults-Rayston, 11 December 1898, Indian Territory Southern District, recorded 1943, County Clerk, Ardmore, Oklahoma.

To answer my question, I did a Google search and came upon an explanation of Indian Territory marriage records by the Oklahoma Historical Society. It turns out that the jurisdiction for this marriage was the United States Federal Court.

"Prior to statehood in 1907, marriages of white citizens in the part of the state known as the Indian Territory were recorded in the Recording districts of the United States Federal Court. The Southern District included the following Chickasaw Nation Court Seats: Ardmore, Purcell, Pauls Valley, Ryan and Chickasha."[2]

William and Dora's daughter, Lorain, had given Pauls Valley as the marriage location. With this information about the jurisdiction, it now made perfect sense. William and Dora had to travel to Pauls Valley for their marriage, probably the closest location of a federal court.

Learn the Boundary Changes

Because United States territories and state boundaries changed as the country grew, it's important to understand how the jurisdictions in your ancestor's location might have changed over the years. His records might be in two or three separate counties. You need to know the parent counties as well as other counties that split off from the parent. How do you even start learning about boundary changes in your location? The Atlas of Historical County Boundaries, (publications.newberry.org/ahcbp/) by the Newberry Library is an interactive website showing United States county border changes.[3]

If you're researching another country, look at the FamilySearch Wiki for information on boundary changes. Being aware of the possibility will make you a better researcher.

Now that we've explored the questions of "What Happened?" and "Where Did it Happen?" it's time to think about the final question.

Ask "Why Did it Happen?"

It might seem obvious to research the history of the place your ancestor lived, but often this is a vital step missed in the hunt for records. County histories, biographical sketches, periodicals, church histories and newspapers can give you insight into the community and provide valuable clues about records that might exist, such as church, school, or business records.

County Histories

County histories reveal the community's origins and background on early settlers. How do you find a county history? A simple *Google Books* search can often yield good results. Another excellent option is to use the *FamilySearch Catalog*, located on *FamilySearch* under the "Search" tab. Do a keyword search, entering the name of your location and "history." Check the bottom left of the screen for "availability" to see if the book has been digitized.

Following this method, I entered "Chickasaw Nation" into the keyword search and was rewarded with 98 results. One book looked especially interesting, *Pioneers of Chickasaw Nation, Indian Territory*, by Nova A. Lemons.[4] On my next visit to the Family History Library in Salt Lake City I located the book and began learning about the history of Chickasaw Nation.

Not only did I discover the history of the specific area where William and Dora Shults lived, I got clear information about how to research and where the records were kept.

I learned that the land was owned by the Chickasaw Nation and as non-citizens the white settlers could lease the land from tribal members. The land was rich and farmers could grow anything. The 1900 census lists all my ancestors there as farmers. The lure of good land probably drew them north from Texas. Knowing that they couldn't own land helped me understand that no deeds would be available to research, but possibly there were records of the leases.

I also learned that after 1898 white settlers were supposed to pay taxes on livestock, but only those who were forced by the collector actually paid up. This tells me that possibly no tax records exist. I did get lots of ideas for further research, both from the county histories and the Family History Library catalog, such as this record collection: "Permits to Non-citizens, 1878-1904." [5]

What if you don't live near the Family History Library? Try using their catalog online at *FamilySearch* (https://www.familysearch.org/catalog/search) to locate records and county history books. More and more of these are being digitized and you can read them from your home computer. If the book isn't digitized yet, try searching online for the title. In the case of *Pioneers of Chickasaw Nation, Indian Territory,* the book is available from the author and I ordered my own copy to peruse at length. A Google search might find the book in a library close by or you could request an interlibrary loan at your local library.

Biographical sketches fill in the gaps between records. Even if your ancestor isn't mentioned, you'll discover more about the history of the community. William and Dora Shults are not included in *Pioneers of Chickasaw Nation, Indian Territory*. But an interview with a settler named W.B. Flick named many details that could very well fit my family. Mr. Flick mentions several locations in his narrative that coincide with my ancestors: Marietta, Ardmore, Maxwell, Pauls Valley and McGee, all in Chickasaw Nation, Indian Territory. [6]

- In 1888, W.B. Flick traveled with his parents and brother from Texas to Indian Territory in a "wagon working 2 horses and 2 oxens [sic]."

- He married Jane Davis in 1889, then "bought a lease from Tom Love, Chickasaw Indian, and built a log house on it, bought 2 oxens [sic] from his father and started to farming."

- In 1891, he moved on to Nebo and went to work for an Indian woman named Lou Brown. Apparently she had married a white man and the Indians didn't like him and killed him. A few nights after Mr. Flick and his wife moved in with her "7 or 8 Indians on horseback surrounded the house and began shooting into the house. He saw that they were all going to be killed, so he got his Winchester and run [sic] out in the yard and began firing from the house."

- W.B. Flick moved at least eight times between 1888 and 1910.

Reading this account revealed a clearer picture of Indian Territory and explained why my ancestors moved so often: because of land leases.

Newspapers

Newspapers give wonderful details of the community but researching them can seem overwhelming with so many websites to search. Three free sites can lead you to online newspapers:

- Chronicling America – Historic American Newspapers
  https://chroniclingamerica.loc.gov/
  The Library of Congress website has newspapers from 1789-1924. You can even search this site on the go if you download the app "OldNews USA" to your smart phone.

- The Ancestor Hunt List of Newspaper Research Links
  http://www.theancestorhunt.com/newspaper-research-links.html
  The Ancestor Hunt website keeps an up-to-date list of links by state of online historical newspapers. This is valuable because newspapers are often digitized by universities or societies.

- Elephind.com
  https://elephind.com/
  Search over 3 million digitized newspapers from libraries and universities across the country. The database is continually growing so check back often to see if your location has been digitized yet.

Summary

To summarize, try these suggestions to put your ancestors in their place:

WHAT: Reexamine the records; look for clues you might have missed and ask yourself questions.

WHERE: Locate the places mentioned in the records; use Google searches to find online map collections.

WHY: Try to understand why your ancestors moved to a particular location: search online first for information, and then try the Family History Library catalog on *Family Search* to find titles of good county histories.

YOUR TASK

Choose one location from your research objective and learn all that you can about the geography, migration into the area, jurisdictions, boundary changes, and the local history.

Compile the information into a locality guide at the best level for your research: town, county, state/province, country.

See Appendix A for the Locality Guide Template and Appendix B for work samples. Link to websites and include any information that will help you plan your research.

Notes for Chapter 3

1   *FamilySearchWiki,* (https://www.familysearch.org/wiki),"Oklahoma Emigration and Immigration," rev. 17:00, 4 April 2017).

2   Oklahoma Historical Society, Research Center "Indian Territory Marriage Records," (http:/www.okhistory.org/research/terrmarriage: accessed 25 February 2016).

3   The Newberry Library, "Atlas of Historical County Boundaries," (http://publications.newberry.org/ahcbp/index.html : accessed 19 February 2018).

4   Nova A. Lemons, *Pioneers of Chickasaw Nation, Indian Territory,* (Miami, Oklahoma : Timbercreek Ltd., 1991).

5   "Chickasaw Nation Records," Oklahoma Historical society, Indian Archives Division (Oklahoma City, Oklahoma: 1971), digital images, *FamilySearch* (https://www.familysearch.org : accessed 15 February 2018); citing "Permits to Non-Citizens, Traders and Doctors, and Related Documents," FHL microfilm 1,666,437; viewable only at a FHC or the FHL.

6   Nova A. Lemons, *Pioneers of Chickasaw Nation Vol. 2,* (Miami, Oklahoma: Timbercreek Ltd., 1997), 280.

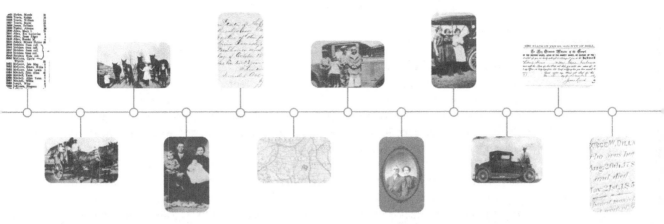

Research Planning

4

Have you ever sat down at your computer to do some genealogy research and two hours later you come up for air? You've found interesting documents and looked at a lot of websites, but you didn't find what you wanted and you don't know where you looked? If so, you are not alone! Disciplining yourself to create a simple research plan and follow through is the hallmark of the true professional.

Now that you've chosen a research objective, analyzed the previously located sources, and created a locality guide, it's time to make your research plan. This entails planning specific strategies and record searches to answer your research question. Five steps will guide you in this task.

1. State your objective with the key identifying information
2. Summarize the known facts
3. Create a working hypothesis
4. Identify sources to search
5. Prioritize your research strategy

Step 1: State Your Objective and Key Identifying Information

Sometimes after you've analyzed all your source documents, you realize you need to tweak your research objective. It might be too narrow or too broad. Perhaps you want to research only one of the children of an ancestor, not all. Make any adjustments to your original objective, and then place it at the head of your Research Project Document. Your objective will guide you in creating your research plan.

I had originally formed a research objective to discover the father of my 3rd great grandmother, Cynthia Dillard Royston. Once I created a timeline analysis of my source documents, I realized that I had a lot of circumstantial evidence pointing to George W. Dillard. I decided to narrow my objective. Notice my use of key identifiers - event dates and places.

> EXAMPLE: The objective of this research project is to determine if George W. Dillard born 1781 in Virginia and died 1854 in Lee County, Alabama, is the father of Cynthia Dillard. Cynthia was born about 1816 in Georgia. She married Thomas Beverly Royston about 1833 in Georgia or Alabama and died in 1882 in Collin County, Texas.

Step 2: Summarize Known Facts

Working from the timeline analysis, list what you know about your ancestor. Include birth, marriage, and death dates and places. Estimate, if needed, based on what's known. For example, I only have an estimated birth date for Cynthia Dillard. Those estimates are important so do your best with the information that you've found.

As well as the vital facts of birth, marriage, and death, include the migration pattern and any other data such as religion, military service, or land ownership. Gather every clue from every document.

Here are the facts I assembled from carefully analyzing each record for George W. Dillard and Cynthia Royston.

EXAMPLE:

Cynthia Dillard Royston

1. *Cynthia Dillard was born about 1815 according to her reported age on the 1850, 1860, 1870, and 1880 census records.*

2. *Cynthia Dillard was born in Georgia, Alabama, or Florida, according to the census records and the death certificates of three of her children.*

3. *Cynthia married Thomas Beverly Royston about 1833 in Georgia or Alabama. No marriage record has yet been located.*

4. *Thomas Beverly Royston was listed in the 1831 tax list of Morgan County, Georgia.*

5. *Thomas and Cynthia Royston owned land in DeKalb County, Alabama, from 1837 – 1842 and are listed on the 1840 census in that county.*

6. *Thomas and Cynthia Royston owned land and resided in Chambers County, Alabama, from about 1842-1872 and are listed on the 1850, 1860, and 1870 census (Cynthia as a widow in 1870).*

7. *Thomas Beverly Royston died in 1868 in Chambers County, Alabama, and his estate file gives the information that Cynthia and some of the children "removed to Texas" about 1872.*

8. *Cynthia Royston and some children are listed on the 1880 census of Collin County, Texas. The birthplace of her parents is given as Virginia.*

9. *The estate file of Thomas Beverly Royston gives Cynthia's date of death in Collin County, Texas, as 2 August 1882.*

George W. Dillard

1. *George W. Dillard was born 26 August 1781 in Virginia and died 21 May 1854 in Auburn, Russell County, Alabama; dates from his headstone inscription, "erected by his children." His listing on the 1850 census of Macon County, Alabama, names his birthplace as Virginia.*

2. *George married Peggy Armour 9 November 1801 in Greene County, Georgia.*

3. *The couple had the following children based on the 1810 and 1820 censuses.*

   a. *1 male born 1795/1805*

   b. *1 male born 1805/1810*

   c. *2 males born 1810/20*

   d. *1 female born 1810/20 - possibly Cynthia*

   e. *1 female born 1805/1810*

4. *G.W. Dillard served in the Creek War of 1813-1814 along with L.D/S.D. Dillard in the same company of the Alabama Mounted Volunteers, Young's Company (spies).*

5. *Peggy Armour died between the 1820 census and George's 2nd marriage on 29 July 1822 to Martha Flournoy Wells in Greene County, Georgia.*

6. *George moved to Muscogee County, Georgia, by 1830 where he is mentioned in the local newspaper, "The Columbus Enquirer" from 1832-1838.*

7. *George purchased land in Chambers County, Alabama, in 1836 and 1840.*

8. *George moved to Russell County, Alabama, and is listed on the 1840 census as head of household.*

9. *George moved to Macon County, Alabama, and is listed on the 1850 census with his wife Martha, and children: Columbus age 21, Alonzo age 15, Leonidas, age 9, and Zenora, age 7.*

10. *George died in 1854 and is buried in Pine Hill Cemetery, Auburn, Alabama. His children erected his headstone, no names of the children or date given.*

Connections between Cynthia Dillard and George W. Dillard

1. *George W. Dillard's birthplace was Virginia, as noted on his headstone and the 1850 Macon County, Alabama, census. Cynthia's father's birthplace was Virginia, noted on the 1880 census of Collin County, Texas.*

2. *George W. Dillard lived in proximity to Cynthia and Thomas B. Royston from 1840 to his death in 1854. George is listed on the 1840 census in Russell County, Alabama and Thomas B. Royston is listed on the 1840 census in DeKalb County, Alabama. By 1850, George has moved to Macon County, Alabama and Thomas and Cynthia to Chambers County, Alabama. They are separated by only one county.*

3. *George purchased land in Chambers County, Alabama, in 1836 and 1840. Thomas and Cynthia Royston settled in Chambers County, Alabama, about 1850 and had a large cotton plantation.*

4. *George had a son named Leonidas, born 1841. Thomas and Cynthia named a son Thomas Leonidas in 1857.*

5. *Cynthia named a daughter Margaret, possibly after Peggy Armour, George W. Dillard's first wife and possible mother of Cynthia.*

6. *The household of George W. Dillard in 1820 and 1830 has a female of the appropriate age to be Cynthia.*

7. *Records of Muscogee County, Georgia, where George Dillard was living in 1833 were destroyed by fire in 1838, possibly why no marriage record for Thomas Royston and Cynthia Dillard has been discovered.*

Step 3: Create A Working Hypothesis

Form an educated guess about your research question using the clues from the known facts. What methodology could you use to test your hypothesis? A search of the census? A land study? Your hypothesis is an educated guess. Do the best with what you've discovered. Use your intuition and choose the most likely scenario to test first. When writing your hypothesis, use specific dates and places.

EXAMPLE:

> *George W. Dillard is the father of Cynthia Dillard. His household contains a female of the appropriate age on the 1820 and 1830 census enumerations. She married Thomas Beverly Royston in Muscogee County about 1833. No marriage record exists because a courthouse fire burned destroying the records before 1838.*

George Dillard purchased land in Chambers County Alabama in 1836 and in 1840. Cynthia Dillard and Thomas B. Royston moved to Chambers County by 1850 and acquired a large amount of land, possibly land deeded to her by George Dillard.

Nathaniel Dillard received a land grant in Chambers County in 1834. He could be Cynthia's brother, and/or George Dillard's son. Lorenzo D Dillard received a land grant in Chambers County in 1837 and could also be Cynthia's brother and/or George Dillard's son.

Cynthia named a son Thomas Leonidas in 1857. George W. Dillard had a son named Leonidas, born 1841. This unusual name could be a connecting link between Cynthia and George Dillard.

In 1850, George Dillard was living in Macon County, Alabama, one county away from Chambers County where Cynthia and Thomas were living. Families often migrated together and the proximity of the Dillards and Roystons could support a father/daughter relationship.

Step 4: Identify Sources to Search

Next identify what sources to search to either prove or disprove your hypothesis. If you need ideas for kinds of records to search for specific information, try the United States Record Finder (https://www.familysearch.org/wiki/en/United_States_Record_Finder) from the *FamilySearch Wiki*. If you're searching in another country, type the name of the country and "record finder" or "record selection" in the search box.

Use your locality guide for ideas on the available records of the time period you'll be researching. Remember to consider county boundary changes and jurisdictions when looking for record collections. Look at the catalogs on *Ancestry.com* and *FamilySearch.org* for digitized books and specific records to search.

EXAMPLE:

- *Marriage records for Thomas Beverly Royston and Cynthia Dillard in Georgia.*

- *Church records for marriage of Thomas B. Royston and Cynthia Dillard in Muscogee Co. Georgia.*

- *1830 and 1840 census records for brothers of Cynthia Dillard in Georgia and Alabama.*

- *Military pension records for George W. Dillard*

- *Probate records for George W. Dillard in Georgia and Alabama.*

- *Court and land records in DeKalb & Chambers County, Alabama, for Dillards - counties where Thomas and Cynthia Royston resided.*

Step 5: Prioritize Your Research Strategy

Now it's time to decide which records to search first. Start with online records as those will be the quickest and easiest to access. Begin with the record most likely to answer your research question, planning specific databases to search.

Since I know that Cynthia Dillard married Thomas Beverly Royston, a marriage record for them could point to her residence and lead to her father. Although I've previously looked for a marriage record I need to check again and track specific searches. Next I could study the land records for Chambers County, Alabama, looking for a Royston/Dillard connection. A probate record search for George Dillard is next, then additional searches. Always check online collections first, and then look for sources in archives, local courthouses, or libraries.

EXAMPLE:

- *Marriage records for Thomas Beverly Royston and Cynthia should be rechecked for the years 1830-1835 in Georgia. As new records are added to online collections, the possibility of discovering the marriage record, if extant, increases.*

    - *"Georgia Marriages, 1699-1944," Ancestry Index, source Hunting for Bears, comp. Georgia Marriages. Includes Morgan County and surrounding counties: Greene, Oconee (Clarke parent county), Walton, Newton, Jasper, and Putnam.*

    - *"Georgia Church Marriages, 1754-1960," FamilySearch.*

    - *Morgan County, Georgia, "Marriages 1821-1854," FHL film 158906, digitized and indexed on FamilySearch.*

- *Land study of Royston and Dillard land in Chambers County, Alabama*

    - *View the land patents of Chambers County, Alabama, for George Dillard, Lorenzo D. Dillard, and Nathaniel Dillard - Chambers County tract books on FamilySearch.*

    - *Compile list of all Royston land in Chambers County, Alabama, from the Deed books of Chambers County.*

    - *Compare land descriptions to determine any Dillard/Royston connections.*

- *Search probate records for George Dillard in Macon County*

    - *"Macon County, Alabama, Probate Records," digitized collection on FamilySearch; search from 1854-1874.*

    - *"Alabama, Wills and Probate Records, 1753-1999;" Ancestry indexed collection*

    - *Mary Jane Galer, "Columbus, Georgia, Lists of People in the Town, 1828-1852: and Sexton's Reports to 1866," (Columbus, Georgia: M.G. Galer, 2000).*

- *Search for a military pension for George W. Dillard: United States Old War Pension Index, 1815-1926.*

- *Search court records of Macon County, Alabama, for George W. Dillard. "Miscellaneous records, wills, estate records, marriages, etc., 1839-1886" is an indexed collection on FamilySearch.*

- *Search the 1830 and 1840 censuses of Alabama for possible brothers of Cynthia - particularly Nathaniel and Lorenzo from the land tract books of Chambers County, Alabama.*

As you can see, this detailed plan will guide my research. I'm starting with what I know – the marriage of Thomas and Cynthia. Next, I'll move on to the land study. Based on what I discover there, I'll move forward with other research.

The more you work on research planning the more confident you'll become. Spend some time on your plan up front and then you're ready to go. You have a focus for your research session. No more surfing the web for hours and coming up empty handed.

YOUR TASK

Working in your Research Project Document, reword your objective if necessary, then summarize the known facts based on your timeline analysis. Create a working hypothesis then identity sources to search. Lastly, prioritize your research strategy. When finished, you'll have a working research plan.

Step 1: State your objective with the key identifying information
Step 2: Summarize the known facts
Step 3: Create a working hypothesis
Step 4: Identify sources to search
Step 5: Prioritize your research strategy

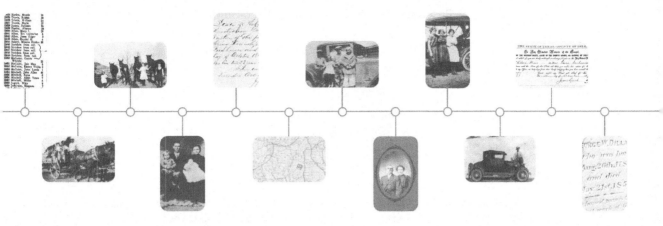

Source Citations

5

How do you keep track of the numerous websites, books, microfilms, and other sources you might consult in your genealogy research? Do you only print or save links to the sources you find? What do you do when you don't locate anything in a database? Learning to keep a research log and use source citations is the next step in your journey to research like a pro.

The terms "research logs" and "source citations" might seem overwhelming but you'll be glad to know that it's not hard to keep a research log that has good source citations attached. In fact, after disciplining yourself to document your searches you won't want to go back to your old methods. This chapter will teach you how to create source citations that clearly state the details of the source that will lead you or anyone else to the source.

Have you ever read a family history with an interesting fact, like "Great Grandma was a full blooded Cherokee"? You're excited to read more and see some proof, but there is nothing: no source citations or documentation of any kind. You're left in the dark, wondering how much to believe in that history.

Figure 5-1:
Eliza Ann
Isenhour

My great grandmother, Eliza Ann Isenhour, supposedly sported Cherokee heritage. Unfortunately, the family history stating this fact neglected to state any proof.

"My father often talked about the "Shults" and he said that his grandmother, Eliza Ann Isenhour (Shults) was a full-blooded Cherokee and she was born in Arkansas, so this is a family story that has been passed down."

How do I document this family story? The source citation I created looks like this:

Don Stagner, "Notes on Eliza Ann Isenhour," 2003, Shults family file, undocumented information; privately held by Diana Elder, Highland, Utah.

Referencing my citation, I am reminded that this information came from my second cousin, Don Stagner and that he shared it with me in 2003. My daughter Nicole and I researched Eliza's parents, found that she actually belonged to the Eisenhower clan, and through that connection discovered our relationship to President Dwight D. Eisenhower. We didn't make any connections to a Cherokee heritage through Eliza Ann Isenhour.

15634	Hyden, Maude	10	F	1-16	272	15718	Beal, William Albert	28	M	1-16	5842
15635	Travis, Robbie	16	F	1-16	3666	15719	Beal, Samantha	9	F	1-32	5843
15636	Travis, William	14	M	1-16	3666	15720	Beal, Bulah	4	F	1-32	5843
15637	Travis, Marie	12	F	1-16	3666	15721	Beal, William D.	2	M	1-32	5843
15638	James, Sallissie	51	F	Full	4915	15722	Dills, Rosa	20	F	1-16	5844
15639	Pusley, Alinton	34	M	Full	4918	15723	Dills, Nora M.	5	F	1-32	5844
15640	Allen, Mary I.	23	F	1-16	46	15724	Dills, Lether Lee	2	F	1-32	5844
15641	Allen, Evi Catherine	6	F	1-32	46	15725	Beal, Reuben, Jr.	24	M	1-16	5845
15642	Allen, Jesse Edger	2	M	1-32	46	15726	Beal, Cora	5	F	1-32	5845
15643	Allen, Randel M.	4	M	1-32	46	15727	Beal, Benj. Lee	4	M	1-32	5845
15644	Askew, Minnie Holder	30	F	1-32	198	15728	Beal, Arthur	17	M	1-16	5846
15645	Stricken from roll.					15729	Beal, Johnnie	15	M	1-16	5846
15646	Stricken from roll.					15730	Beal, John Peter	17	M	1-16	5846
15647	Stricken from roll.					15731	Beal, Pony	15	M	1-16	5847
15648	Stricken from roll.					15732	Beal, Roy May	13	F	1-16	5847
15649	Stricken from roll.					15733	Moore, Ada Bell	18	F	1-16	5848
15650	McGuire, Carrie					15734	Beal, Annie	16	F	1-16	5848
	Whittle	23	F	1-4	236	15735	Moore, Roy L.	1	M	1-32	5848
15651	McGuire, Isie May	5	F	1-8	236	15736	Beal, William T.	13	M	1-16	5849
15652	McGuire, Emery Willis	3	M	1-8	236	15737	Meek, Jacob	60	M	1-4	5850
15653	McGuire, John Lewis	1	M	1-8	236	15738	Meek, James H.	26	M	1-8	5850
15654	Mitchell, John Allen	40	M	1-16	238	15739	Meek, Calvin W.	15	M	1-8	5850
15655	Mitchell, Enna	8	F	1-16	238	15740	Edgar, Rhoda M.	21	F	1-32	5851
15656	Mitchell, Allen Yates	7	M	1-16	238	15741	Edgar, Earnest	5	M	1-64	5851
15657	Mitchell, Willie	6	F	1-16	238	15742	Edgar, Sarah Ettie	1	F	1-64	5851
15658	Joseph, Wicy	8	F	Full	720	15743	Moran, James E.	24	M	1-16	5852
15659	Jefferson, Simpson	7	M	Full	1202	15744	Moran, Maude Ola	3	F	1-32	5852

Figure 5-2: "U.S., Native American Enrollment Cards for the Five Civilized Tribes, 1898-1914," entry for Jacob, James H. and Calvin W. Meek, Ancestry (www.ancestry.com : accessed 10 February 2016), image 572.

Several years later I stumbled upon evidence that proved her second husband, Jacob Meek, was one-quarter Choctaw with his enrollment in the Dawes Rolls, lists of people accepted as eligible for tribal membership in the "Five Civilized tribes: Cherokees, Creeks, Choctaws, Chickasaws, and Seminoles," shown in Figure5-2.[1]

Also listed were Jacob and Eliza's sons, James and Calvin Meek; each with one-eighth Choctaw heritage. They didn't inherit any Native American ancestry from their mother, Eliza Ann Isenhour, proving that she was not full-blooded Cherokee.

Somewhere along the way, Eliza's marriage to the Choctaw, Jacob Meek, morphed into Great Grandma being a full-blooded Cherokee. Mystery solved! Now I could fully document that information and lay the story to rest. What did I use for documentation? Information gleaned from sources. And when I put this information into *FamilySearch*, *Ancestry*, and my personal database, I used a source citation.

When is the best time to create a source citation? When you're looking at the source! Don't fool yourself that you'll go back and add details like the book title, page number, or image number. You'll be lucky to even find the source again.

First of all, you might ask: "Why would I need to learn about creating source citations? I just add record hints from *FamilySearch* or *Ancestry* and the citation is automatically created." Good point.

Our modern technology makes it easy to add source documentation for those digitized, indexed records, but what about the family bible pages you own or the local history book on your shelf? What if you find a record on one of the numerous state websites and you want to add it to your family tree on *Ancestry*, *FamilySearch*, or your personal database? You'll need to create your own source. Even the readymade citations on the major websites like *Ancestry* and *FamilySearch* might need to be tweaked to meet your specific needs.

Perhaps you are adding source documentation to your personal database. You've ordered several death certificates and need to clearly state where each came from. If you share one of those documents with a fellow researcher, a source citation attached would explain where it originated.

You could be writing a family history book and in order for it to be credible, you must include a source citation for each genealogical fact. After years of research, you might have finally proven a difficult relationship. Writing a proof summary with complete source citations will enable you to share your findings with confidence. Perhaps you wish to publish your findings. All genealogical publications require complete source citations. To summarize, you might need to create a source citation when:

- Creating a new source on the *FamilySearch* Family Tree or another online tree
- Entering a source into your personal database
- Sharing a source document
- Writing a family history book
- Writing a proof statement
- Writing an article for publication

Besides giving your research credibility, citing your sources can also help you evaluate and analyze each source you locate. Having to dig into the source will aid you in truly understanding the information that it contains. You'll discover clues that you might have overlooked with a cursory scan for facts.

As genealogists, we often return to our research and need to view a source document again. A complete source citation will lead us straight back to our source and will also enable anyone else to locate the source. Complete source citations will show that you've thoroughly researched each possible source to answer your research question.

Evidence Explained: Citing History Sources from Artifacts to Cyberspace by Elizabeth Shown Mills is the definitive source about citation and should be included in every serious genealogist's library.[2] I'll give you several references for more in-depth study at the end of this chapter. Now that we've made the case for source citations, let's define the terms.

Source

What is a source? A document, book, article, microfilm, photograph, website, etc. that gives you information, which becomes evidence in proving a conclusion.

Source Citation

What is a source citation? A statement identifying the specific location of a source and details about that source.

How to Create a Source Citation

Genealogy Standards names five elements that a complete citation should include.[3] Tom Jones elaborates on those elements and explains that a source citation can be created by answering five questions.[4]

1. **Who** created the source?
2. **What** is the source?
3. **When** was the source created or when did the event occur?
4. **Where in** the source?
5. **Where is** the source?

To answer these five questions you must understand the source. You need to closely examine it, note the information it contains, and discover who created it.

Example

Let's explore the five questions using the example of a Florida land record I discovered on the *MyFlorida* website, shown in Figure 5-3.[5]

Figure 5-3: Screenshot of Florida armed occupation land patents for Arthur Dillard

Viewing the image of the original document, I abstracted the information that this contained:

- Land Office at Newnansville
- Under the armed occupation act for settlement in East Florida
- Arthur Dillard, head of a family
- Resident of Florida from July 1843
- SW ¼ of Section 25 Township 14 S Range 21 East

The website provided more information about this source document but did not provide a neat and tidy source citation. I had to create my own, answering the five questions: Who, What, When, Where in, and Where is.

1) Who? This refers to either the author of the source, the creator (often a religious or government entity), or the informant.

The land permit for Arthur Dillard didn't say who created this record, but under the FAQ on the website, I discovered it was the Florida Department of Environmental Protection that collected the data and images.

Who? Florida Department of Environmental Protection

2) What? A description of the source comes next, located at the top of the website. I also included "entry for Arthur Dillard." Identifying the specific individual listed in a source clarifies the source.

What? "Armed Occupation Act of 1842, Florida Land Permits," entry for Arthur Dillard

3) When? Typically cite the year a book or microfilm was published. If it is a journal or magazine, add the month or season. For a website, add the access date. If the source is unpublished, use the date it was created or the date of the event it reported, 26 July 1843 in the land record. Because I accessed this source on the web, I also used the access date of 9 February 2016.

When? 26 July 1843 and 9 February 2016

4) Where in the source? This could be a page number, an image number, or any other way to explain to others how to find the source again. Not sure how the website organized the information, I included all the locator information at the top of the web page:

Wherein? DM ID: 148527 Legacy Doc. Locator: AOP3815

5) Where is the source? This could be the publisher's city and state, the URL, or the physical location if the source is unpublished. An easy one here – I copied and pasted the URL of the website.

Where is? MyFlorida.com (http://tlhdslweb.dep.state.fl.us)

My finished citation looks like this:

> Florida Department of Environmental Protection, "Armed Occupation Act of 1842, Florida Land Permits," entry for Arthur Dillard, 26 July 1843, online database, *MyFlorida.com* (http://tlhdslweb.dep.state.fl.us : accessed 9 February 2016), DM ID: 148527, Legacy Doc. Locator: AOP3815.

Practice

Next, let's look at the marriage license and certificate of my great grandparents, William Shults and Dora Royston, Figure 5-4. I inherited this source document from my father. I had to carefully analyze the record and do some investigating to understand this source.

The license and certificate are the source holding information of their names, residence, and date and place of marriage. I used that information as evidence to prove their marriage as well as their residence in Indian Territory in 1898. Below the image is the source citation answering the five questions above.

No. _____

MARRIAGE LICENSE

UNITED STATES OF AMERICA,)
Indian Territory,   ) SS.
Southern District.   )

TO ANY PERSON AUTHORIZED BY LAW TO SOLEMNIZE MARRIAGE-GREETING-

You are hereby commanded to solemnize the Rite and publish the Bans of Matrimony between Mr. _W. H. Shults_____ of _Elmore_____, in the Indian Territory, aged ___20___ years, and M_ _A. D. Rayston_ of _Elmore_ in the Indian Territory, aged _16_____ years, according to law, and do you officially sign and return this License to the parties herein named.

Witness my hand and official seal, this __7th___ day of __December__ A. D. _1898_____.

C. M. CAMPBELL,
Clerk of the United States Court.

By _____ Deputy

CERTIFICATE OF MARRIAGE

UNITED STATES OF AMERICA,)
Indian Territory,   ) SS.
Southern District.   )

I, A. B. Hughes_____ a _M. of G.___ do hereby certify that on the __11th__ day of_December_ A. D. 1898 I did duly and according to law, as commanded in the foregoing License, solemnize the Rite and publish the Bans of Matrimony between the parties therein named.

Witness my hand, this __11th__ day of __December__ A.D._1898_

A. B. Hughes_____

a __M. of G._____

My Credentials are recorded in the office of the Clerk of the United States Court in the Indian Territory, _____ Judicial Division, Book __A.__ Page _108_.

Filed and duly recorded, this__10th_day of _January_____ 1898

- - -   - - -

Certificate of True Copy

STATE OF OKLAHOMA)
) ss.
CARTER COUNTY   )

I, Willie Maddox, do certify that I have compared the foregoing copy of a Marriage License with the original now remaining on file in this office, and that the same is a full, true and exact copy thereof.

In witness whereof I have hereunto set my hand and affixed my official seal this ___6th___ day of __March_____ 1942X3

Willie Maddox Court Clerk

By _____
                    Deputy

Figure 5-4: Carter County, Oklahoma, copy of original marriage license and certificate, unpaginated, Shults-Rayston, 11 December 1898, Indian Territory Southern District, recorded 1943, County Court Clerk, Ardmore, Oklahoma.

Let's look at each part of the source citation to discover how it answers the five questions.

WHO?

This refers to either the author of the source, the creator (often a religious or government entity), or the informant. In the example below, Carter County, Oklahoma, is the government entity that issued the marriage license and certificate.

> **Carter County, Oklahoma,** copy of original marriage license and certificate, unpaginated, Shults-Rayston, 11 December 1898, Indian Territory Southern District, recorded 1943, County Court Clerk, Ardmore, Oklahoma.

WHAT?

If this is a published work such as a book, include the full title in italics. Websites are publications and should be italicized. The individual collections on a website are like chapters in a book and are set apart by quotation marks. If the source is not published, such as a personal history, use quotes around the title. If there is no title, describe the record, as shown here.

> Carter County, Oklahoma, **copy of original marriage license and certificate,** unpaginated, **Shults-Rayston,** 11 December 1898, Indian Territory Southern District, recorded 1943, County Court Clerk, Ardmore, Oklahoma.

WHEN?

Typically cite the year a book or microfilm was published; for a journal or magazine, add the month or season. For a website, add the access date. Because URLs change, the date could help to relocate the source using the *Internet Archive* Wayback Machine (http://archive.org/web/).This website has over 310 billion web pages saved from the past. If the source is unpublished, use the date it was created or the date of the event it reports. In some cases it might be necessary to include both, as shown below.

> Carter County, Oklahoma, copy of original marriage license and certificate, unpaginated, Shults-Rayston, **11 December 1898,** Indian Territory Southern District, **recorded 1943,** County Court Clerk, Ardmore, Oklahoma.

WHERE IN?

In a published source, this could be a volume or page number. In an online database, cite the image number, or any other way to explain to others how to find the source again. For a government certificate, this would be the document number.

If a source is not published, such as an unbound collection of documents, try to identify an order and describe it: "folio 3, page 25." In the example below, the marriage record has no document number nor do I know an order to describe it, so it is designated as "unpaginated."

> Carter County, Oklahoma, copy of original marriage license and certificate, **unpaginated,** Shults-Rayston, 11 December 1898, Indian Territory Southern District, recorded 1943, County Court Clerk, Ardmore, Oklahoma.

WHERE IS?

If the source is published, such as a book, this would be the publication location. If an unpublished source, such as a manuscript, letter, or document, name the location where the event took place and where the source is held.

Cite a website's URL. Because some URLs can be overly long, you can use the URL of the home page and include enough information to locate the source, such as the record collection, image number, or waypoints.

The example below shows the location of both the original marriage jurisdiction and where the marriage record is currently located.

> Carter County, Oklahoma, copy of original marriage license and certificate, unpaginated, Shults-Rayston, 11 December 1898, **Indian Territory Southern District**, recorded 1943, County Court Clerk, **Ardmore, Oklahoma.**

Layered Citations

What about a source that is now digitized and accessed through a website such as *FamilySearch* or *Ancestry*? Elizabeth Shown Mills coined the phrase "layered citations" to describe digital sources that contain digital images of original records.[6] Include both the physical source citation, then all of the digital source citation information, separating the two sections with a semicolon. A third section might be necessary if referencing the original microfilm reproduction of the source, as shown below.

> Mason County, Kentucky, "Marriage Bonds, Book 4, 1855-1857," Scott–Frank bond (2 September 1857); database and digital images, "Kentucky Marriages, 1797-1954," image 305, *FamilySearch* (https://familysearch.org : accessed 24 Jun 2012); citing FHL microfilm 281,846.

Citation Formats

Different citation formats are used depending upon the project. These include reference notes and source list entries.

Reference Notes

Reference notes are used to prove a fact such as the date or place of an event. The previous examples used this format, which would also be used when uploading a source to *FamilySearch* or *Ancestry.* Reference notes in a report can appear in two places.

- Footnotes: inserted throughout the article, referenced by number and appearing at the bottom of the page

- Endnotes: listed at the end of a chapter, article, or book

The following example shows a citation referencing a specific page in a book.

> Thaddeus Brockett Rice, *History of Greene County Georgia*, (Macon, Georgia: J.W. Burke Company, 1961), 394.

Shortened reference notes are used after the first full citation in a report, as shown below.

> Rice, *History of Greene County Georgia,* 394.

Source List Entries

Source list entries, often called bibliographies, are master lists of books, microfilm, or other sources we have consulted for our research. This is generally used at the end of a book or an article. See Appendix C for this book's source list. No specific mention is made of page numbers or other details. Authors are listed alphabetically by last name.

> Rice, Thaddeus Brockett. History of Greene County Georgia. Macon, Georgia : J.W. Burke Company, 1961.

Where do you create and record your source citation? On your research log! Once you have it saved there, you can use it anywhere that you share the source. I used the citation for the marriage certificate of William Shults and Dora Royston in several places: adding the marriage license and certificate to my Ancestral Quest database, uploading the document as a source on *FamilySearch* and *Ancestry*, and proving this marriage in my four-generation Royston report for accreditation.

YOUR TASK

As you follow your research plan, document each source searched with a source citation in your research log. Create each citation by answering the 5 questions: Who, What, When, Where in, Where is. Remember to be clear and consistent in formatting your citations. The best time to create your citation is the first time you look at the source. You may be tempted to skip this step, but don't. Taking the time to form the citation will force you to understand the source and help you make connections in your research.

TIPS
1. Make a citation template. Each time you form a good citation, add it to your template to be used again. See my example in Appendix A.
2. Create the citation the first time you look at a source.

To learn more about source citations, see the resources in Appendix C.

Notes for Chapter 5

1   "Dawes Rolls," Native American Heritage, *National Archives*
(https://www.archives.gov/research/native-americans/dawes/tutorial/intro.html : viewed 20
February 2018).

2   Elizabeth Shown Mills, *Evidence Explained: Citing History Sources from Artifacts to
Cyberspace.* Third Edition, (Baltimore: Genealogical Publishing Company, 2015).

3   Board for Certification of Genealogists, *Genealogy Standards,* 50th Anniversary Edition,
(Nashville and New York: Turner Publishing Company, 2014), 7.

4   Thomas W. Jones, *Mastering Genealogical Proof,* (Arlington, Virginia: National Genealogical
Society, 2013), 33-35. For an in-depth discussion of each question see Thomas W. Jones,
Mastering Genealogical Documentation, (Arlington, Virginia: National Genealogical Society, 2017).

5   Florida Department of Environmental Protection, "Armed Occupation Act of 1842, Florida
Land Permits," entry for Arthur Dillard, 26 July 1843, online database, *MyFlorida*
(http://tlhdslweb.dep.state.fl.us : accessed 9 February 2016), DM ID: 148527, Legacy Doc.
Locator: AOP3815.

6   Elizabeth Shown Mills, "Fundamentals of Citation," *Evidence Explained: Citing History Sources
from Artifacts to Cyberspace,* 3rd ed. (Baltimore: Genealogical Publishing Company, 2015), 2.33:
Citation Layers, 58.

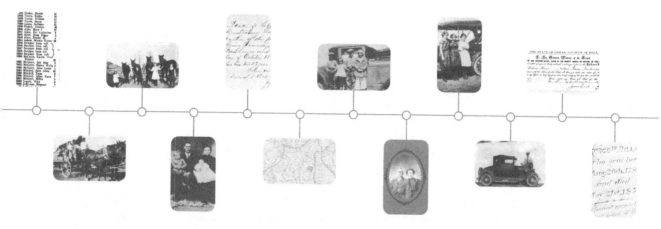

Research
Logs

6

Now that you've created your research plan from Chapter 4 and learned about source citations in Chapter 5, you're ready to learn how to put order into your work using a research log.

Family History work has come a long way in the last fifteen years. When I first started research in 2003, I kept all my documents in paper file folders, my family tree on PAF (Personal Ancestral File) and *Ancestry* was new.

Now we have the collaborative Family Tree on *FamilySearch*, record hinting, the ability to attach sources with a few clicks of our mouse, need I go on? Searching for our ancestors has never been easier, and organizing our research should be getting easier, right? Or do the many options available paralyze us and we do nothing?

I'm continually looking for ways to make better use of my research time. Efficiency is key with a limited amount of hours in the day. I don't want to spin my wheels looking for the same information over and over because I neglected to record my searches.

When I work on the collaborative *FamilySearch* Family Tree attaching record hints and doing easy searches for sources, I don't fill out a formal research log. Instead I use a simple research notebook to track the family I'm working on and my research questions.

What about those difficult research projects where I'm trying to break through brick walls in my family history? That is where a research log comes in handy. If I'm searching land records on microfilm or browsing an entire county in a census, I don't want to repeat that search and I need to record it somewhere safe.

A professional genealogist uses a research log to track searches both positive and negative. The client wants to know what records have been searched and the professional knows the value of a research log. You can also learn to track your searches and utilize this important tool.

If you're new to the world of family history research, a research log is where you simply record what you're looking for, where you looked, and what you found. Before the computer age, genealogists kept these logs by hand. Now we have multiple options, everything from a simple research notebook to complex computer programs. Each has a purpose.

Figure 6-1 is an example of a basic research log. If this looks too complicated, don't panic. I'm going to break it down for you and show you several different options for a research log so you can choose the best fit for you. I'll give you some tips about each option. You can pick one or try them all. It takes time and experience to find the perfect fit so be patient and keep trying!

Ancestor	Everett Cline			
Objective	What is the death date and place of Everett Cline, born 1875 in Missouri?			
Locality	Missouri			
Date of Search	Location / Call Number	Source	Results/ Comments	Document Number
24 Nov 2015	FindAGrave.com	Missouri cemeteries	Searched for all Clines in Missouri, born 1875; also Eve* Cline in Missouri, all years, NIL	

Figure 6-1: Basic research log

Basic Components of a Research Log

Some research logs may be simple and others complex. Most research logs have the following features in common:

- *Ancestor's name*: This can be an individual, a couple, or a family, depending on your objective. For example, on the *FamilySearch* Family Tree, I'm currently researching the family of Jacob Cline. One of his sons has "deceased" for his death information, and no spouse or children. Everett is a good candidate for a research project so I write:

    Everett Cline

- *Objective:* This is your research question. What do you want to find out? I have many questions about Everett, but I'm going to focus on one.

    What is the death date and place of Everett Cline, born 1875 in Missouri?

- *Locality*: Where are you going to look for the information? You'll be more efficient if you've narrowed down the place. Doing a global search for Everett Cline would bring up too many results and waste my time. The 1940 census record shows him living in Missouri, so I specify my locality as:

    Missouri

- *Date of Search:* Enter the actual day you performed the search. Online databases are occasionally updated, so it's possible that your record might show up at a later date.

    24 November 2015

- *Location / Call Number:* Where is the source located? If it is a book or microfilm, enter the call number and the library: Family History Library (FHL) 974.56 or FHL Film 80321. If it is a computer database, enter the title of the website:

    FindAGrave.com

- *Description of Source:* What is the title of the book or record set on the microfilm or database?

    Missouri cemeteries

- *Comments:* What variations of the name did you search and for what years? What specifics do you need to remember about the search? What were your results? My search of "Eve*" told the system to search all varieties of spellings. The search returned: "Evea, Evelyn, Everett, and Evert." None of them were correct, so I write "NIL" meaning not in location.

    Searched for all Clines in Missouri, born 1875; also Eve Cline in Missouri, all years, NIL*

- *Document Number:* You can use this column if you're preparing a client report and numbering the documents for an appendix or separate document file. You could also use this if you use a numbered filing system. I have no results from this source, so I leave it blank.

Types of Research Logs

Now that we've explored the basic components of a research log, let's look at different types of research logs: a paper research log, a research notebook, an electronic research log in a document table or spreadsheet format, or a web-based research log like *Research Ties*.

Paper Research Log

A printed research log is useful in visiting an archive that allows only pencil and paper for note-taking. If you choose to use paper research logs, file them alphabetically in a binder or file folders. When returning to the research for an individual or family, you'll quickly locate your log and easily pick up your research again.

The Research Notebook

I keep a research notebook with the date, what I hope to accomplish, and what I did accomplish during that research session. I use this simple method for working on the collaborative *FamilySearch* Family Tree or my *Ancestry* tree. Because the hints generated by the two websites make research as simple at times as attaching a source, I record that I "attached a marriage record for _____." I also note the ID numbers and names of any individuals I want to explore in the future so that when I come back to working on that tree I remember my thought process. Any records that I attach automatically have a source citation created by the website so no need to write it in my notebook unless there's a special circumstance I want to record.

The Electronic Research Log

When I'm working on a more involved research project I use an electronic research log. I've tried out the table feature of Microsoft Word and Google Docs and that works fine, but I've settled on Google Sheets as my preferred method. The ability to sort by various columns makes it easy for me to evaluate my findings. Everything I enter is automatically saved and I can refer to past versions if I make a major error. My research log is available on all my devices through my Google account: my smart phone, tablet, laptop, or any computer that has internet access.

I have created a research log template and whenever I start a new research project I make a copy of my template, rename it, and save it in the file of the individual I'm researching. My research log template has the research objective and localities I'm researching at the top. This helps me stay on track with my research and not head off in another direction.

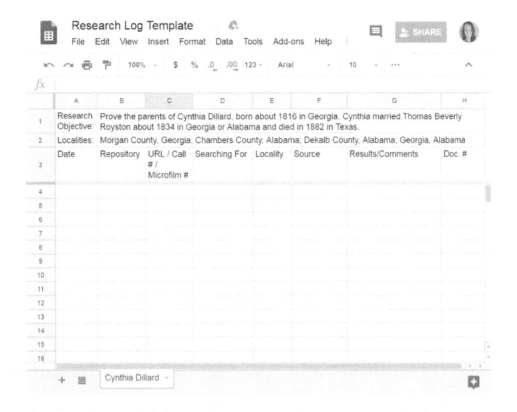

Figure 6-2: Screenshot of Google Sheets spreadsheet research log for Cynthia Dillard

In this example, my research objective is to prove the parents of Cynthia Dillard, born about 1816 in Georgia. My plan includes a search for her marriage record, census, probate, court, and land records for possible fathers in the areas that she lived. First on my list is locating a marriage record for Cynthia and Thomas Beverly Royston. I've searched previously for this marriage, but didn't record my searches, so I'll do it again. This time the search will be recorded on my research log. Here is a breakdown of the elements of my electronic research log and how I fill them out.

- Date: *29 Aug 2017*

  Because you'll be saving this research log and may not return to it for a few months or even years, it is important to note the date you performed the research. As stated previously, some databases are updated periodically and need to be rechecked at a later date.

- Repository: *Ancestry*

  The repository is the library, archive, or other physical location that holds the source. It might even be your own files if it is a letter or photocopy you've inherited. What about a website? Technically the internet is the repository and individual websites are publications. I use the website name here because it is more descriptive.

- URL/Call#/Microfilm#: *http://search.ancestry.com/search/db.aspx?dbid=7839*

  In this column I copy and paste the URL from the website. Because *Ancestry's* URLs can be really long, I often use the BITLINKS website (https://app.bitly.com) to create much shorter links for my research logs. If I'm researching at a library or archive, this is where the unique call number or microfilm number goes.

- Searching for: *Marriage of Cynthia Dillard and Thomas Beverly Royston*

  This column tells me exactly what I am looking for. With a spreadsheet, I can sort all of my marriage searches, or all of the census searches. It helps me organize as I'm researching if I am careful to be consistent with my entries always listing the source type first.

- Locality: *Georgia*

  Be specific here. If you're checking a general statewide index, just the state is fine. But, if you're looking in a specific county or township, list that. Using descending place names: state, county, city will let allow you to sort and view the locations you have searched.

- Source: *"Georgia Marriages, 1699-1944," search for Dillard-Royston marriage, Ancestry (http:ancestry.com : accessed 29 August 2017).*

  This is where I create the source citation. Because I didn't find anything in this database, I don't have any specifics of a marriage to list, so I just name the database, where it is located and the date I checked it.

- Results/Comments: *NIL, found other Dillard marriages 1833-1835 in Oglethorpe, Jefferson, Bibb, Stewart, Telfair counties; not all Georgia counties are included in this database and not all of the counties that are listed have marriage records for the correct time frame.*

  For a negative search I use NIL, recognized as "not in location." I also add comments that explain why a record might not have been found. If I did locate the record, I would detail all of the information in this column. At a glance I can see exactly what I found. Using the copy and paste function makes it easy.

  That's all there is to it. As I work down my research plan I add each search. In the midst of my research if I discover another website to search for the marriage record I enter it into my research log as well. It holds every site that I've searched. It takes some discipline to start using a research log, but once you start you'll love the feeling of accomplishment. An hour of research where you didn't find anything doesn't feel wasted. Instead you have all of your searches entered and you've discovered that you need to rethink your hypothesis.

In the case of Cynthia Dillard and her marriage, I found a possible father, George W. Dillard. The county in Georgia where he was living in the 1830s had a courthouse fire that destroyed the marriage records for that era; possibly the reason I can't locate a marriage for Cynthia and Thomas Royston.

Research Ties

Another type of research log that I use is a website named *Research Ties* (http://researchties.com). I use this online research log when extracting multiple results from the same source. This is especially helpful when searching all entries of a surname from a microfilm. You may not know how everyone is related, but while you're looking at that film you might as well record the information to save time in the future.

With *Research Ties* I can enter in the source information once, and then add each result as I find it with specific details. In the screenshot below, I've used the program to log all the entries for the surname Royston found in the Chambers County deed book index. The source information is repeated and I just added the specifics. This particular index had entries for about 20 Royston individuals. *Research Ties* made the task of recording each entry fast and easy.

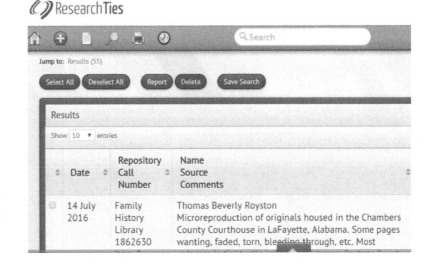

Figure 6-3: Screenshot of Research Ties

I can export all the information that I've added either as a PDF or spreadsheet. Entries for the individual I'm specifically researching can then be copied and pasted into my Google Sheet research log. When I begin researching another individual, the information is there waiting for me.

Research Ties has a nice feature that allows you to upload images of the sources you locate and the URLs so that you can easily view them straight from the program. It syncs with *FamilySearch* so you can quickly create a new source for your ancestor using the information that you've already entered.

YOUR TASK

Following your research plan, search each source, recording the search in a research log. Try using the research log template in Appendix A, or create your own. Appendix B contains two sample research logs to give you ideas on recording different types of searches. Formulate a source citation as you look at each source and record the results. Start a research notebook to track your research sessions.

As you search, a helpful practice is to write your research report as you go. You can do this in your Research Project Document. Describe the source, what information it holds, and your analysis. This will become the body of your report. Often it is easier to write about the source as you are researching. If you choose this method, read Chapter 7 for ideas on how to write up your research.

Another option is to complete your research, then write your report. Try both options and decide what works best for you. Because I need to be as efficient as possible, I write as I go. When my research time is up, I go back and reorganize the report to make the most sense for a client.

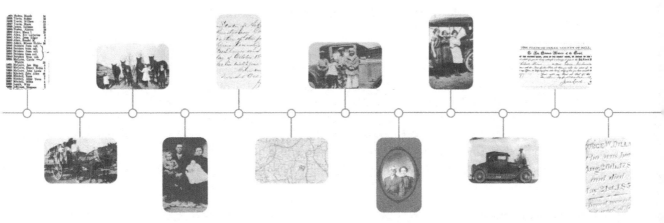

Report Writing

What do you do when you come to the end of your research project? How do you record your results, proof, and ideas for future research? A professional finalizes a research project by writing a report detailing what records were searched, what was found, what the evidence proved, and what to search next. You don't necessarily need to write a full-scale report every time you finish a particular project, but you do need to write something! Several options make this a fun and rewarding task and one you'll thank yourself for in the future.

Why Write up Your Results?

As you research you analyze your findings. You create hypotheses and correlate the evidence, whether you know it or not. The simple act of looking at a census and thinking, "great grandpa's parents are listed as born in Virginia so I need to look there for records" is analysis. If you don't record your thoughts and ideas, when you come back to researching this family, you'll waste time going through your findings again.

The process of writing helps your brain form connections. Having to concisely describe a record forces you to look at it more closely and helps you find all of the clues it holds. Often one of those clues will lead to another piece of evidence to prove your hypothesis.

Having your research written up in a simple proof summary makes it very easy to share with family members. You don't have to take the time to write an email explaining your thought process. You can copy the proof summary out of your files and send it off in a matter of minutes. You can also easily upload it to your online tree lending credibility to your research.

Who Is Your Reader?

Before you write, decide who will be reading your research findings. Will you be sharing a proof summary on the *FamilySearch* Family Tree or another online tree? Are you recording your personal research notes? Are you writing a formal research report for a client? You might be writing an article or family history book for publication. Keeping your audience in mind will help you write in the appropriate style. Be clear and accurate in any case.

Once you've determined your reader, decide what voice to use. Be consistent throughout your writing with first, second, or third person voice. Not sure what those terms mean? Here is a brief example of each.

Write in **first person** if you're sending an email to a family member or fellow researcher describing what you found.

> EXAMPLE: I discovered the marriage record of Florence Creer. She was married . . .

Using the **second person** voice works well for an informal report or email to a client.

> EXAMPLE: Your grandmother, Florence Matilda Creer, married Edward Raymond Kelsey on . . .

Writing in **third person** is more formal and appropriate for family history books, proof summaries, journal articles, and research reports.

> EXAMPLE: Florence Creer married Edward Raymond Kelsey on. . .

TIP: Write first, then go through the rough draft and make the needed changes so the voice is consistent throughout.

How to Start?

Begin by writing a report. This will help you make sense of your research. The report can be for your own research notes or for a client. As you add to your research, the report might become the basis of a proof summary or proof argument that could be published on the *FamilySearch* Family Tree or another online tree. You could submit your work to a genealogical journal or incorporate it into a family history book.

If you have a writing phobia left over from school days, this may not seem like a very fun part of your research. But as you start writing up your research, analyzing the records, and making connections, you'll discover that it's extremely helpful.

Preparing the four-generation report for accreditation taught me the value of each element of a genealogy research report. Knowing what to write provides a solid basis for the report. To illustrate, I'll use portions of a research report that became a proof argument proving the parents of Mary, wife of Ignatius Bryan of Hardin County, Kentucky. See Appendix B for the finished proof argument. In my work as a professional genealogist, I write 2-3 research reports a month and having a set template greatly facilitates the process.

Elements of a Research Report

- Research Objective
- Background Information
- Body of the Report
- Conclusion
- Summary of Evidence
- Future Research Suggestions

Research Objective

If you're using the Research Project Document template, then you've already written your research objective and tweaked it as needed. As you learned in Chapter One, your objective could focus on identifying an individual, proving a relationship, or discovering an action. It needs to clearly state the focus of your research project and contain key identifiers of names, dates, and places of the main ancestor.

The objective for the sample research project was focused on proving a relationship and clearly identifies Mary Ann.

> EXAMPLE: The objective of this report was to prove the parents of Mary Ann, wife of Ignatius Bryan, resident of Hardin County, Kentucky, in 1800. Mary Ann was born about 1782 and died after 1835.

Background Information

Begin with some background on the individual or family. You could include what had previously been known, including any family myths. A little about the time period or location might be helpful. Maybe the courthouse burned so records were scarce for the family. Was there a major event like the Civil War, Depression, or Dust Bowl that the family lived through? Include whatever you feel sets the stage for your findings. Be creative and think of what might catch the interest of your audience. Think of what will help your reader better understand the research you're going to present.

> EXAMPLE: Determining the maiden name and parents of a woman born in the late 1700s is one of the most difficult genealogical undertakings. Because women were

not mentioned in many of the records of the era, few sources exist to prove their parentage. Combine that with record loss and the task becomes even more difficult. Descendants of Ignatius Bryan, born about 1775 in Maryland and died 1803 in Hardin County, Kentucky, have long wondered about the origins of his wife Mary.

Body of the Report - Organization

The body of your writing can have several subheadings or even chapters if your report becomes a book. You might have sections discussing the census records, land records, the pension file, or other documents. Arranging the research chronologically or geographically could make sense if following the migration of an individual. Perhaps you're researching men of the same name in a location; in that case each man could have his own subheading.

The beauty of our modern technology is that you can rearrange your sections at the end to make the most sense. You might only have a few sections or many depending on the extent of your research. In the example, you'll see that the subheadings are record types and not arranged chronologically. This type of research report works well if you write as you research. As you research a record set, you would write about what you found or didn't find.

> *EXAMPLE: Organization by Record Types*
> - *Land Records of Hardin County*
> - *Marriage Records*
> - *Probate of the Estate of Ignatius Bryan*
> - *County Histories and Church Records*
> - *1835 Parish Census*
> - *1799 Layton - French Marriage*
> - *1815 Will of James French*

For more ideas on how to use subheadings in your report, read articles in the *National Genealogical Society Quarterly* or another genealogical publication. Note the topics and organization flow.

Body of the Report - Evidence Analysis

As you discuss the research, explain the reasoning behind searching a certain record type. Your reader may not know why a census was taken or why you'd search land records. A professional genealogist strives to educate the client through the report and you can do the same. Help your reader understand the importance of the record type and what information could be found.

> *EXAMPLE: Marriage records are some of the earliest vital records available and are generally recorded in the county of the marriage. A marriage record will list the bride's maiden name if it's her first marriage and can have her father's name as well, so that would be the first place to search for Mary's maiden name and possibly father.*

Include negative as well as positive searches. In order to perform reasonably exhaustive research, you must show that you performed the necessary research. Give an explanation for the absence of the record and ideas for future research that might locate the record. In the example, the previous paragraph discussed the two counties where Mary and Ignatius had lived and could have been married. The source citation detailed the collections and indexes searched.

EXAMPLE: A thorough search of both locations in online collections and published marriage indexes were searched but no record was found for Mary and Ignatius in either county. It would seem that the marriage took place in another location, or quite possibly the marriage record was lost. Tracing the couple beyond Kentucky might result in a marriage record, if they were married before their migration to the newly formed state.

Body of the Report - Presenting Information

When presenting complicated information used as evidence, consider ways to clarify the details. Use bullet points, bold print, and other formatting tools to be clear. The example below shows the presentation of a deed abstract that lists family relationships.

Because name variations will occur in original documents, when abstracting, spell the names as they are used in the document. In the following example of an abstract included in a report, "Bryan" is spelled as "Bryant" and "Bryan." The abstract reflects the actual spelling in the original deed. Throughout the rest of the report use one consistent spelling of the name. When quoting from an original record, use quotation marks around the actual spelling of the name in the document. Another method to clarify name variations is to add the usual spelling of the name in brackets after the spelling on the original record. For example: Barton Rheuby [Roby].

EXAMPLE:

On 15 August 1826, the heirs of Ignatius Bryant deeded the 85 acres of land on the Rolling Fork to James Crawford. An abstract of the deed gives valuable genealogical information for the family of Ignatius Bryan and Mary listing three children and their spouses.

Indenture made 15 August 1826

Hardin County, Kentucky [Bullet points inserted for clarity and children of Ignatius and Mary Bryant bolded]
- *George Atwood & Mary his wife late Mary Bryan Widow of Ignatius Bryant deceased*
- *William Norris & Elizabeth his wife late **Elizabeth Bryant***
- *John Atwood Medly and Elen his wife late **Elen Bryant***
- ***Benjamin Bryant** and Treacy his wife*

Heirs of Ignatius Bryan deceased of Hardin County, (except Norris & wife of Bullitt) and James Crawford of Hardin County for consideration of $85 the *tract of land situated on the waters of the Rolling Fork near the mouth of Clear Creek containing 85 acres. Being the same land conveyed by James Murdough to Ignatius Bryan, 6 November 1800, recorded in Deed Book B, page 191. The said Ignatius Bryan having departed this life intestate the same hath ascended to his heirs the parties of the first part to this indenture.*

Help the reader understand the information by putting it in context, explaining any terms, laws or history that has bearing on the situation. Present the evidence that supports the conclusion.

EXAMPLE: The 1826 deed states that Ignatius Bryan died intestate, meaning that he left no will. In this circumstance, if there was property involved, the probate proceedings were set in motion. At a county court for Hardin County, Kentucky, on Monday, the 19th of September 1803, "Mary Brian & Barton Rheuby" applied for and were granted the right of administration of the estate of "Ignatius Brian," deceased. Together with "James French and Isaac Irwin," they gave bond of £200 with securities for the faithful performance of administration.

Posing a question can break up the text and add focus to the next portion of the report.

EXAMPLE: Generally, those applying for administration of an intestate estate are the surviving spouse and next of kin, so what relationship to Mary Bryan are Barton Rheuby [Roby], James French, or Isaac Irwin?

You can then answer the question, analyzing the information and explaining how it provides evidence to prove your conclusion.

EXAMPLE: Examining further probate records showed that Barton Roby acted as administrator for all further actions for the estate of Ignatius Bryan and also for the estate of James French. He received payment for his service and appears throughout the court records administering various estates. He seems to have been the family attorney.

Research proved that Isaac Irwin was born in 1774 and would have been about age 30 when he gave security for the estate bond, too young to be Mary's father. He was also named in another court order with Ignatius in 1802 as potential appraisers of an estate. Hence they were probably just friends. There is no indication that he is related to Mary Bryan. James French therefore seems the most likely candidate for Mary's father.

Adding information on the history and laws throughout the report keeps the reader's interest as well as helping to support the evidence.

EXAMPLE: Who was the James French mentioned in the probate of Ignatius Bryan? County histories became popular in the late 1800s and can be valuable sources of information about early settlers in an area. In the 1887 publication of "The Centenary of Catholicity in Kentucky," author Benedict Joseph Webb discusses early Catholic settlers in the area of Hardin County, Kentucky. "The first church station at this point was the house of one James French where mass was said by Father Badin as early as the years 1804-5."

Body of the Report - Source Citations

To give your report credibility, you'll need to use source citations for each genealogical statement. Save time by creating the source citation in your research log when you first view the source, not only will it help you to understand the source and the information it contains, it will help to organize your research. Create a template by keeping a spreadsheet of citations commonly used – census, *FindAGrave*, books, etc.

Once the source citation is created in your research log, it can be copied and pasted into your report. Using the format features of your word processing program makes it simple. CTRL+ ALT+ F is the shortcut for adding a footnote.

Source Citation Tips:

- Create a source citation in the research log the first time a source is searched.
- Use complete source citations throughout the report until finished.
- Shorten subsequent citations only when satisfied with the flow of the report.
- Create a citation template sheet for commonly used records.

For a client report, include references to the documents in the citations. Add the documents to an appendix or add to a separate document file. Label documents with the citation so that the reader knows the important details and how to locate that document.

The 1835 Barrens Parish Census shown below holds valuable information relating to the research project, so it is included in the document folder. Notice the citation and document number attached to the record.

1835 Barrens Parish Census

Comm.	Confir.	Family Members	Age
		# 5. continued	
x	x	**Mary RINEY**, wife, daughter of Thomas, years	
x	x	**LAYTON**, John, son, 25 years	
x	x	Appollinaris, son, 18 years	
x	x	Christina, daughter, 17 years	
x	x	Felix Joseph, son 14 years	
x	x	Andrew, son 21 years	
x	x	Marcellus, son, 10 years	
		# 6.	
x	x	**John LAYTON, Sr.**, son of John, 56 years	
x	x	**Monica FRENCH**, wife, daughter of James, 50 years	
x	x	**LAYTON**, Louis, son, 24 years	
x	x	Augustine, son, 20 years	
x	x	Mary, daughter, 18 years	
x	x	Amatus Alexander, 13 years	
x	x	**Mary Ann FRENCH**, sister of Monica, 52 years	
		# 7.	
x	x	**Ignatius LAYTON**, son of John, 61 years	
x	x	**Elizabeth MILES**, wife, daughter of Joseph, 53 years, deceased	
x	x	**LAYTON**, Bede, son, 24 years	
x	x	Rosa Ann, daughter, 23 years	
x	x	Felix Augustine, son, 16 years	
x	x	Vincent, son, 14 years	
x	x	Matilda Amelia, daughter, 12 years	
		Ann Elizabeth, daughter, 8 years	
x		_____, Peter, servant, with the family of Simon DUVALL, 34 years	

Figure 7-1: 1835 Barrens Parish Census, Church of the Assumption of the Blessed Mary, John Layton, Sr household, Perry County, Missouri Historical Society, image of original; originally shared 15 November 2009 on Ancestry.com by mikeELBB. Document 1

Tips for Documents:

- Saving documents throughout the project enables you to quickly view the document and saves time by not having to look it up again and download at the end of the project.
- Create a document folder for the research project at the beginning of research.
- Download each document and give it a descriptive file name: 1835_Census_Mary-French_Perry-County_MO.
- Assemble documents at the end of the project, following the order in the report.
- Create a PDF of the document images by inserting them into a Google or Word Document. Copy the source citation from the report and paste it under each image. Once all images are in the document, download it as a PDF.

Body of the Report - Make Connections

As you write your report, you'll need to discuss possibilities that the records suggest and make connections. Help the reader understand why you came to a certain conclusion. This example refers to the 1835 Barrens Parish Census, Document 1 shown in Figure 7-1.

> *EXAMPLE: If Mary Ann French is the sister of Monica, her father would also be James French. Why are the women listed by their maiden names? It appears from the rest of the listings on the page that this was careful record keeping on the part of the parish. All women on the page are listed by their maiden names and their father is identified.*

Body of the Report - Tables, Maps & Charts

Use tables, maps, and charts to help your reader make sense of the evidence you're sharing. A simple table can illustrate your point very effectively. A map could show the proximity of two families or the land. Charting the family's migration might illustrate it better than an entire paragraph of writing.

Tables are very useful for census information, showing land records, indirect evidence, etc. In the following example, the table assembles the evidence that connects Mary French with her sister Monica and parents, James and Susan.

Evidence connecting Mary with sister Monica and parents, James and Susanna

RECORD	DATE	PLACE	DETAILS
Marriage of Monarca French and John Layton	1799	Hardin County, Kentucky	Names parents James French and Susanna
Probate of Ignatius Bryan	1803	Hardin County, Kentucky	James French provided security for bond with Mary Bryan, widow of Ignatius Bryan
Will of James French	1815	Hardin County, Kentucky	Names daughter, Mary French, and wife, Susanna
Barrens Parish Census	1835	Perry County, Missouri	Names James French, father of Monica French and Mary Ann French, sister of Monica French (women listed by maiden name in household of John Layton)

Figure 7-2: Sample table included in a report showing a summary of evidence.

Summary of Findings and Conclusion

You'll want to summarize your findings with a good solid conclusion. Create bullet points of key items using action verbs. Simply and clearly lead your reader through the research again.

EXAMPLE:

The objective of this research project was to determine the parents of Mary, wife of Ignatius Bryan. Numerous original records were located that provided information on the couple. Although records listing females are not frequent in the early 1800's, Mary does appear in several of those records. Land, tax, probate, and a second marriage record established her as a resident of Hardin County, Kentucky.

- *Land and tax records for both Ignatius and Mary Bryan show the purchase, taxation, and sale of 85 acres on the Rolling Fork water course of Hardin County, Kentucky.*
- *Probate records for the estate of Ignatius Bryan detail key actions in the administration of the estate. Importantly, the initial motion lists James French with Mary as putting up bond for the administration of the estate.*
- *Marriage records for Hardin and Nelson Counties do not show a marriage for Ignatius Bryan and Mary, but the 1813 marriage of Mary Bryan and George Atwood in Hardin County was located.*

Several important sources provided indirect evidence for Mary, daughter of James French of Hardin County, Kentucky.

- *The 1815 will of James French of Hardin County names his wife Susanna and daughter, Mary.*
- *The 1799 marriage record of Mary's sister, Monica French, in Hardin County names parents James and Susanna.*
- *The 1835 Barren Parish census of Perry County, Missouri, shows Mary Ann French, the sister of Monica French, in the household of John Layton, Monica's husband. Monica's father is listed as James French, and thus indirectly proves James French as the father of Mary.*

Future Research Suggestions

Whether you're writing a client report or a research report for yourself, always end with recommendations for future research. When you return to this particular individual or family, you'll know exactly where to begin again. If you're writing for a client, you will be giving him a reason to hire you in the future.

EXAMPLE: Suggestions for Future Research
- *Search for the marriage record of Ignatius Bryan and Mary in Washington County, Kentucky (where Mary's sister Monica was married): 1795-1800.*
- *Search for a marriage record for Ignatius Bryan and Mary in St. Mary's County, Maryland: 1795-1800.*
- *Search probate records in Hardin County, Kentucky, for George Atwood: 1813-1826.*
- *Search probate records in Hardin County, Kentucky, for Isaac and James Irwin: 1810-1830, to see if they were relatives or just associates.*
- *Search probate records in Perry County, Missouri for John Layton: 1835-1860*
- *Search 1850 census for John Layton and wife, Monica French Layton in Perry County, Missouri.*
- *Search for a marriage record for Mary Atwood in Perry County, Missouri: 1835-1860.*

That's it! Your research report is done - or almost. Perhaps the most important aspect of writing is to proofread zealously. Look for grammar and punctuation, then edit for wording. Also edit for analysis. A good practice is to print out the report, then use a red pen to make changes. Let your writing sit at least overnight before returning to edit. Develop your own style – read other articles, books, reports to see how others write up their research but trust in your own style.

Tips for Excellent Writing

- After writing the rough draft, go back through and circle the passive "be" verbs: is, are, and were.
- Rewrite the sentences using action verbs when possible.

- Keep a list of good action verbs to use: determined, revealed, searched, discovered, found, etc.
- Eliminate trite phrases and take out excess words.
- Be consistent with the voice - first, second, or third person.
- Proofread for grammar, spelling, and punctuation.
- Edit for content.
- Did you analyze each source thoroughly?
- Did you explain the reasoning behind searching a particular source?
- Did you present the evidence clearly?
- Set aside your writing for a few days, then look at it with fresh eyes.
- Print out a paper copy of your report and edit with a red pen.
- Develop your own style.

YOUR TASK

Try your hand at writing up your research. Whether or not you were able to prove your hypothesis, writing a report will help you make connections in your research. You'll know what to do for your next research project and using your future research suggestions, you'll easily be able to formulate a research plan. If you did solve your mystery and prove your hypothesis, you can start over again with a new research objective.

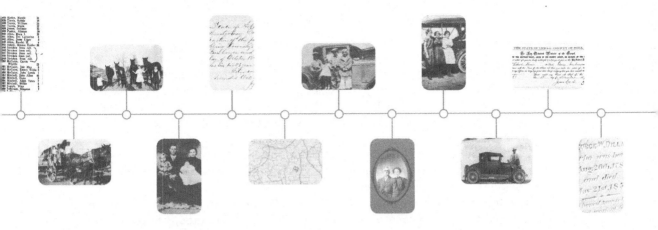

What's Next

8

Congratulations! You've worked your way through this book and you've learned how to take a research question from start to finish. You may have solved a long-standing family mystery or perhaps your research came up dry. Don't despair. Negative results simply point you to rethinking your hypothesis.

Begin with your list of future research ideas. Your next step is to repeat the research process by taking those ideas and forming a new objective and research plan. Evaluate what you found. If you discovered the father of your ancestor, now you can research his children, or his origins. Every discovery leads to new avenues of research.

You'll want to continue your genealogy education, both in learning about the records, locality, and research methods. Take advantage of the many learning opportunities available through books, webinars, conferences, institutes, blog posts, and journals. Soak up tips from the experts. Your genealogy journey is just beginning.

As you learn, return to difficult research problems. Possibly a new record set will be available or you've discovered another way to approach your brick wall. Reviewing your past research will be much easier. You'll refer to the timeline analysis, research log, research report, and future research suggestions. Without wasting time, you'll be able to pick up the research and start again.

Now that you've learned the secrets of professional genealogy, what's holding you back? Keep practicing the research process. You'll learn from each project and you will leave a legacy of solid research for future generations.

Interested in learning more about the Research Like a Pro Study Groups? Go to our website, http://familylocket.com/services/research-like-a-pro-study-group/ to read more. Subscribe to the FamilyLocket newsletter to receive advance notice of new groups and ways you can participate. Go to http://familylocket.com/sign-up/ to subscribe. Thanks for joining me in the effort to be a better genealogist every day!

Diana

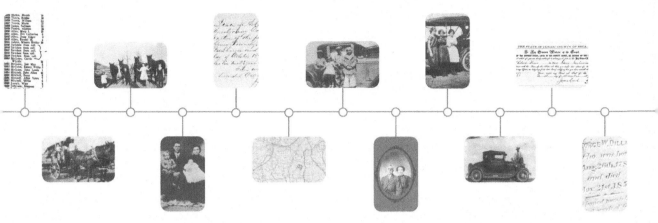

APPENDIX A
Templates

To aid your quest to research like a pro, several templates are included here for your use as you complete each step of the research process. You can download electronic versions of these forms online at http://familylocket.com/RLP

- **Research Project Template**: Follow the steps outlined in each section as you plan and carry out your research project.
- **Timeline Analysis Template:** Fill in the information suggested in each column. Add events and columns as needed for your specific project.
- **Locality Guide Template:** Create your own locality guide by researching the main location of your project and adding the information for the suggested headings.
- **Research Log Template:** Track your searches and record your source citations in one place.
- **Source Citation Template:** View examples of source citations for major record types and add citations for the sources you commonly use.

Research Project Template

Objective

Complete name and key identifiers: birth dates, places, or residence. Does this question ask for relationship, identity or activity?

Summary of Known Facts

Chronological table of known facts and analysis of sources

Background Information

Create a quick reference guide for the locality or check the FamilySearch Wiki for information on available records, maps, gazetteer, historical facts, etc.

Working Hypothesis

Methodology, clues from the known facts

Identified Sources

Use locality guide to identify available sources to search

Prioritized Research Strategy

Five best sources most likely to answer the research question, specific details

Findings & Analysis - Research Report

State the purpose for searching the records and what valuable information was expected to be found. What does this mean to the objective? What is the significance of key findings? Discuss whether information is primary (eyewitness) or secondary (hearsay) or indeterminable. Discuss sources -whether authored work, original or derivative. Discuss evidence, whether direct, indirect, or negative. Address conflicting evidence. Add clues from records located to future research immediately.

Conclusion

Address the research objective, summarize the research results with bullet points, state how the objective was or was not met

Suggestions for Future Research

Specific records with dates and places, all items from research plan not researched, all items suggested by the research

Results Summary

Create at the end of the project, use action verbs, include what you analyzed, searched, found, etc. You may want to put this first in the report.

Timeline Analysis Template

Objective:						
Event	Date	Place	Source	**Source** Original / Derivative / Authored	**Information** Primary / Secondary / Undetermined	**Evidence** Direct / Indirect / Negative	Notes
Birth							
Baptism							
Residence							
Marriage							
Birth of child							
Military							
Birth of child							
Immigration							

Marriage of child							
Taxation							
Land deed							
Land sale							
Death of spouse							
Death							
Burial							
Probate administration							
Death of child							
[add or remove events as needed]							

Locality Guide Template

Background

Quick Facts

Capital, dates of county formation, state formation, type of land (state land vs. federal land) when registration of births and deaths began, etc.

Online Research Guides

Links to the FamilySearch wiki guide about the locality and other guides online

Geography and Maps

Boundary changes, neighboring counties/towns, links to gazetteers, historical maps

Timeline of Major Events

Timeline of the area including major government changes and events

History

History of settlement, links to history articles and books about the locality, major periods, military engagements, etc.

Migration Routes

Main migration routes through the locality; links to maps and articles about migration

Law and Government

Books, articles, and blog posts about the laws and statues of the locality – Google Books, Archive.org, The Legal Genealogist blog, library websites, etc.

Libraries and Archives

Repositories, courthouses, public libraries, genealogical libraries; located within the locality or specific to the locality; research aids published by the libraries and archives; "America's Best Genealogy Resource Centers" by William Dollarhide and Ronald A. Bremer identifies the top 10 in each state and includes contact information and a summary of the record collections.

Genealogical Societies and Publications

Genealogical societies, their websites and publications

Record Loss

Record sets lost due to courthouse fires, floods, etc.; record substitutes, if any

Local History

Local history books, county histories, town histories, etc.

Reference Books

Additional books pertaining to research in this locality

Record Collections

General Collections

Catalog listings for the locality at Ancestry.com, FamilySearch.org, MyHeritage.com, FindMyPast.com, etc.

Bible Records and Compiled Genealogies

Links to websites that have Bible records for the locality and other family Bible collections

Cemetery Records

Links to cemetery records in the locality

Census Records and Substitutes

Links to different types of censuses: federal, state, town, colonial, territorial, census substitutes, etc.

Church Records

Various denominations and where their records are kept

Court Records

Court record collections and descriptions of what they contain

Ethnic Records

Various ethnic groups in the locality and the unique record collections available about them

Immigration and Naturalization

Immigration in the locality and associated record collections

Land Records

Collections about land grants, patents, bounty lands, and other land records

Legislative Records

Collections about legislative records, if applicable, i.e. Virginia's legislative petitions

Military Records

Colonial, militia, war, regimental histories, etc.

Newspapers and Directories

List of newspapers in the locality and the dates they were published; links to digitized newspapers and availability of non-digitized newspapers

Probate Records

Record collections about wills, probate, estate files, etc.

Vital Records (Birth, Marriage, Death)

Links to vital record collections including birth, marriage, and death records; list of Gretna Greens if applicable

Tax Records

Tax record collections, personal property tax, land tax, etc.

[Add additional sections depending on your locality and what types of records exist]

Research Log Template

Objective:							
Localities:							
Date	Repository / Website	URL / Call # / Microfilm #	Searching For	Locality	Source	Results/Comments	

Source Citation Templates

Category	Type	Citation	Short Form
Cemetery	Find a Grave	*Find A Grave*, database with images (http://www.findagrave.com : accessed 4 April 2016), memorial 57822585, Charles Leslie Shults, (1904-1996), gravestone photographed by D.A.R., member 46604592.	*Find A Grave*, memorial 13395707, R.C. Royston (1948-1915), gravestone photograph by Debbie.
Census	1900 Census	1900 U.S. Census, Chickasaw Nation, Indian Territory, population schedule, township 2 S. range 5W, enumeration district (ED) 166, sheet 24B (penned), dwelling 378, family 393, W.H. Shults; digital image, *Ancestry*, (http://www.ancestry.com accessed 17 February 2016); citing NARA microfilm publication T623, roll 1849.	1900 U.S. Census, Chickasaw Nation, Indian Terr., pop. sch., ED 166, sheet 24B, (penned), fam. 396, Robert C Royston household.
Census	1880 Census	1880 U.S. Census, Johnson County, Texas, population schedule, precinct 3, enumeration district (ED) 83, sheet 293C (stamped), p. 14 (penned), dwelling 161, family 166, Robt Royston household; digital image, *FamilySearch* (https://familysearch.org : accessed 28 April 2016); citing NARA microfilm publication T9, roll 1313.	1880 U.S. Census, Johnson Co., Texas, pop. sch., ED 83, p. 14 (penned), dwell. 161, fam. 166, Robt Royston household.
Census	1870 Census	1870 U.S. Census, Chambers County, Alabama, population schedule, Beat No 2, p. 4 (penned), p. 22 (stamped), dwelling 24, family 24, Cynthia Royston household; digital image, *Ancestry* (http://www.ancestry.com : accessed 26 April 2016); citing NARA microfilm publication M593, roll 6.	1870 U.S. Census, Chambers Co. Alabama, pop. sch., p. 4 (penned), p.22 (stamped), dwell. 24, fam. 24, Cynthia Royston household.
Census	1860 Census	1860 U.S. Census, Chambers County, Alabama, population schedule, Northern Division, Milltown Post Office, p. 130 (penned), dwelling 915, family 895, Thomas B. Royston household; digital image, *FamilySearch* (https://familysearch.org : accessed 29 April 2016); citing NARA microfilm publication M653.	1860 U.S. Census, Chambers Co., Alabama, pop. sch., p. 130 (penned), dwell. 915, fam. 895, Thomas B. Royston household.

Census	1850 Census	1850 U.S. Census, Chambers County, Alabama, population schedule, 19th District, p. 318 (stamped), dwelling 749, family 749, Thomas B. Royston household; digital image, *Ancestry* (http://www.ancestry.com : accessed 17 August 2016); citing NARA microfilm publication M432, roll 2.	1850 U.S. Census, Chambers Co., Alabama, pop. sch., p. 318 (stamped), dwell. 749, fam. 749, Thomas B. Royston household.
Census	1840 Census	1840 U.S. Census, DeKalb County, Alabama, population schedule, Northern District, S.C. Newnan, p. 7 (penned), line 31, F.B. Royston household; digital image, *Ancestry* (http://www.ancestry.com : accessed 27 September 2016); citing NARA microfilm publication M704, roll 4.	1840 U.S. Census, DeKalb Co., Alabama, pop. sch., Newnan, p. 7 (penned), line 31, F.B. Royston household.
Death	Death Certificate - image online	Texas State Board of Health, death certificate, Dora Algia Shults, Reg. Dis. No 3184, Registered No. 476. Lubbock, 1925; digital image, "Texas, Death Certificates, 1903–1982," database, *Ancestry*, Lubbock 1925, Jan–Mar image 11 (http://search.ancestry.com: accessed 20 February 2016).	Texas death certificate no. 3184-476, 1925, Dora Algia Shults.
General	Document provided by another party	Polly Royston vs John Royston, Divorce Petition, Greene County, Georgia, Superior Court, September Term 1814, No. 11, p. 435; photocopy provided by Betty Royston Brooks [ADDRESS FOR PRIVATE USE,] Royston, Georgia, 2016.	Polly Royston vs John Royston, Divorce Petition, Greene County, Georgia, Superior Court, September Term 1814, No. 11, p. 435.
General	DNA	Donald Robert Royston, "The Results of the 46 Marker DNA Male Y Chromosome Tests," 24 October 2009 (revised 21 June 2010), report prepared for author [ADDRESS FOR PRIVATE USE,] privately held by author, 2017.	Donald R. Royston, The Results of the 46 Marker DNA Male Y Chromosome Tests," 21 Jun 2010, Summerfield, Florida.
General	Personal History	Effie Lorain Shults Bassett, "Memories," personal history p.1 -5, between 1971 and 2000, photocopy of typescript from Bobby Gene Shults, [ADDRESS FOR PRIVATE USE], Burley, Idaho; files of author.	Effie Lorain Shults Bassett, "Memories."

Land	Unbound headright and Bounty Document File	Georgia, Surveyor General Department, "Unbound Headright and Bounty Document Files 1783-1909," Document # 4139, John Royston, Warrant, Bulloch County, 3 January 1814, Georgia Division of Archives and History, Morrow.	Georgia, Surveyor General Department, "Unbound Headright and Bounty Document Files 1783-1909," Document # 4139, John Royston, Warrant, Bulloch County, 3 January 1814.
Military	Pension File	Isabell D. Royston, widow of Robert C. Royston, application no. A6942, 1929-1942, pension no. P5893, Record Group 5, Commissioner of Confederate Pensions, Oklahoma State Archives, Oklahoma Department of Libraries, Oklahoma City, OK.; digital images, Oklahoma, "Confederate Pension Records Database," *Oklahoma Digital Prairie* (http://www.digitalprairie.ok.gov) : accessed 15 July 2016) .	Isabell D. Royston, widow of Robert C. Royston, application no. A6942, 1929-1942, pension no. P5893, Record Group 5, Commissioner of Confederate Pensions, Oklahoma.
Probate	Will as a digital image on Ancestry	Chambers County, Alabama Estates, box 26 folder 24, Thomas Beverly Royston, for will of 1867; "Alabama, Wills and Probate Records, 1753-1999," case file for Thos B Royston, 1867-1883, *Ancestry* (http://www.ancestry.com: accessed 19 August 2016), digital images 138-140.	Chambers Co. Al. Estates, box 26 folder 24, Thos Beverly Royston, will of 1867, images 138-140.
Tax	Tax Records - County	Morgan County, Georgia, Superior Court, 1831 Tax Digest, page 2, entry for Thomas B. Royston, Morgan County, Archives, Madison, Georgia.	Morgan County, Georgia, Superior Court, 1831 Tax Digest, page 2, entry for Thomas B. Royston.

APPENDIX B
Work Samples B

As you work through your research project, you will find it helpful to view examples of complete projects. Discover how Nicole and I set an objective, analyzed previous research, created a locality guide, made a research plan, tracked our research in a log using source citations, then wrote a research report of findings. Follow our work from start to finish with the two complete research projects provided in this section.

When you've complete your research and you've proved identify, relationship, or ancestor actions, what is the final step? Writing a proof summary (for simple cases using direct evidence) or a proof argument (for complex cases using indirect evidence) clarifies your conclusions and helps others to follow your reasoning. Read Diana's proof argument for an example of assembling indirect evidence to prove the father of Mary, wife of Ignatius Bryan.

To view the full versions of these work samples, complete with maps and other images, go to http://familylocket.com/RLP .

List of Work Samples

Work Sample 1: Research Project for Determining a Relationship
Is George W. Dillard the Father of Cynthia (Dillard) Royston?
By Diana Elder, AG
- Chronology and Evidence Analysis
- Timeline Comparison and Evidence Analysis
- Alabama Locality Guide
- Research Log
- Research Plan
- Research Report

Work Sample 2: Research Project for Discovering Actions
Moses W. Isenhour Confederate Service
By Nicole Dyer
- Chronology and Evidence Analysis
- Montgomery County, Arkansas, Locality Guide
- Research Log
- Research Plan
- Research Report

Work Sample 3: Proof Argument
Determining the Father of Mary Ann (French) Bryan Atwood: A Case of Indirect Evidence
By Diana Elder, AG
    Discover how Diana assembled several pieces of indirect evidence to prove the father of Mary, the wife of Ignatius Bryan, residents of Hardin County, Kentucky 1800 - 1830.

Work Sample 1: Research Project

Is George W. Dillard the Father of Cynthia (Dillard) Royston?

Diana Elder, AG

Introduction

Over the years of researching my third great grandparents, Thomas Beverly Royston and Cynthia Dillard, I had accumulated a lot of information on George W. Dillard. He stood out as the prime suspect for Cynthia's father, but I didn't know if I had enough proof. For the second Research Like a Pro Study Group, I decided to tackle the research question, "Is George W. Dillard the father of Cynthia (Dillard) Royston?" I would follow all the steps I was teaching the study group members.

I wrote a clear objective and analyzed the evidence I had previously gathered. First, I created a chronology just for George W. Dillard, starting with his gravestone and moving back in time. I created this in a document format so that I could analyze the source, information, and evidence in detail. Then I did a side-by-side timeline analysis for George W. Dillard and Cynthia (Dillard) Royston. This helped me see how she could have fit in with his family and became my summary of known facts. Next, I reviewed the Alabama locality guide I had created for Accreditation to refresh my memory of the history, geography, and records of the time. With this background information in mind, I created a working hypothesis, identified sources to search, and made my research plan.

I followed my research plan which meant digging into the land records for a thorough comparison of the Royston and Dillard land. Writing up the research report helped me to put the pieces of this complicated puzzle together in a logical fashion. Although the evidence continues to point to George W. Dillard as the father of Cynthia (Dillard) Royston, I have additional research to perform before I can write a proof argument. I have several avenues for future research suggested from this research project. I can't wait to get started!

Chronology and Evidence Analysis - George W. Dillard

The following sources are arranged chronologically, working backwards from George's cemetery record to his first marriage, the earliest located record. This analysis is part of a project to prove George W. Dillard as the father of Cynthia Dillard. His migration from Greene County, Georgia to Macon County, Alabama provides clues that will help in finding connections between him and possible daughter, Cynthia.

   The sources support that George W. Dillard was born 26 August 1781 in Virginia and died 21 May 1854 in Lee County, Alabama. He married first, Peggy Armour in Green County, Georgia, on 9 November 1801. He married next, Martha Wells on 29 July, 1822 in Greene County, Georgia. The sources establish his residence in Green County and Muscogee County, Georgia; and Russell, Macon, and Lee County, Alabama.

1. Find A Grave Memorial for George Wellington Dillard, Lee County, Alabama
2. 1850 Census, Macon County, Alabama
3. 1850 Alabama State Census, Macon County, Alabama
4. 1840 Census, Russell County, Alabama for G.W. Dillard
5. Selection from the online journal, *DILLARD ANNUAL,* "Dillards and Johnsons, Early Alabama Pioneers"
6. 1840 News article, Columbus, Muscogee County, Georgia for George W. Dillard
7. 1837 News article, Columbus, Muscogee County, Georgia for G.W. Dillard
8. 1836 News article, Columbus, Muscogee County, Georgia for G.W. Dillard
9. 1835 News article, Columbus, Muscogee County, Georgia for G.W. Dillard
10. 1832 News Article, Columbus, Muscogee County, Georgia for Capt. Geo. W. Dillard
11. 1830 Census, Muscogee County, Georgia for G.W. Dillard
12. 1822 Greene County, Georgia Marriage for George W. Dillard and Martha F. Wells
13. 1820 Census, Greene County, Georgia for George W. Dillard
14. 1801 Marriage of George Dallard and Peggy Armour, Greene County, Georgia

1. *Find A Grave* Memorial for George Wellington Dillard, Lee County, Alabama[1]

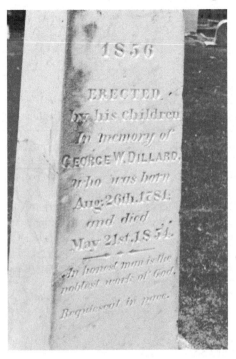

Birth: Aug. 26, 1781
Virginia, USA
Death: May 21, 1854
Auburn, Lee County, Alabama, USA

Married twice;
1st Wife: Margaret Armour
Married Nov. 4, 1804
Greene County, Georgia

2nd Wife: Martha Flournoy Wells
Married July 29, 1822
Greene County, Georgia

Burial: Pine Hill Cemetery, Auburn
Alabama

Inscription: "1856 Erected by his children in memory of George W. Dillard who was born August 26, 1781; and died May 21st 1854. An honest man is the noblest work of God. Requiescat in peace."

Analysis:

- **Source:** *Original and Derivative.* The headstone inscription was written by his children and the photograph shows it in its original form. The memorial information was derived from the inscription and other non-sourced records.
- **Information:** *Primary* (death and burial from the headstone). *Secondary (*birth from headstone*). Undetermined* (middle name and marriages from the memorial). Because the inscription states that the headstone was erected by "his children, they would likely have witnessed his death. Their knowledge of his birth date is secondary. No sources are given for the middle name of "Wellington" and the marriages.
- **Evidence:** *Indirect.* The inscription does not state which children erected the headstone, but Cynthia Dillard lived in nearby Chambers County and could be one of the children who helped erect it. Chambers County borders Lee County to the north.

---

[1] *Find A Grave*, database with images (https://www.findagrave.com: accessed 6 June 2017), memorial 8971146, George Wellington Dillard, (1781-1854), gravestone photographed by JC, member 46615432.

2. 1850 Census, Macon County, Alabama [2]

Date/Locality	1850 Census of Alabama, Macon County, District 21			
ED, Sheet No.	Page 272 a			
House, Family	House # 1088, Family #1096			
Family Member	**Sex**	**Age**	**Occupation**	**Birthplace**
George W. Dillard	M	68	None	Virginia
Martha Dillard	F	42		Virginia
Columbus Dillard	M	21	Clerk	Georgia
Alonzo Dillard	M	15		Georgia
Leonidas Dillard	M	9		Alabama
Zenora Dillard	F	7		Alabama

Analysis:
- **Source:** Image of *Original.* The census record appears to be the original copy of the census, written in the handwriting of Thos. McGunn, Ass't Marshal. The writing is faded in spots, but still fairly legible.
- **Information:** *Undetermined.* The informant for the census information cannot be determined, but given the specifics of the names, birthplaces, and ages it could be surmised that either George or Martha provided the household information. George's age of 68 matches well with the 1781 birthdate.
- **Evidence:** *Indirect.* The census provides indirect evidence for the relationship between Cynthia and George Dillard. George's residence in Macon County is a clue that their families followed similar migration patterns. In 1850, Cynthia's family lived in Chambers County, just one county away from Macon County to the northeast. The names of George's children may also provide indirect evidence linking the families.

---

[2] 1850 U.S. Census, Macon County, Alabama, population schedule, 21st District, p. 272 (stamped), dwelling 1088, family 1096, George W. Dillard household; digital image, *Ancestry* (http://www.ancestry.com : accessed 10 March 2017); citing NARA microfilm publication M432, roll 9.

3. 1850 Alabama State Census, Macon County, Alabama[3]

AN ENUMERATION OF THE INHABITANTS OF *Macon* COUNTY, 1850. 23										
NAMES OF INDIVIDUALS, OR Heads of Families. *Printed at the Advertiser and Gazette Office, Montgomery, Alabama.*	White males under 21.	White males over 21.	White males between 18 and 45.	White males over 45.	White females under 21.	White females over 21.	Insane within county.	Insane sent abroad.	Number of slaves.	Number of free persons of color.	TOTAL INHABITANTS.
John McGehee	2	1	1		2	1			19		20
Jesse Taylor	1	3	1	1	2	2			8		13
J. M. Taylor		1	1		4	1					6
J. C. Crosley		3	1	1		2			10		14
Jno. Ward	2	1	1		3	1					6
J. J. McCormick		1	1								1
George W. Dillard	3	2	2	1	1	1			12		18
S. M. Grayson		1	1		2	1			2		6
F. W. Dillard		1	1			1			3		5

George W. Dillard
- 3 white males under 21
- 2 white males over 21
- 2 white males between 18 and 45
- 1 white male over 45
- 1 white female under 21
- 1 white female over 21
- 12 slaves
- 19 total inhabitants

Analysis:
- **Source:** *Original.* Image of original state census record, original image digitized from microfilm at the Alabama Department of Archives and History.
- **Information:** *Undetermined.* Although it is highly likely that George W. Dillard gave the number of individuals for each age and gender category, it can't be certain. An F.M. Dillard, two lines below his entry is a possible relative and could have given the information. George would be 69 in 1850, calculating from his birth year of 1781, matching the male over 45.
- **Evidence:** *Indirect.* The census provides indirect evidence for the relationship between Cynthia and George Dillard. George's residence in Macon County is a clue that their families followed similar migration patterns. In 1850, Cynthia's family

---

[3] 1850 Alabama State Census, Macon County, p. 23 (penned), line 7, George W. Dillard; "Alabama State census, 1820-1866," digital image, *Ancestry* (http://www.ancestry.com : accessed 6 June 2017); citing Alabama Department of Archives & History.

lived in Chambers County, just one county away from Macon County to the northeast.

4. 1840 Census, Russell County, Alabama for G.W. Dillard[4]

GW Dillard household:
- Free White Persons - Males - 5 thru 9: 2
- Free White Persons - Males - 15 thru 19: 2
- Free White Persons - Males - 20 thru 29: 1
- Free White Persons - Males - 60 thru 69: 1
- Free White Persons - Females - 15 thru 19: 1
- Free White Persons - Females - 30 thru 39: 1
- Slaves - Males - Under 10: 1
- Slaves - Males - 10 thru 23: 3
- Slaves - Males - 36 thru 54: 2
- Slaves - Females - 10 thru 23: 3
- Slaves - Females - 24 thru 35: 1
- Slaves - Females - 36 thru 54: 1
- Persons Employed in Agriculture: 4
- Free White Persons - Under 20: 5
- Free White Persons - 20 thru 49: 2
- Total Free White Persons: 8
- Total Slaves: 11
- Total All Persons - Free White, Free Colored, Slaves: 19

Analysis:
- **Source:** *Original.* The digital image is clear and doesn't appear to be tampered with. Faint marks from the opposite page have bled through, but the writing is easily discerned. The handwriting appears to differ at times, possibly some of the men signed their own names and another individual signed for any who were unable to write. G. W. Dillard's signature is distinctive.
- **Information:** *Undetermined.* It is highly likely that G.W. Dillard gave the household information, especially if the signature proves to be his. Born in 1781, George would have been 59, close to the male age 60-69 on the census.
- **Evidence:** *Indirect.* The census provides indirect evidence for the relationship between Cynthia and George Dillard. George's residence in Russell County is a clue

---

4 1840 U.S. Census, Russell County, Alabama, population schedule, p. 35 (penned), line 25, G.W. Dillard household; digital image, *Ancestry* (http://www.ancestry.com : accessed 7 June 2017); citing NARA microfilm publication M704, roll 15.

that their families followed similar migration patterns. In 1840, Cynthia's family lived in DeKalb County, Alabama, to the north of Russell County, Alabama. No female of appropriate age for Cynthia is listed in the household indicating a possible marriage for the female age 15-19 on the 1830 census.

5. Selection from the online journal, *DILLARD ANNUAL,* "Dillards and Johnsons, Early Alabama Pioneers"[5]

Ruth Royal Crump the present historian of Chambers County, Alabama has diligently copied every original land sales transaction which took place in Chambers County. She has published these transactions in a book entitled, The Original Tract Book for Chambers County.

This book lists the following transactions involving persons named Dillard: [only those for George W. Dillard are listed below]

In Township 21, Range 25, Sections 29 and 35, **George W. Dillard** purchased at auction in 1836 478 acres and in the same year Samuel Morrell and Lorenzo D. Dillard purchased 40 Acres."

In 1840 **George W. Dillard** purchased from E-Far-Emarthle or E-Molly (a Creek Chief) 320 acres.

Analysis:

- **Source:** *Authored.* The author uses a *derivative source* when he lists the land transactions, but he has combined this into an *authored narrative* that is part of a larger work dealing with Dillard pioneers in early Alabama.
- **Information:** *Undetermined.* It is impossible to determine from this document who recorded the land transaction and if he had firsthand knowledge of the event.
- **Evidence:** *Indirect.* The selection provides indirect evidence for the relationship between Cynthia and George Dillard. George purchased land in Chambers County in 1840, and Thomas and Cynthia (Dillard) Royston settled in Chambers County, Alabama by 1850.

---

[5] Hugh S. Johnson, "Dillards and Johnsons, Early Alabama Pioneers," *DILLARD ANNUAL,* Volume 5; January, 1998, (http://www.dillardfamilyassociation.com/dannuals/da1998/da98hs4.htm : accessed 6 June 2017), 6.

6. 1840 News article, Columbus, Muscogee County, Georgia for George W. Dillard[6]

The Subscriber has located himself four miles from Columbus, on the road leading to LaFayette, Chambers county, and Auburn, Macon county, Ala.—It will give him great pleasure in entertaining all persons that may feel disposed to favor him with a call.

George W. Dillard

Analysis:

- **Source:** *Original.* The digital images of the newspaper appear to be complete and untampered. The image is clear and legible.
- **Information:** *Primary.* George W. Dillard, the subscriber, wrote the advertisement.
- **Evidence:** *Indirect.* The selection provides indirect evidence for the relationship between Cynthia and George Dillard. Cynthia's husband, Thomas B. Royston, was also named in the Columbus Enquirer in 1840 for a letter remaining at the post office. Although Thomas and Cynthia Royston were homesteading in DeKalb County, Alabama, in 1840, the listing of both men in the newspaper points to a connection.

7. 1837 News article, Columbus, Muscogee County, Georgia for G.W. Dillard[7]

The following ticket has been handed us for publication. The men are all well known, and could receive no strength from any recommendation of ours.

Mayor.
James S. Calhoun.
For Aldermen.
Ward No. 1.
James C. Holland
Buckner Beasley,
No 2.
H.S. Smith.
Sam'l R. Anders.
No. 3.
Allen Lawhon.
A.K.Ayer.

---

6 *Columbus Enquirer,* 14 October 1840, p. 3, col. 4, para. 6, George W. Dillard advertisement, *Georgia Historic Newspapers:* Columbus Enquirer (enquirer.galileo.usg.edu : accessed 19 June 2017).

7 *Columbus Enquirer,* 21 December 1837, p. 2, col. 6, para. 2, Geo.W. Dillard, Alderman; Columbus Enquirer (enquirer.galileo.usg.edu : accessed 19 June 2017).

No. 4.
Wm. P. Yonge.
James Kivlin.
No. 5.
Geo. W. Dillard
Capt. John Peabody.
No. 6.
Thos. G Godron.
Benj. F. Coleman

Analysis:
- **Source:** *Original.* The digital images of the newspaper appear to be complete and untampered.
- **Information:** *Undetermined.* It is impossible to determine from the news article who provided the information. The plural "we" is used throughout the article describing the politics of the time and the election.
- **Evidence:** *Indirect.* The selection provides indirect evidence for the relationship between Cynthia and George Dillard. Cynthia's husband, Thomas B. Royston, was named in the same newspaper, the Columbus Enquirer, in 1840 for a letter remaining at the post office. The listing of both men in the newspaper points to a connection.

8. 1836 News article, Columbus, Muscogee County, Georgia for G.W. Dillard[8]

But we have said that victory has perched upon the insulted banner of our party. Here is the proof. On Saturday last, *John Fontaine,* was elected Mayor of the city, by a majority of 25 votes over Gen. Watson, and *G.W. Dillard, Thos. G. Gordon, Tho's. C. Evans E. Sigourney Norton, H.S. Smith,* and *E.L. Wittick,* were at the same time elected Aldermen, all by handsome majorities.

Analysis:
- **Source:** *Original.* The digital images of the newspaper appear to be complete and untampered.
- **Information:** *Undetermined.* It is impossible to determine from the news article who provided the information. The plural "we" is used throughout the article describing the politics of the time and the election.

---

[8] *Columbus Enquirer,* 8 January 1836, p. 2, col. 4, para.4, G.W. Dillard elected Alderman; *Georgia Historic Newspapers:* Columbus Enquirer (enquirer.galileo.usg.edu : accessed 19 June 2017).

- **Evidence:** *Indirect.* The selection provides indirect evidence for the relationship between Cynthia and George Dillard. Cynthia's husband, Thomas B. Royston, was named in the same newspaper, the Columbus Enquirer, in 1840 for a letter remaining at the post office. The listing of both men in the newspaper points to a connection.

9. 1835 News article, Columbus, Muscogee County, Georgia for G.W. Dillard[9]

On Monday last, the election for Intendant and Commissioners was held at the Court House, in Columbus. The following gentlemen were elected.

Gen. Jas. C. Watson, Intendant
Col. S. R. Bonner,
Dr. A.s. Clifton,
Col. Asa Bates,
J.P.H. Campbell, Esq.
Geo. W. Dillard, Esq.
Lewis C. Allen, Esq.

Analysis:
- **Source:** *Original.* The digital images of the newspaper appear to be complete and untampered.
- **Information:** *Undetermined.* It is impossible to determine from the news article who provided the information. No author is listed anywhere in the paper.
- **Evidence:** *Indirect.* The selection provides indirect evidence for the relationship between Cynthia and George Dillard. Cynthia's husband, Thomas B. Royston, was named in the same newspaper, the Columbus Enquirer, in 1840 for a letter remaining at the post office. The listing of both men in the newspaper points to a connection.

---

[9] *Columbus Enquirer*, 9 January 1835, p. 3, col. 2, para.3, Geo. W. Dillard elected commissioner; *Georgia Historic Newspapers*: Columbus Enquirer (enquirer.galileo.usg.edu : accessed 8 June 2017).

10. 1832 News Article, Columbus, Muscogee County, Georgia for Capt. Geo. W. Dillard[10]

> FOR SALE
> A comfortable two-story Dwelling, with convenient out-houses and garden, at the upper end of Oglethorpe street now in the occupancy of Capt. Geo. W. Dillard, in a healthy and beautiful part of Columbus.

This exact advertisement ran for three consecutive weeks: 13, 20, and 27 October 1832.

Analysis:
- **Source:** *Original.* The digital images of the newspaper appear to be complete and untampered.
- **Information:** *Primary.* Thos. G. Gordon's name appears at the end of the advertisement and he describes himself as an agent for the owner. He would almost certainly have firsthand knowledge of the dwellings occupants.
- **Evidence:** *Indirect.* The selection provides indirect evidence for the relationship between Cynthia and George Dillard. Cynthia's husband, Thomas B. Royston, was named in the same newspaper, the Columbus Enquirer, in 1840 for a letter remaining at the post office. The listing of both men in the newspaper points to a connection.

11. 1830 Census, Muscogee County, Georgia for G.W. Dillard [11]

G.W. Dillard Household
- Home in 1830 (City, County, State): Columbus, Muscogee, Georgia
- Free White Persons - Males - Under 5: 3
- Free White Persons - Males - 20 thru 29: 5
- Free White Persons - Males - 30 thru 39: 7
- Free White Persons - Males - 40 thru 49: 1
- Free White Persons - Females - Under 5: 1
- Free White Persons - Females - 15 thru 19: 1
- Free White Persons - Females - 20 thru 29: 1
- Slaves - Males - Under 10: 1

---

[10] *Columbus Enquirer,* 27 October 1832, p. 4, col. 1, para.3, Capt. Geo. W. Dillard occupancy of dwelling; *Georgia Historic Newspapers*: Columbus Enquirer (enquirer.galileo.usg.edu : accessed 19 June 2017).

[11] 1830 U.S. Census, Muscogee County, Georgia, population schedule, p. 277 (penned), line 2, G.W. Dillard household; digital image, *Ancestry* (http://www.ancestry.com : accessed 7 June 2017); citing NARA microfilm publication M19, roll 19.

- Slaves - Males - 10 thru 23: 2
- Slaves - Males - 55 thru 99: 1
- Slaves - Females - Under 10: 4
- Slaves - Females - 24 thru 35: 2
- Free White Persons - Under 20: 5
- Free White Persons - 20 thru 49: 14
- Total Free White Persons: 19
- Total Slaves: 10
- Total - All Persons (Free White, Slaves, Free Colored): 29

Analysis:

- **Source:** *Original.* The image is clear and doesn't appear to be tampered with. Faint marks from the opposite page have bled through, but the writing is easily discerned. It appears that the same individual wrote each name. G.W. Dillard's name here doesn't seem unique from any of the other names and doesn't match the handwriting from the 1840 census.
- **Information:** *Undetermined.* It is highly likely that GW Dillard gave the household information.
- **Evidence:** *Indirect.* The census record provides indirect evidence for George Dillard as the father of Cynthia. The household includes a female age 15 -19 that could be Cynthia (Dillard) Royston. George's reported age of 40-49 would be appropriate for her father.

12. 1822 Greene County, Georgia Marriage for George W. Dillard and Martha F. Wells[12]

Georgia, Greene County: George W. Dillard of the one part and Martha F. Wells of the other part, according to the rites of your church, provided there be no lawful cause to obstruct the same, and this shall be your authority for so doing. Given under my hand as the clerk of the court of ordinary of the county aforesaid, this 29th day of July 1822.

   Ebenezer Torrence Clk.

I do certify that George W. Dillard and Martha F. Wells were joined together in the holy bands of Matrimony by me, on the 29th day of July 1822.

   Lovick Pierce M.G.

Recorded 8th August 1822. Ebenezer Torrence, Clk.

---

12   Greene County, Georgia Marriages 1829-1849, Dillard - Wells, 29 July 1822, p. 186; "Georgia, Marriage Records from Select Counties, 1828-1978," image 201, *Ancestry,* (http://www.ancestry.com : accessed 10 March 2017).

Analysis:
- **Source:** Image of *Original* marriage record from the Greene County, Georgia marriage book.
- **Information:** *Primary.* The minister who performed the marriage certified that he married the couple on 29 July 1822 and it was recorded by the county clerk on 8 August 1822, just a week later.
- **Evidence:** *Indirect.* The marriage record is indirect evidence of the relationship between Cynthia and George W. Dillard. Cynthia's daughter, Martha, could have been named for her stepmother, Martha F. Wells.

13. 1820 Census, Greene County, Georgia for George W. Dillard[13]

George W. Dillard Household
- Home in 1820 (City, County, State): Capt E Woodhams District, Greene, Georgia
- Enumeration Date: August 7, 1820
- Free White Persons - Males - Under 10: 2
- Free White Persons - Males - 10 thru 15: 1
- Free White Persons - Males - 16 thru 25: 1
- Free White Persons - Males - 26 thru 44: 1
- Free White Persons - Females - Under 10: 1
- Free White Persons - Females - 10 thru 15: 1
- Free White Persons - Females - 26 thru 44: 1
- Slaves - Males - Under 14: 6
- Slaves - Males - 14 thru 25: 1
- Slaves - Males - 26 thru 44: 5
- Slaves - Females - Under 14: 8
- Slaves - Females - 14 thru 25: 5
- Slaves - Females - 26 thru 44: 4
- Number of Persons - Engaged in Agriculture: 11
- Number of Persons - Engaged in Commerce: 1
- All Other Persons Except Indians not Taxed: 37
- Free White Persons - Under 16: 5
- Free White Persons - Over 25: 2
- Total Free White Persons: 8

---

13   1820 U.S. Census, Greene County, Georgia, Capt E Woodhams District, population schedule, p. 202, line 2, George W. Dillard household; digital image, *Ancestry* (http://www.ancestry.com : accessed 7 June 2017); citing NARA microfilm publication M33, roll 8.

- Total Slaves: 29
- Total All Persons - White, Slaves, Colored, Other: 37

Analysis:

- **Source:** *Original.* The image is clear and doesn't appear to be tampered with. Faint marks from the opposite page have bled through, but the writing is easily discerned. The handwriting seems to be the same throughout, indicating that the census taker recorded all the names.
- **Information:** *Undetermined.* It is highly likely that George W. Dillard gave the household information.
- **Evidence:** *Indirect.* The census record provides indirect evidence for George Dillard as the father of Cynthia. The household includes a female age 0-10 that could be Cynthia (Dillard) Royston. George's reported age of 26-44 would be appropriate for her father.

14. 1801 Marriage of George Dallard and Peggy Armour, Greene County, Georgia [14]

Different Dates: Nov. 9th 1801
Persons married: George W. Dallard to Peggy Armour
Voucher by: self & Nicholson

Analysis:

- **Source:** *Original.* The microfilmed book has all pages included. This marriage is also listed at the beginning in the index. The page image is clear and doesn't appear to be tampered with.
- **Information:** *Undetermined.* The handwriting is consistent throughout the book and this style of marriage recording is consistent until April 1806, when the county clerk, Henry Carleton, began to record the entire marriage license. Because no information is giving regarding who married the couple, it is unknown who gave the marriage date and names of the couple and the voucher information.
- **Evidence:** *Indirect.* The marriage record is indirect evidence of the relationship between Cynthia and George W. Dillard. Cynthia's daughter, Margaret, could have been named for her mother, Margaret Armour.

---

[14] Greene County, Georgia, "Marriage Licenses 1786 To 1810," p. 9, Dallard-Armour marriage, 9 November 1801; "Georgia, County Marriages, 1785-1950," image 21 of 659, *FamilySearch* (https://familysearch.org : accessed 7 June 2017); citing "Marriage Records 1786-1849," FHL microfilm # 159,052.

Timeline Comparison George W. Dillard and Cynthia (Dillard) Royston

Event & Date	Place	Source	Evidence Analysis	Comments	Thos B. Royston / Cynthia Dillard	Place	Source	Evidence Analysis	Comments
George W. Dillard born 1781	Virginia	Find A Grave George Wellington Dillard, (1781-1854)	Original source (gravestone), secondary information, indirect evidence	Pine Hill Cem, Auburn AL, "1856 Erected by his children ...born August 26, 1781; and died May 21st 1854.					
1801 marriage to Peggy Armour	Greene County, Georgia	Greene County, Georgia, "Marriage Licenses 1786 To 1810," p. 9, Dallard-Armour	Original source, undetermined information, indirect evidence	Different Dates: Nov. 9th 1801 Persons married: George W. Dallard to Peggy Armour Voucher by: self & Nicholson					Peggy Armour would be the possible mother of Cynthia. Cynthia did name her oldest daughter, Margaret, a possible connection to this family.
1813-14 Creek war	Alabama	"U.S. Army Indian Campaign Serv. Index, 1815-1858" Ancestry	Original source, undetermined information, indirect evidence	Dillard, G.W. Young's Co. (Spies), AL Mtd. Vols. (Creek War) Pvt., also Dillard, L.D or S.D. in the same company.					
					1816 Birth of Cynthia	Georgia			
1820 census	Greene County, Georgia	1820 U.S. Census,	Original source, undetermined information, indirect evidence	Males under 10: 2 Males 10-15:1 Males 16-25: 1 Males 26-44: 1 **Females under 10: 1** Females 10-15:1 Females 26-44:1	Cynthia possibly in 1820 census in household of George W. Dillard	Greene County, Georgia	1820 U.S. Census	Original source, undetermined information, indirect evidence	Based on information from the 1850, 1860, 1870, and 1880 censuses. Males under 10: 2 Males 10-15: 1 Males 16-25: 1 Males 26-44: 1 **Females under 10: 1** Females 10-15: 1 Females 26-44: 1

Event & Date	Place	Source	Evidence Analysis	Comments	Thos B. Royston / Cynthia Dillard	Place	Source	Evidence Analysis	Comments
1821, death of Margaret Armour	Greene County, Georgia	1820 U.S. Census and Greene County, Georgia Marriages 1829-1849, Dillard - Wells	Indirect evidence derived from the presence of a female age 26-44 on the 1820 census & the remarriage in 1822.						
1822 marriage to Martha F. Wells	Greene County, Georgia	Greene County, Georgia Marriages 1829-1849, Dillard - Wells	Original source, primary information, indirect evidence	29 July 1822					
1830 census	Muscogee County, Georgia	1830 U.S. Census	Original source, undetermined information, indirect evidence	G.W. Dillard household: Free White Persons Males under 5: 3 Males 20-29: 5 Males 30-39: 7 Males 40-49: 1 Females under 5: 1 **Females 15-19: 1** Females 20-29: 1	Cynthia possibly in the 1830 census, household of George W. Dillard		1830 U.S. Census	Original source, undetermined information, indirect evidence	G.W. Dillard household: Free White Persons Males under 5: 3 Males 20-29: 5 Males 30-39: 7 Males 40-49: 1 Females under 5: 1 **Females 15-19: 1** Females 20-29: 1
					1831 Tax record for Thomas B. Royston	Morgan County, Georgia		Original source, undetermined information, indirect evidence	
1832-35 News articles	Muscogee County, Georgia	Elizabeth Evans Kilbourne, Columbus, GA Newspaper Clippings	Original source, primary information, indirect evidence	For Sale: dwelling on Oglethorpe street, now in the occupance of Capt. Geo. W. Dillard, in Columbus					

Event & Date	Place	Source	Evidence Analysis	Comments	Thos B. Royston / Cynthia Dillard	Place	Source	Evidence Analysis	Comments
					Marriage Abt 1833	Georgia	unsourced	Date based on birth of oldest daughter, Mary about 1834.	Muscogee County records lost with fire on 8 October 1838
1836 land purchase	Chambers County, Alabama	Ruth Royal Crump, Chambers County, Alabama, Tract Book.	Authored source, undetermined information, indirect evidence	"In Township 21, Range 25, Sections 29 and 35, George W. Dillard purchased at auction in 1836 478 acres"					
1836-38 News articles	Muscogee County, Georgia	Columbus, GA, Newspaper Clippings	Original source, primary information, indirect evidence	George W. Dillard elected commissioner, etc.					
1840 census	Russell County, Alabama	1840 U.S. Census	Original source, undetermined information, indirect evidence	GW Dillard household: Free White Persons Males 5-9: 2 Males 15-19: 2 Males 20-29: 1 Males 60-69: 1 Females 5-19: 1 Females 30-39: 1	1840 Census	DeKalb County, Alabama	1840 U.S. Census	Original source, undetermined information, indirect evidence	Males 0-5:2 (Ulysses, Charles Baldwin) 30-40: 5 (Thomas and ????) Females 5-10: 1 (Mary) 20-30: 1 (Cynthia)
1840 land purchase	Chambers County, Alabama	Ruth Royal Crump, Chambers County, Alabama Tract Book.	Authored source, undetermined info, indirect evidence of land purchase	"In 1840 George W. Dillard purchased from E-Far-Emarthle or E-Molly (a Creek Chief) 320 acres."					
1850 census	Macon County, Alabama	1850 U.S. Census	Original source, undetermined information, indirect evidence	George W. Dillard 62, Martha F 42, Columbus 21, Alonzo 15, Leonidas 9, Zenora 7	1850 Census	Chambers County, Alabama	1850 U.S. Census	Original source, undetermined information, indirect evidence	Macon and Chambers counties are separated by Lee County, Alabama

Event & Date	Place	Source	Evidence Analysis	Comments	Thos. B. Royston / Cynthia Dillard	Place	Source	Evidence Analysis	Comments
					6 Oct 1852 Wm Ingram to Thomas Royston	Chambers County, Alabama	Chambers Co., AL Deed book 11:256; Wm Ingram to Thomas B. Royston	Original source, primary information, indirect evidence	Section 24 Township 24 Range 26 Section 13 of same township and range containing 40 acres containing 450 acres for $1500.
					1852 Thomas & Cynthia Royston to John Daniels	Chambers County, Alabama	Chambers Co., AL, "Deeds v. 11 1852-1854," page 639, Royston to Daniels	Original source, primary information, indirect evidence	Section 33 Township 24 Range 26; 420 acres for $2,200
George W. Dillard death	Lee County, Alabama	Find A Grave George Wellington Dillard, (1781-1854)	Original source (gravestone), secondary information, indirect evidence	Pine Hill Cemetery, Auburn AL, "1856 Erected by his children ...born August 26, 1781; and died May 21st 1854.					
					1857 birth of son Thomas Leonidas	Chambers County, Alabama	unsourced	Date derived from 1860, 1870, and 1880 censuses	Name on the 1860 and 1870 census, then Thomas L. on the 1880.
1860 census	Macon County, Alabama	1860 U.S. Census	Original source, undetermined information, indirect evidence	Location for son of George: Alonzo Dillard	1860 census	Chambers County, Alabama	1860 U.S. Census	Original source, undetermined information, indirect evidence	Thos B. Royston 54, Cynthia 44 GA, Charles B 21, Adeline 19, Sarah 17, Joseph 16, Benjamin 16, Robert C 14, Thomas B 12, **Margt 8 AL, Leonidas 3, Infant F 8/12**

Alabama Locality Guide

BACKGROUND

Quick Facts

[*The Handybook for Genealogists,* (Draper, Utah: Everton Publishers, 2002), 29-33.]
- Alabama became a state on 14 December 1819
- Prior to statehood Alabama was Alabama Territory
- Statewide registration of births and deaths began in 1908
- County marriage records begin with the formation of each county
- After 1936, marriage records are located at the State Dept of Health: Bureau of Vital Statistics
- Alabama is a Federal Land State
- State/Territorial Censuses taken in 1816, 1818, 1820, 1831, 1850, 1855, 1866, and 1880

General Online Alabama Research Guides and Collections

- *FamilySearch* Alabama Wiki: clickable map for counties, migration routes, and more https://www.familysearch.org/wiki/en/Alabama,_United_States_Genealogy
- *FamilySearch* Record Collection: indexed and browse-only collections https://www.familysearch.org/search/collection/location/33
- *FamilySearch* Catalog "Alabama": list of books and microfilm by category http://bit.ly/2Iz9X22
- *FamilySearch* "Alabama Online Genealogy Records": by record type, with links https://www.familysearch.org/wiki/en/Alabama_Online_Genealogy_Records
- *Ancestry* Alabama family history research page: record collections and resources https://search.ancestry.com/Places/US/Alabama/Default.aspx
- *Ancestry* "Alabama State Research Guide": history, resource, records https://www.ancestrycdn.com/support/us/2016/11/researchguidealabama.pdf
- Saffold Berney, *Handbook of Alabama: A Complete Index to the State, with Map,* (Mobile, Alabama: Roberts & Son, 1892).
  - Includes tax laws of Alabama, business laws and statutes, education, insane hospital, convict system, counties, sketches of cities and town, railroad, geology, industry, agriculture, etc.
  - Digitized at *FamilySearch* https://dcms.lds.org/delivery/DeliveryManagerServlet?dps_pid=IE6424082

County Information

Alabama Department of Archives and History: http://www.archives.alabama.gov
- "Alabama Counties" http://www.archives.alabama.gov/counties.html
  Includes county seat, date established, original counties, and links to the record collections for each county: very helpful in determining what records should be searched
- "Alabama County Historical and Genealogical Societies
  http://www.archives.alabama.gov/referenc/societies.pdf#Chambers
  Addresses, phone #'s and web links
- "Alabama Courthouses Destroyed by Fire" Shows county and dates of fire
  http://www.archives.alabama.gov/REFERENC/firemap.gif

Maps and Geography

- *Atlas of Historical County Boundaries*, "Alabama," The Newberry Library
  http://publications.newberry.org/ahcbp/pages/Alabama.html
  - Interactive map of Alabama county boundaries and chronologies
  - Map with historical borders begins with 3 March 1817
- "Map Database," *Alabama Department of Archives and History*
  http://www.archives.alabama.gov/mapbase/mapbase.cfm
  Includes a wide variety of maps: counties, fire insurance
- Department of Geography, "Alabama Maps," *The University of Alabama*
  http://alabamamaps.ua.edu/
  Wonderful collection of maps; easily searched and downloaded
- "Maps of Alabama," *Map of US*, interactive map of Alabama Counties Formation
  https://www.mapofus.org/alabama/
- "Alabama Gazetteers," *FamilySearch* Wiki
  https://www.familysearch.org/wiki/en/Alabama_Gazetteers
  - Louis A. Adams, *Adam's Directory of Points and Landings on Rivers and Bayous in the States of Alabama, Arkansas, Florida, Georgia, Indiana, Illinois, Kentucky, Iowa, Louisiana, Minnesota, Mississippi, Missouri, Nebraska, Ohio, Tennessee, Texas and Wisconsin*, (New Orleans : W.L. Murray, 1877).
    Digital version at Internet Archive:
    https://archive.org/details/cu31924095607135
  - Samuel R. Brown, *The Western Gazetteer or Emigrant's Directory, Containing a Geographical Description of the Western States and Territories, viz. The States of Kentucky, Indiana, Louisiana, Ohio, Tennessee and Mississippi: and the Territories of Illinois, Missouri, Alabama, Michigan, and North-Western.* (Auburn, N.Y.: H.C. Southwick, 1817). Available on Google Books.

    o   Thomas and Marie Owen, *History of Alabama and dictionary of Alabama biography,* (Chicago, Illinois : S.J. Clarke Pub. Co., 1921). 4 Digital volumes digitized at *FamilySearch:* https://www.familysearch.org/search/catalog/192472

Timelines

- "Alabama History," *FamilySearch Wiki* Timeline of important events in Alabama's history that affected political jurisdictions, family movements, and record keeping. https://www.familysearch.org/wiki/en/Alabama_History
- "Alabama History Timeline: From Prehistory to Modern Day" is interactive with links to articles, photographs, maps and much more. http://www.archives.alabama.gov/timeline/index.html

History

- Thomas McAdory Owen, LL.D., *History of Alabama and Dictionary of Alabama Biography,* (Marie Bankhead Owen: 1921). Digitized book at *MyHeritage.com*
- Mary Elizabeth Young, *Redskins, Ruffleshirts and Rednecks: Indian Allotments in Alabama and Mississippi, 1830-1860* (Norman, Oklahoma: University of Oklahoma Press, 1961).
- Lester Jesse Cappon, *The History of Alabama During the Civil War,* (University of Wisconsin: 1922). Digitized on *Hathitrust.org* https://babel.hathitrust.org/cgi/pt?id=wu.89086023215
- Judy Russell, "State Constitutions: Alabama," *The Legal Genealogist* - Excellent article describing the jurisdictions and history of the Alabama area before statehood. http://www.legalgenealogist.com/2012/07/05/state-constitutions-alabama

French Period: 1710-1763

The first permanent European settlers in Alabama were French. By 1702, Fort Louis (on the present site of Mobile) had been settled as the capital of the French colony known as Louisiana. With the Treaty of Paris in 1763, the French ceded most of Louisiana to Great Britain. Settlers during this period came from South Carolina and Georgia, as well as England, France, and Spain.

British Period: 1763-1783

Britain controlled the Alabama area until 1783 when the Treaty of Paris ceded British holdings in the Mobile area to Spain. During the Revolutionary War, many British sympathizers left Georgia to settle in the British controlled Alabama area. Planters from Virginia and the Carolinas followed in 1783.

Multiple Claims to the Alabama area: 1783-1817 [shortened version of the FS Wiki timeline]

- 1783: Britain ceded the southern region, around Mobile, to Spain. The area further north of the Alabama region was claimed by Georgia. The boundary between the two areas was in dispute until 1795, when it was set at the 31st parallel, a few miles north of Mobile.
- 1798: U.S. Congress created the Mississippi Territory from the land north of the 31st parallel, the area previously claimed by Georgia.
- 1802: Choctaw Indians ceded land.
- 1805: Choctaw Indians ceded land.
- 1806: Cherokee Indians ceded land.
- 1812: The area below the 31st parallel was added to Mississippi Territory in 1812.
- 1812–1814: During the War of 1812, on 15 April 1813 American forces captured Mobile from the Spanish. General Andrew Jackson defeated the Creek Indians in several battles, including the Battle of Horseshoe Bend, 27 March 1814. Removal of the Creeks and other Indian tribes commenced and European settlers began flooding into the region, bringing African-American slaves with them.
- March 29, 1814: Creek Indian War ended as General Andrew Jackson defeated the Creeks under Chief Weatherford at the battle of Horseshoe Bend, Alabama where nearly 900 - 1000 Indians engaged were killed.
- 1814: Creek Indians ceded land.
- 1816: Chickasaw, Choctaw and Cherokee Indians ceded land.
- 1817: Cherokee Indians ceded land.
- March 3, 1817: The Mississippi Territory was divided into the state of Mississippi, and the Alabama Territory at that time. The Alabama Territory was composed of the following seven counties: Baldwin, Clarke, Madison, Mobile, Monroe, Montgomery, and Washington.

Mississippi Territory (1798–1817)

When established by Congress in 1798, the Mississippi Territory encompassed the present-day state of Mississippi and seven present-day counties in Alabama. Following the West Florida Revolution of 1810, the Mississippi counties of Hancock, Harrison, and Jackson were added to the territory. For the one hundred years preceding U.S. control, however, France, Spain, and Great Britain exercised authority in the Mississippi Territory.

For more details see: Mrs. Dunbar Rowland, *Mississippi Territory in the War of 1812*, (Baltimore : Genealogical Publishing Co., inc. 1996). Digitized book on *Ancestry* http://search.ancestry.com/search/db.aspx?dbid=48048

Alabama Territorial Period (1798–1819)

Following the Revolutionary War, the United States acquired British claims to all lands east of the Mississippi River. This included the Alabama area. Congress created the Alabama Territory out of the eastern half of the Mississippi Territory on March 3, 1817 "The population grew so rapidly in the Alabama Territory that statehood became imminent

For more details see: Thomas Chase Hagood, "Territorial Period and Early Statehood," *Encyclopedia of Alabama.* http://www.encyclopediaofalabama.org/article/h-1548

Statehood: 1819

During the early years of statehood the most significant genealogical event was the opening of lands formerly held by Native Americans to white settlers between 1802 and 1838. By 1840, all but a few scattered remnants of tribes had been moved west beyond the Mississippi River.

These developments are detailed in Mary Elizabeth Young's, *Redskins, Ruffleshirts and Rednecks: Indian Allotments in Alabama and Mississippi, 1830–1860* (Norman, Okla.: University of Oklahoma Press, 1961).

Law and Government

- Judy Russell, "State Constitutions: Alabama," *The Legal Genealogist* - Excellent article detailing the jurisdictions of Alabama before statehood and the various constitutions after statehood.
  http://www.legalgenealogist.com/2012/07/05/state-constitutions-alabama/
- Abram Joseph Walker, *The Revised Code of Alabama,* (Alabama : Clerk's office of the District Court of the United States, 1867). Digital version on *Google Books*
- Saffold Berney, "Constitution of the State of Alabama," *Handbook of Alabama: A Complete Index to the State, with Map,* (Mobile, Alabama : Roberts & Son, 1892), p. 9-58. Digitized at *FamilySearch*
  https://dcms.lds.org/delivery/DeliveryManagerServlet?dps_pid=IE6424082

Libraries and Archives

- For contact information see "Alabama Archives and Libraries," *FamilySearch Wiki*
  https://familysearch.org/wiki/en/Alabama_Archives_and_Libraries
- Alabama Department of Archives and History (ADAH)
  http://www.archives.alabama.gov/
    - Reference requests: $25 out-of-state fee; will search one surname and four sources
    - Catalog of collections includes online indexes and digital collections

- o ADAH (closed Mondays) has the following records: federal and state censuses; vital records (birth, death, marriage, and divorce); county records (deeds, wills, and other probate records); land, military, and military discharge records (DD214s); surname files; city directories; African-American records (Reconstruction to the present); American Indian records; and immigration and naturalization records. [*FamilySearch* Wiki]
- Mobile Municipal Archives (http://www.cityofmobile.org/archives/)
  - o Includes records of early Alabama/Florida settlers: Spanish, French, and Anglo especially during the Spanish period. Good reference for Gulf Coast settlers.
- Huntsville-Madison County Public Library (http://hmcpl.org/departments/hhr)
  - o Contains a large genealogical collection for Alabama families and is a starting point in all time periods of Alabama
  - o Special Collections houses unique collections relating to Huntsville, Madison County, and Alabama history.
- Samford University Library (http://library.samford.edu/)
  - o Holds original and secondary sources primarily for Alabama and the Southeast USA.
  - o Irish manuscript and local histories for Kerry and Cork.
  - o The Baptist collection includes congregational and mission records, maps, local histories, genealogical periodicals, and newspapers.

Genealogical Societies and Publications

- The Alabama Historical Quarterly
  http://digital.archives.alabama.gov/cdm/search/collection/quarterly
  - o Hosted by the Alabama Dept of Archives & History (digitized and word searchable)
  - o Dates from 1930 - 1982
- Alabama Genealogical Society (http://algensoc.org/) publishes the AGS Magazine twice a year

Manuscripts, Biographical Sources, and Personal Papers

- "WPA Index to Alabama Biography," *Birmingham Public Library*
  http://bpldb.bplonline.org/db/biographies
  - o This is a Works Progress Administration project begun in the 1930's then abandoned when funding for the WPA was curtailed.
  - o "Although the index was never completed, over 97 titles such as Who's Who in America, other biographical dictionaries, and local histories were

indexed by the workers. It is an invaluable tool for researching Alabama
biographical sources."

- "Alabama Biography," *FamilySearch Wiki*
  https://familysearch.org/wiki/en/Alabama_Biography
  The wiki article lists online resources, and the Family History Library titles for
  Alabama
- Thomas and Marie Owen, *History of Alabama and Dictionary of Alabama
  Biography,* (Chicago, Illinois : S.J. Clarke Pub. Co., 1921). 4 Digital volumes on
  FamilySearch
- Thomas McAdory Owen, LL.D., *History of Alabama and Dictionary of Alabama
  Biography,* (Chicago, Illinois : S.J. Clarke Pub. Co. : 1921). Digitized book at
  MyHeritage

Migration Routes

- The Old Federal Road website (http://oldfederalroad.aum.edu/) provides an
  interactive map as well as information on this route from Georgia into Alabama;
    - In 1805, the U.S. Government got permission from the Creek Nation for a
      "horse path" from the Ocmulgee River to the Mobile River, through the
      Creek Nation. This became the Federal Road that thousands of settlers
      would use to move into Mississippi Territory (present-day Alabama and
      Mississippi.)
    - The Old Federal Road was begun in 1811 and connected Fort Stoddert,
      Alabama to Ford Wilkinson, Georgia.
    - Became a major military road; was the highway of its day, directly
      contributed to the increase in Alabama's population between 1810 and
      1820.
- "Alabama Migration," *FamilySearch Wiki*: Links and maps
  https://familysearch.org/wiki/en/Alabama_Migration
    - Fall Line Road: Colonial road from Philadelphia to Montgomery, Alabama;
      as Indians were removed from 1790-1826, the Fall Line Road extended
      further west until the 1831 final treaty that allowed settlers to settle as
      far as Montgomery.
    - Natchez Trace: "Old Natchez Trace" or "Chickasaw Trail" was a 450 mile
      long trail connecting what were originally American Indian settlements on
      the Cumberland and Tennessee Rivers with settlements near the
      Mississippi River (Natchez, Mississippi, Grand Village of the Natchez
      Indians.) It became a road in 1801 making it possible for a wagon to go
      overland from the east coast to the Mississippi River. It declined in
      importance after 1816 when rival roads and steamboats grabbed much of
      its traffic.

- Indian Trails
  - William E. Meyers, *Indian Trails of the Southeast: Extract from the 42nd Annual Report of the Bureau of American Ethnology.* Map covers 125 individual Southeast trails from Kentucky to Florida, the Atlantic to Texas. http://www.gustavslibrary.com/setrails.htm
  - Great Indian Warpath or Seneca Trail: A network of ancient Indian pathways with many branches. From Mobile, Alabama northeast to Tennessee and on. Many settlers used sections of the trail. https://www.familysearch.org/wiki/en/Great_Indian_Warpath
- Dorothy Williams Potter, *Passports of Southeastern Pioneers, 1770–1823: Indian, Spanish, and Other Land Passports for Tennessee, Kentucky, Georgia, Mississippi, Virginia, North and South Carolina,* (Baltimore, Maryland: Gateway Press, 1982).
  - Digitized book available at Family History Centers.
  - A source listing persons traveling through Indian lands during the period from 1798 to 1819 Alabama was part of the Mississippi Territory. These records list people going from the Mississippi Territory elsewhere or coming into the Mississippi Territory from other states. The records also mention people who obtained passports from the Chickasaw, Choctaw, and Cherokee Indian agencies to pass through their land. The book is well indexed.

RECORDS

Bible Records and Compiled Genealogies

- Jeannette Holland Austin, *Alabama Bible records,* (Riverdale, Georgia: J.H. Austin, 1987). Database available at the Family History Library.
- MariLee Beatty Hageness, *Abstracts of Georgia - Alabama Bible and family records,* (Anniston, Alabama: MLH Research, 1995-1998). 7 volumes
- Sharry Crofford-Gould, *Bible records index,* (San Antonio, Texas: Limited Editions, c1982). FHL 973 V2; digitized book available at Family History Centers. Surname index to some 3000 family Bibles which were printed in published sources, such as periodicals, books, etc. These published sources came from Arkansas, Texas, Alabama, Virginia, Tennessee, Utah, New York, Washington D.C., South Carolina (actually for Georgia), but may cover a much broader area.
- Index to Early Bible Records: http://www.learnwebskills.com/patriot/biblerecords.htm Free index to over 17,000 online and offline pre-1830 Bible records. Use the names and dates in the index to identify a Bible record of interest
- DAR GRC Index http://www.learnwebskills.com/patriot/documentingthelineage.htm#dargrc

- o For more than 100 years, DAR members have been researching, transcribing, and compiling thousands of "reports" containing vital records, cemetery records, family Bibles, military records, court records, obituaries, and probate records.
  - o Known as the DAR GRC (Genealogical Records Committee) Reports, the entire collection is housed at the DAR Library in Washington DC.
- Pauline Myra Jones Gandrud, *Alabama Records* (Easley, South Carolina: Southern Historical Press, 1981). 245 volumes, each individual indexed.

Census Records and Substitutes

Colonial and Territorial Censuses

- 1786, 1787, and 1789 Spanish Censuses on the Baldwin County website http://baldwincountyal.gov/departments/archives-history/online-eresources/census-records
- Lawrence H. Feldman, *Anglo-Americans in Spanish Archives: Lists of Anglo-American Settlers in the Spanish Colonies of America: a Finding Aid,* (Baltimore, Maryland: Genealogical Pub. Co., 1991).
  - o From source materials available in some of the major Spanish archives, the author has abstracted from original census documents genealogical data about individuals and families who settled in the French territories of Louisiana and the Floridas after they came under Spanish rule in 1766.
  - o The areas settled correspond to the present-day states of Florida, Alabama, Mississippi, Louisiana, and Missouri in the US and to Belize, formerly British Honduras, in Central America. The time period of the tabulated census data is 1781-1797.
- *Alabama early settlers, 1816: Alabama counties----Mississippi territory,* (Hanceville, Alabama : Briarwood Press, 1983).
- Daughters of the American Revolution, Broken Arrow Chapter, *Inhabitants of Alabama in 1816,* (Pell City, Alabama: Daughters of the American Revolution. Broken Arrow Chapter, 1955). Digital version, *FamilySearch,* https://familysearch.org/search/catalog/215867

State Censuses

- "Alabama State Census, 1820-1866" https://search.ancestry.com/search/db.aspx?dbid=1576
  - o Images of state censuses from Alabama for the years 1820, 1850, 1855, and 1866. Each of these censuses recorded the names of the head of households and the number of other household inhabitants according to gender and age categories.
  - o Some years also included race categories and distinguished between individuals who were free and slave. Unfortunately, records do not exist

for every county that existed at the time. See the webpage for a listing of counties and years available.

- "Alabama State Census, 1855": index to the census taken in 1855, no images
https://www.familysearch.org/search/collection/1915984
- "Alabama State Census, 1866": Index to the census taken in 1866, no images
https://www.familysearch.org/search/collection/1915987
  - ○ This census lists head of household and has statistical information about the makeup of the household. In some counties, the records indicate whether there were soldiers in the household who were killed, disabled, or died of sickness.
- "Alabama Voter Registration, 1867": one of the first records to list African American males living in Alabama
https://search.ancestry.com/search/db.aspx?dbid=60968
  - ○ The Alabama 1867 voter registration records were created as a direct result of a Reconstruction Act passed by the United States Congress on March 23, 1867.
  - ○ The act required the commanding officer in each military district to hold, before September 1, 1867, a registration of all male citizens, 21 years and older, in each county who were also qualified to vote and who had taken the loyalty oath. Each registrant visited the local registration office, took the oath, and was listed in the Voter Registration record.
  - ○ 1867 Voter Registration database from ADAH: indexed and with images
http://www.archives.alabama.gov/voterreg/search.cfm
- "Alabama, Census of Confederate Soldiers, 1907, 1921"
https://search.ancestry.com/search/db.aspx?dbid=1998
  - ○ *Ancestry* collection from ADAH of two censuses of Confederate Soldiers residing in Alabama in the early 1900s. Both were carried out more for pension purposes than for numbering purposes, but the census counted any Confederate veterans residing in Alabama, not just those who served for a regiment or company from Alabama.
- "Alabama, Compiled Census and Census Substitutes Index, 1810-1890" *Ancestry* collection from a variety of records: Alabama State Census, 1820-1866, U.S. Federal Census Mortality Schedules, 1850-1885, U.S. Census Reconstructed Records, 1660-1820, Alabama, Homestead and Cash Entry Patents, Pre-1908.
https://search.ancestry.com/search/db.aspx?dbid=3531

Federal Censuses

Alabama Non-Population Schedules table at *FamilySearch* Wiki
https://www.familysearch.org/wiki/en/Alabama_Census

Cemetery Records

- "Alabama Cemeteries," *FamilySearch Wiki*
  https://familysearch.org/wiki/en/Alabama_Cemeteries
    - Links to online Alabama cemetery records
    - Links to Family History Library collection of Alabama cemetery records
- Gazetteer of Alabama cemeteries by ePodunk.com > Alabama > Cemeteries
- Hazle R. Collins Ivison, *Alabama Tombstone Inscriptions,* (Mobile, Alabama: Dorothy J. Moffett, 1987). Digitized book on *FamilySearch* includes index

Church Records

- Alabama Church and Synagogue Records Collection Database. ADAH index to the collection searchable by denomination and county; can also browse by denomination http://www.archives.alabama.gov/AlChurchRecs/search.cfm
- "U.S., Evangelical Lutheran Church of America, Records, 1875-1940," *Ancestry* collection; browse Alabama counties and cities; membership, baptismal records and more https://search.ancestry.com/search/db.aspx?dbid=60722
- "Alabama Church Records." Specific denominations in Alabama and where the records are housed.
  https://www.familysearch.org/wiki/en/Alabama_Church_Records
- Alabama Church Records by County at
  https://www.accessgenealogy.com/alabama/alabama-church-records.htm

Court Records

Colonial Period

"Original Spanish, French and English documents, 1788-1798; index, 1788-1798, 1788-1798." Microfilm of original housed at the Probate Court of Mobile County, in Mobile, Alabama. Documents deal with land and property matters, criminal and civil matters, bills of sales, slavery matters, military items and vital information. Many records are from the city of Mobile. https://www.familysearch.org/search/catalog/976666

Territorial and Statehood

- Original court records are kept either in the county courthouse or in the State Archives. The Family History Library and the Alabama Department of Archives and History have microfilm copies of court records from many counties. Few of the records are well indexed. Some court records have been transcribed and published in books or periodicals.

- Alabama State Court Organization: flow chart of courts and jurisdictions
  http://www.courtstatistics.org/other-
  pages/state_court_structure_charts/alabama.aspx
- Alabama Blacksheep Ancestors:
  http://www.blacksheepancestors.com/usa/alabama.shtml
  - Search for Blacksheep Ancestors in Genealogical Prison and Convict
    Records, Historical Court Records, Executions, Insane Asylum Records and
    Biographies of Famous Outlaws, Criminals & Pirates in the United States,
    United Kingdom and Canada
- "Alabama Court Records" at *FamilySearch*. List of the major Alabama courts that
  kept records of genealogical value.
  https://www.familysearch.org/wiki/en/Alabama_Court_Records

Ethnic Records

African Americans
- "Alabama Voter Registration, 1867": one of the first records to list African
  American males living in Alabama. The Alabama 1867 voter registration records
  were created as a direct result of a Reconstruction Act passed by the United States
  Congress on March 23, 1867.
  https://search.ancestry.com/search/db.aspx?dbid=60968
- Freedmen Bureau Records on *FamilySearch*: indexes and available online
  https://www.familysearch.org/search/catalog/1193947
  - United States Records of Freedmen
  - United States Freedmen's Bureau Labor Contracts, Indenture and
    Apprenticeship Records
  - United States Freedmen's Bureau, Records of Freedmen's Complaints
  - United States Freedmen's Bureau Claim Records
  - United States Freedmen's Bureau Hospital and Medical Records
  - Alabama, Freedmen's Bureau Field Office Records
- "U.S., Southeast Coastwise Inward and Outward Slave Manifests, 1790-1860,"
  Ancestry database with images, search by first names.
  https://search.ancestry.com/search/db.aspx?dbid=1714

Native Americans
"Indians of Alabama" https://www.familysearch.org/wiki/en/Indians_of_Alabama
- Tribes and Bands of Alabama
- Alabama State Recognized Tribes
- Details and resources for Cherokee, Choctaw, Chickasaw, and Creek research

Immigration and Naturalization Records

- "Alabama Emigration and Immigration" Links and information about southern ports
  https://www.familysearch.org/wiki/en/Alabama_Emigration_and_Immigration
- "Alabama Immigration & Travel" collections on *Ancestry*
  https://search.ancestry.com/Places/US/Alabama/Default.aspx?category=40&ldf=1
  - "U.S., Applications for Seaman's Protection Certificates, 1916-1940"
  - "Alabama, Naturalization Records, 1888-1991"
  - "Alabama, Passenger Lists, 1904-1962," database with images, provided by NARA; can browse by series description
  - "U.S., Southeast Coastwise Inward and Outward Slave Manifests, 1790-1860," database with images, search by first names

Land Records – Federal Land State

"Alabama Land and Property," Information on land records for the various countries, states, and territories that governed Alabama before statehood
https://www.familysearch.org/wiki/en/Alabama_Land_and_Property

Colonial and Territorial Records

- Clifford Neal Smith, *Spanish and British Land Grants in Mississippi Territory, 1750-1784,* (Baltimore: Genealogical Publishing Co., Inc., 2004) Searchable digitized book; includes index; derived from the "public lands" and "claims" records found in the "The American State Papers": consists of grants or patents made to Americans and subsequently recorded in the Register's office for the Mississippi Territory. http://search.ancestry.com/search/db.aspx?dbid=49216
- *First settlers of the Mississippi Territory : Grants Taken from the American State Papers, Class VIII, Public Lands, Volume I,* (St. Louis: Ingmire Publications). Digitized book, indexed;
  https://search.ancestry.com/search/db.aspx?dbid=26397

Federal Government Land Sales - beginning 1806
- United States Bureau of Land Management Tract Books, 1800 – circa 1955
  https://www.familysearch.org/search/collection/2074276
  - *FamilySearch* collection, browse only; organized by state, then volume; the books are organized by township number and range number
  - "Tract Books": https://www.familysearch.org/wiki/en/Tract_Books : History, content, arrangement and search strategies
  - Tract Books Coverage Table designates the township and range for each volume
    https://www.familysearch.org/wiki/en/United_States,_Bureau_of_Land_

Management_Tract_Books_Coverage_Table_(FamilySearch_Historical_Re cords)

- Search Land Patents at Bureau of Land Management General Land Office Records to obtain Township and Range (https://glorecords.blm.gov/default.aspx)
    - 8 million successful federal land applications are indexed here
    - 2 million applications were left unfinished or were rejected and not in this database; to locate, a page-by-page tract book search is necessary, then the application can be sent for from the National Archives
    - 3,907 tract books containing official records of the land status and transactions involving surveyed public lands arranged by state and then by township and range.
    - These books indicate who obtained the land and include a physical description of the tract and where the land is located. The type of transaction is also recorded such as cash entry, credit entry, homesteads, patents (deeds) granted by the Federal Government, and other conveyances of title such as Indian allotments, internal improvement grants (to states), military bounty land warrants, private land claims, railroad grants, school grants, and swamp grants.
    - Additional items of information included in the tract books are as follows: number of acres, date of sale, purchase price, land office, entry number, final Certificate of Purchase number, and notes on relinquishments and conversions. Original documents are located at the Bureau of Land management in Springfield, Virginia.

Land Claims by Choctaw Indians

Choctaw Indians who chose to remain in the east could receive land allotments or, later, scrip for public lands in Mississippi, Louisiana, Alabama, or Arkansas. The records are in the National Archives, Records Group 75. These are the records of the claims commission connected with the 1830 Treaty of Dancing Rabbit Creek. The records of scrip certificates surrendered for land are in the Bureau of Land Management, Records Group 49. Most of these records have been microfilmed.

- Joe R. Goss, *A Complete Roll of All Choctaw Claimants and Their Heirs Existing Under the Treaties Between the United States and the Choctaw Nation as Far as Shown by the Records of the United States and of the Choctaw Nation,* 1889 Reprint, (Conway, Arkansas: Oldbuck Press, 1992). Lists those who filed for land allotments or scrip.
- Angie Debo,*The Rise and Fall of the Choctaw Republic. The Civilizations of the American Indians Series*; 6 (Norman, Oklahoma: University of Oklahoma Press, 1961). A helpful history of the Choctaw people from the 1500s to about 1930.

Military Records

- Many federal military records of Alabama are found at the Family History Library, the National Archives, and the National Archives Southeast Region (Atlanta) (Morrow, Georgia).
- The Alabama Department of Archives and History has the most complete collection of Alabama military records. Their collection includes military records and soldiers' correspondence from all wars in which Alabama has participated. "Alabamians at War," is a list of all collections at the Alabama Archives for the Revolutionary War through the Vietnam War. http://www.archives.alabama.gov/referenc/military.html
- "Alabama Military" on *Ancestry* - large collection of records, many from ADAH https://search.ancestry.com/Places/US/Alabama/Default.aspx?category=39

Civil War
- "Alabama Civil War Service Cards" file at ADAH; most collections have been digitized by Ancestry.com http://www.archives.alabama.gov/civilwar/index.cfm
- "Alabama Civil War Service Records of Confederate Soldiers, 1861-1865" *Family Search* collection Confederate service records of soldiers who served in organizations from Alabama. https://www.familysearch.org/search/collection/1932139
- "Alabama Civil War Service Records of Union Soldiers, 1861-1865" *FamilySearch* collection, Union service records of soldiers who served in the First Regiment of Alabama Cavalry. https://www.familysearch.org/search/collection/1932389
- "Alabama, Confederate Pension and Service Records, 1862-1947" This *Ancestry* collection contains records held at ADAH that relate to Confederate veterans' pensions in Alabama between 1865-1940. During the 35 years after the Civil War until 1900, only disabled soldiers were receiving a pension from the state of Alabama for their service. In 1899, the State Legislature authorized pensions for Confederate veterans who weren't disabled and resided in Alabama or for their widows. https://search.ancestry.com/search/db.aspx?dbid=1593
- "Alabama Civil War Muster Rolls, 1861-1865" https://search.ancestry.com/search/db.aspx?dbid=1736
  - These rolls are for Confederate units formed in Alabama during the Civil War—though many operated outside of the state over the course of the war. The records include rolls for infantry, cavalry, artillery, reserves, navy, marines, and even out-of-state regiments.
  - *Ancestry* collection from original data at ADAH. The rolls in this database are searchable by roll date, name, and estimated birth year. Only muster rolls and similar records (such as payroll records) have been indexed for this collection, but other records from the source collection are included and are grouped by unit.
  - Browse once the individual's unit is determined

World War I

World War I Gold Star Database at ADAH found at:
http://www.archives.alabama.gov/goldstar/info.html This database contains information on individuals who died during the war or who had been awarded recognition, biographical sketches, photographs, newspaper articles, and correspondence from family members.

Newspapers and Directories

- "Alabama Online Historical Newspapers" at *The Ancestor Hunt*: description of newspaper, county and city, years covered, where to access.
  https://sites.google.com/site/onlinenewspapersite/Home/usa/al
- "Alabama Online Historical Directories"
  https://sites.google.com/site/onlinedirectorysite/Home/usa/al listed by county
- "Alabama Newspapers on Microfilm" at ADAH; search newspapers by county for name of newspaper and dates available.
  http://www.archives.alabama.gov/newsmicro/search.cfm
- Alabama "Hardbound Newspapers" hardbound - ADAH; search newspapers by county for name of newspaper and dates available.
  http://www.archives.alabama.gov/newshard/search.cfm
- Pauline Myra Jones Gandrud and Lucille Smith Craddock, *Marriage, Death and Legal Notices From Early Alabama Newspapers, 1819-1893*, (Easley, South Carolina: Southern Historical Press, 1981). Newspapers from neighboring states as well.
- Tad Evans, *Alabama Newspaper Clippings: Taken from Georgia Newspapers, 1814-1907* (Savannah, Georgia: Tad Evans, 2007). Digitized book on *FamilySearch*
- Alabama Newspapers & Publications at *Ancestry*
  https://search.ancestry.com/Places/US/Alabama/Default.aspx?category=38&ldf=2
  Ancestry record collection

Probate Records

- "Alabama Estate Files, 1830-1976"
  https://www.familysearch.org/search/collection/1978117
  - *FamilySearch* collection: Index and images of estate files created by the probate courts of various Alabama counties.
  - Probates were generally recorded in the county of residence. This collection covers probate records created 1830-1976, but the content and time period of the records will vary by county.
- "Alabama, Wills and Probate Records, 1753-1999," *Ancestry* collection: images of probate records from the state of Alabama. 99% of Alabama counties included.
  https://search.ancestry.com/search/db.aspx?dbid=8799

Vital Records

The Center for Health Statistics operates the vital records system and collects and tabulates health-related statistical data for the state of Alabama.
http://www.alabamapublichealth.gov/vitalrecords/

Birth Records

- How to Find Alabama Birth Records
  https://www.familysearch.org/wiki/en/How_to_Find_Alabama_Birth_RecordsFamilySearch WIKI information with links
- The Alabama Center for Health Statistics began filing birth certificates in 1908 for persons born in Alabama.
- Restrictions: By Alabama law, birth certificates are confidential records with restricted access for 125 years from the date of birth. They may be obtained by the following persons, upon payment of the proper fee: individual, parent, grandparent, spouse, child, sibling, guardian or anyone with a legal interest in the certificate.
- "Alabama Births and Christenings, 1881-1930" *FamilySearch* Collection - Name index to birth, baptism, and christening records from the state of Alabama. Microfilm copies available at the Family History Library and Family History Centers. Due to privacy laws, recent records may not be displayed. The year range represents most of the records. Not complete for any time period or area.
  https://www.familysearch.org/search/collection/1661470
- "Alabama Births and Christenings, Coverage Table (*FamilySearch* Historical Records)"
  https://www.familysearch.org/wiki/en/Alabama_Births_and_Christenings,_Coverage_Table_(FamilySearch_Historical_Records)

Death Records

- "How to Find Alabama Death Records" Strategies and links
  https://www.familysearch.org/wiki/en/How_to_Find_Alabama_Death_Records
- For copies of Alabama death records after 1908, contact: Center for Health Statistics; State Dept. of Public Health; P.O. Box 5625 ; Montgomery, AL 36103-5625; Tel: 202-242-503 Center for Health Statistics
  http://www.alabamapublichealth.gov/vitalrecords/
- "Alabama Deaths and Burials, 1881-1952" *FamilySearch* Collection; Name index to death and burial records from the state of Alabama. Microfilm copies of these records are available at the Family History Library and Family History Centers. This set contains 110,202 records. The year range represents most of the records.
  https://www.familysearch.org/search/collection/1674670

- "Alabama Deaths, 1908-1974," *FamilySearch* collection: Name index to death certificates from the state of Alabama, 1908-1974. https://www.familysearch.org/search/collection/1307888
- "Alabama, Death Index, 1908-1959" https://search.ancestry.com/search/db.aspx?dbid=5188
  - *Ancestry* collection: This database is an index of deaths recorded by the state of Alabama from 1908 to 1959. The registration of births and deaths on the county level began in 1881; however, state-level registration of deaths in Alabama did not begin until 01 January 1908.
  - The index includes name of the deceased, county of death, date of death, and the state certificate number (volume and page).
  - Alabama deaths, 1908-1974; index to deaths, 1908-1959 *FamilySearch* catalog listing of microfilm of death certificates; use with death indexes on *FamilySearch* or *Ancestry*. https://www.familysearch.org/search/catalog/683729

Marriage Records

- The Alabama Center for Health Statistics began filing marriage certificates in 1936 for marriages that occurred in Alabama. (Information for marriages prior to 1936 must be obtained from the probate office in the county where the marriage license was issued.)
- "How to Find Alabama Marriage Records" links and strategies https://www.familysearch.org/wiki/en/How_to_Find_Alabama_Marriage_Records
- "Alabama Marriages, Coverage Table (*FamilySearch* Historical Records)" https://www.familysearch.org/wiki/en/Alabama_Marriages,_Coverage_Table_(FamilySearch_Historical_Records)
- "County Marriage Holdings Map, Alabama": interactive map http://user.xmission.com/~jsvare/FR/AL_FRM.html
- "Alabama, Select Marriages, 1816-1942," *Ancestry* collection: This index is not complete for any particular place, region or time period. This collection may include information previously published in the International Genealogical Index or Vital Records Index collections. https://search.ancestry.com/search/db.aspx?dbid=60000
- "Alabama County Marriages, 1809-1950" *FamilySearch* collection: This collection of marriage records for Alabama counties includes: a) indexed records with images; b) indexed records without images; and c) images which can be browsed but do not have searchable indexes. The indexed records without images display a message "Image is Unavailable" when you attempt to view the image. The browse records are grouped by film number / digital film number (DGS). Each film is arranged by county, volume and date. https://www.familysearch.org/search/collection/1743384

- "Alabama Marriages, 1816-1957"
  https://www.familysearch.org/search/collection/1674672 *FamilySearch* collection: Name index to marriage records from the state of Alabama. Microfilm copies of these records are available at the Family History Library and Family History Centers. Due to privacy laws, recent records may not be displayed. The year range represents most of the records. A few records may be earlier or later.

Research Plan - George W. Dillard

Objective

The objective of this research project is to determine if George W. Dillard born 1781 in Virginia and died 1854 in Lee County, Alabama is the father of Cynthia Dillard. Cynthia was born about 1816 in Georgia. She married Thomas Beverly Royston about 1833 in Georgia or Alabama and died in 1882 in Collin County, Texas.

Summary of Known Facts

Cynthia Dillard Royston

1. Cynthia Dillard was born about 1815 according to her reported age on the 1850, 1860, 1870, and 1880 census records.

2. Cynthia Dillard was born in Georgia, Alabama, or Florida, according to the census records and information from the death certificates of three of her children.

3. Cynthia married Thomas Beverly Royston about 1833 in Georgia or Alabama, no marriage record has yet been located.

4. Thomas Beverly Royston was listed in the 1831 tax list of Morgan County, Georgia.

5. Thomas and Cynthia Royston owned land in DeKalb County, Alabama from 1837 – 1842 and are listed on the 1840 census in that county.

6. Thomas and Cynthia Royston owned land and resided in Chambers County, Alabama from about 1842-1872 and are listed on the 1850, 1860, and 1870 census (Cynthia as a widow in 1870).

7. Thomas Beverly Royston died in 1868 in Chambers County, Alabama and his estate file gives the information that Cynthia and some of the children "removed to Texas" about 1872.

8. Cynthia Royston and some children are listed on the 1880 census of Collin County, Texas. Birthplace of her parents is given as Virginia.

9. The estate file of Thomas Beverly Royston gives Cynthia's date of death in Collin County, Texas as 2 August 1882.

George W. Dillard

1. George W. Dillard was born 26 August 1781 in Virginia and died 21 May 1854 in Auburn, Russell County, Alabama; the dates are taken from his headstone inscription, "erected by his children."

2. George married Peggy Armour 9 November 1801 in Greene County, Georgia.

3. The couple had the following children based on the 1810 and 1820 censuses.

   a. 1 male born 1795/1805
   b. 1 male born 1805/1810
   c. 2 males born 1810/20
   d. 1 female born 1810/20 - possibly Cynthia
   e. 1 female born 1805/1810

4. G.W. Dillard served in the Creek War of 1813-1814 along with L.D / S.D. Dillard in the same company of the Alabama Mounted Volunteers, Young's Company (spies).

5. Peggy Armour died between the 1820 census and George's 2nd marriage on 29 July 1822 to Martha Flournoy Wells in Greene County, Georgia.

6. George moved to Muscogee County Georgia by 1830 where he is mentioned in the local newspaper, *The Columbus Enquirer* from 1832-1838.

7. George purchased land in Chambers County, Alabama, in 1836 and 1840.

8. George moved to Russell County, Alabama, and is listed on the 1840 census there with his household.

9. George moved to Macon County, Alabama, and is listed on the 1850 census with his wife Martha, and children: Columbus age 21, Alonzo age 15, Leonidas, age 9, and Zenora, age 7.

10. George died in 1854 and is buried in Pine Hill Cemetery, Auburn, Alabama. His children erected his headstone, no names of the children or date given.

Connections between Cynthia Dillard and George W. Dillard

1. George W. Dillard lived in proximity to Cynthia and Thomas B. Royston from 1840 to his death in 1854. George is listed on the 1840 census in Russell County, Alabama, and Thomas B. Royston is listed on the 1840 census in DeKalb County, Alabama. By 1850, George had moved to Macon County, Alabama and Thomas

and Cynthia to Chambers County, Alabama. They were separated only by one county.

2. George purchased land in Chambers County, Alabama, in 1836 and 1840. Thomas and Cynthia Royston settled in Chambers County, Alabama, about 1850 and had a large cotton plantation.

3. George had a son named Leonidas, born 1841. Thomas and Cynthia named a son Thomas Leonidas in 1857.

4. Cynthia named a daughter Margaret, possibly after Peggy Armour, George W. Dillard's first wife and possible mother of Cynthia.

5. The household of George W. Dillard in 1820 and 1830 has a female of the appropriate age to be Cynthia.

6. Records of Muscogee County, Georgia where George Dillard was living in 1833 were destroyed by fire in 1838, possibly why no marriage record for Thomas Royston and Cynthia Dillard has been discovered.

Background Information

Muscogee County, where George W. Dillard resided from 1830-1840 lost its early records in a courthouse fire of 1838. No land, probate, or marriage records survived. If Cynthia was married in the county the record would not be extant.

Working Hypothesis

George Wellington Dillard is the father of Cynthia Dillard. His household contains a female of the appropriate age on the 1820 and 1830 census enumerations. She married Thomas Beverly Royston in Muscogee County about 1833. No marriage record exists because a courthouse fire burned destroying the records before 1838.

George Dillard purchased land in Chambers County Alabama in 1836 and in 1840. Cynthia Dillard and Thomas B. Royston moved to Chambers County by 1850 and acquired a large amount of land, possibly land given to her by George Dillard.

Nathaniel Dillard received a land grant in Chambers County 1834 and could be a brother to Cynthia as well as George Dillard's son. Lorenzo D Dillard also received a land grant in Chambers County in 1837 could be a brother to Cynthia and George Dillard's Son.

Cynthia named a son Thomas Leonidas in 1857. George W. Dillard named a son Leonidas in 1841. This unusual name could be a good connecting link between Cynthia and George Dillard.

In 1850, George Dillard is living in Macon County, Alabama, one county away from Chambers County where Cynthia and Thomas are living. Families often migrated together and the proximity of the Dillards and Roystons could support a father/daughter relationship.

Identified Sources

- Marriage records for Thomas Beverly Royston and Cynthia Dillard in Georgia.

- City directory for Columbus, Georgia - possible mention of George W. Dillard, mentioned as a commissioner in the Columbus Enquirer from 1832-1838.

- 1830 and 1840 census records for possible older brothers of Cynthia Dillard in Georgia and Alabama.

- Military pension records for George W. Dillard.

- Probate records for George W. Dillard in Macon County, Alabama.

- Court and land records in DeKalb & Chambers County Alabama for Dillards - counties where Thomas and Cynthia resided.

- Land study of Chambers County land for both Dillard and Royston surnames.

Prioritized Research Strategy

1. Marriage records for Thomas Beverly Royston and Cynthia should be rechecked for the years 1830-1835 in Georgia. As new records are added to online collections, the possibility of discovering the marriage record, if extant, increases.

    a. "Georgia Marriages, 1699-1944," *Ancestry* Index, source Hunting For Bears, comp. Georgia Marriages. Includes Morgan County and surrounding counties: Greene, Oconee (Clarke parent county), Walton, Newton, Jasper, and Putnam.

    b. "Georgia Church Marriages, 1754-1960," *FamilySearch*.

    c. Morgan County, Georgia, "Marriages 1821-1854," FHL film 158906, digitized and indexed on *FamilySearch*.

2. Land study of Royston and Dillard land in Chambers County, Alabama.

    a. View the land patents of Chambers County, Alabama for George Dillard, Lorenzo D. Dillard, and Nathaniel Dillard - Chambers County tract books on *FamilySearch*

    b. Compile list of all Royston land in Chambers County, Alabama from the deed books of Chambers County.

    c. Compare land descriptions to determine any Dillard/Royston connections

3.   Search probate records for George Dillard in Macon County, Alabama

    a.   "Macon County, Alabama, Probate Records, 1834-1930," digitized microfilm, *FamilySearch* (https:/www.familysearch.org). Search from 1854-1874.

    b.   "Alabama, Wills and Probate Records, 1753-1999," indexed and digitized microfilm, *Ancestry* (https://search.ancestry.com).

4.   Search for George W. Dillard in: Mary Jane Galer, *Columbus, Georgia, Lists of People in the Town, 1828-1852 : and Sexton's Reports to 1866,* (Columbus, Georgia: M.G. Galer, 2000).

5.   Search for a military pension for George W. Dillard: "United States Old War Pension Index, 1815-1926," *FamilySearch* (hhttps://www.familysearch.org/search/collection/1979425).

6.   Search court records of Macon County, Alabama for George W. Dillard. "Miscellaneous records, wills, estate records, marriages, etc., 1839-1886" FHL microfilm 1391868 is indexed on *FamilySearch.*

7.   Search the 1830 and 1840 censuses of Alabama for possible brothers of Cynthia - particularly Nathaniel and Lorenzo from the land tract books of Chambers County, Alabama.

Research Log Sample

George W. Dillard

DATE	REPOSITORY URL, Call # Film #	SEARCHING FOR	LOCALITY	SOURCE CITATION	RESULTS
7 Jun 2017	*Ancestry* http://ancstry.me/2 rVSNGJ	1820 Census George W. Dillard	Georgia, Greene County	1820 U.S. Census, Greene County, Georgia, Capt E Woodhams District, population schedule, p. 202, line 2, George W. Dillard household; digital image, *Ancestry* (http://www.ancestry.com: accessed 7 June 2017); citing NARA microfilm publication M33, roll 8.	Free White Persons Males 0/10 2 Males 10/15 1 Males 16/25 1 Males 26/44 1 Females 0/10 1 Females 0/15 1 Females 26/ 44 1
11 Feb 2018	*General Land Office Records* http://bit.ly/2HhYW 5R	Land Patents for George W. Dillard	Alabama, Chambers County	George W. Dillard,(Chambers County, Alabama), 1837, cash entry patents no. 3733, 3768, 3770, 3771, "Land Patent Search," images, *General Land Office Records* (www.glorecords.blm.gov : accessed 17 March 2018).	State Volume Patents, dated 10 April 1837, St Stephens Meridian, Section 29, Chambers County, Alabama: # 3733, 3768, 3770, 3771.
7 Jun 2017	*FamilySearch* https://familysearc h.org/ark:/61903/3: 1:33SQ-GPP6-94XQ	Marriage record for George W. Dillard and Margaret Armour	Georgia, Greene County	Greene County, Georgia, "Marriage Licenses 1786 To 1810," p. 9, Dallard-Armour marriage, 9 November 1801; "Georgia, County Marriages, 1785-1950," image 21 of 659, *FamilySearch* (https://familysearch.org : accessed 7 June 2017); citing "Marriage Records 1786-1849," FHL microfilm # 159,052.	Nov. 9th 1801 George W. Dallard to Peggy Armour; self & Nicholson [vouchers]
19 Jun 2017	Family History Library Salt Lake City, UT 978.8473/C1 B3k v.1	Newspaper mention of George W. Dillard	Georgia, Muscogee County	Elizabeth Evans Kilbourne, *Columbus, Georgia, Newspaper Clippings (Columbus Enquirer Volume I, 1832-1834),* (Savannah, Georgia : E. Evans Kilbourne, 1997-2009), 4.	Saturday, March 26, 1831: "Candidates for Office: We are authorized to announce George W. Dillard as a candidate for Clerk of the superior Court of the county of Muscogee. . ."

Cynthia (Dillard) Royston

DATE	REPOSITORY URL, Call # Film #	SEARCHING FOR	LOCALITY	SOURCE CITATION	RESULTS
17 Aug 2016	*Ancestry* http://bit.ly/2iF8opX	1850 Census – Cynthia in household of Thomas B. Royston	Alabama, Chambers County	1850 U.S. Census, Chambers County, Alabama, population schedule, 19th District, p. 318 (stamped), dwelling 749, family 749, Thomas B Royston household; digital image, *Ancestry* (http://www.ancestry.com : accessed 17 August 2016); citing NARA microfilm publication M432, roll 2.	Thomas B Royston 47 Syntha 35 Mary 15 Ulissus 13 Baldwin 10 Adaline 8 Sarah 6 Joseph 4 Benjamin 4 Robert 2 Thomas B 0
18 Nov 2016	*Ancestry* http://bit.ly/2iFt4vS	Death Certificate for Adeline (Royston) Spears	Texas, Montague County	Texas State Board of Health, death certificate, Mrs. Adeline Spears, No 27410 (stamped), Registered No. 105 (penned). Bowie, 1920; digital image, "Texas, Death Certificates, 1903–1982," database, *Ancestry*, Montague 1920, Jul-Sep image 10 (http://search.ancestry.com: accessed 18 November 2016).	Mrs Adeline Spears, born 5 May 1841, in Alabama; died 19 August 1920 Informant M.C. Lovelady, Father - Thomas Royston, unknown birthplace, Maiden name of Mother - Dillard born Florida
27 Sep 2016	National Archives 8601 Adelphi Road College Park, MD	Land Case File for Thomas B. Royston, DeKalb County, Alabama	Alabama, DeKalb County	Thomas B. Royston (DeKalb County) cash entry file, 1842, state volume patent no. 5969, Lebanon, Alabama, Land Office; Land Entry Papers 1800-1908, Record Group 49: Records of the Bureau of Land Management; National Archives, Washington, D.C.	SE ¼ of Section 20, Township 9 of Range 7E under Act of 22 June 1838
1 Oct 2016	Family History Library Salt Lake City, UT 976.V2	Marriage Record for Thomas B. Royston and Cynthia Dillard	Alabama	Pauline Myra Jones Gandrud and Lucille Smith Craddock, *Marriage, Death and Legal Notices From Early Alabama Newspapers, 1819-1893*, (Easley, South Carolina: Southern Historical Press, 1981).	NIL for Royston in index

Is George W. Dillard the Father of Cynthia (Dillard) Royston? Research Report

Diana Elder, AG

RESEARCH SUMMARY

OBJECTIVE

The objective of this research project was to determine if George W. Dillard born 1781 in Virginia and died 1854 in Lee County, Alabama was the father of Cynthia (Dillard) Royston. Cynthia was born about 1815 in Georgia. She married Thomas Beverly Royston about 1833 in Georgia or Alabama and died 2 August 1882 in Collin County, Texas.

SUMMARY OF RESULTS

- Estimated the birth year of Cynthia (Dillard) Royston as 1815 based on the 1850-1880 census records. Also noted her birthplace of Georgia on the same census years and the birthplace of her father as Virginia from the 1880 census.
- Searched marriage records of Georgia and Alabama for a marriage of Cynthia (Dillard) Royston and Thomas Beverly Royston. No results.
- Studied Thomas B. Royston's land ownership in DeKalb County and Chambers County, Alabama.
- Confirmed the death dates of Cynthia (Dillard) Royston and Thomas B. Royston in the administration of his estate papers.
- Verified the fourteen children of Thomas and Cynthia Royston from census and probate records.
- Discovered Cynthia's maiden name of Dillard from the death certificates of three of her children: Martha Ann (Royston) Hogge, Richard A. Royston, and Adeline (Royston) Spears.
- Examined the records for George W. Dillard, candidate for father of Cynthia (Dillard) Royston.

- Noticed the presence of a female of appropriate age in the 1820 and 1830 households of George W. Dillard.
- Found two marriage records for George W. Dillard: the 1801 marriage to Peggy Armour and the 1822 marriage to Martha F. Wells. Determined that Peggy Armour would be the mother of Cynthia if George W. Dillard was her father.
- Researched newspaper articles for more information on the actions of George W. Dillard. Found several references to him in the community of Columbus, Muscogee County, Georgia, from 1828-1836.
- Noted the proximity of Thomas B. Royston's land in Lee County, Georgia, to Muscogee County, Georgia, providing a possible meeting for Thomas and Cynthia (Dillard) Royston.
- Researched newspaper articles for Thomas B. Royston. Found references to him in the *Columbus Enquirer* for 1841, putting him in the same location as George W. Dillard.
- Discovered the Muscogee County courthouse burned in 1838, destroying all records. If Cynthia (Dillard) Royston and Thomas B. Royston had married in the county, no record would exist, explaining the lack of a marriage record for the couple.
- Examined the land descriptions for George W. Dillard's land patents in Chambers County, Alabama.
- Compared the Dillard land descriptions to the Royston land descriptions using original deeds and land patents. No connection was made.
- Searched probate records for George W. Dillard in the general Alabama probate index and in the Macon County, Alabama, probate indexes, no results. Future research could expand the probate search to neighboring counties.
- Noticed the unique name of "Leonidas" in both the households of George W. Dillard (1850) and Thomas and Cynthia Royston (1860). Researching the descendants of George W. Dillard could uncover further naming patterns.

FUTURE RESEARCH SUGGESTIONS

- Search the probate records of Lee County, Alabama, for George W. Dillard.
- Order the land case entry files from the National Archives for George W. Dillard's land patents in Alabama between 1834 and 1841. The case entry files might have further clues that could uncover a relationship between Cynthia (Dillard) Royston and George W. Dillard.
- Build up the FAN club (friends, associates, and neighbors) for George W. Dillard and Thomas and Cynthia (Dillard) Royston looking for connections.
- Research the possible children of George W. Dillard from the 1850 census: Columbus, Alonzo, Leonidas, and Zenora. Note naming patterns among their descendants.

- Research Lorenzo and Nathaniel Dillard. They also patented land in Chambers County, Alabama, and could be related to George W. Dillard and/or Cynthia (Dillard) Royston.
- Research other Dillard men in Alabama from 1830-1860 to discover possible brothers to Cynthia from George W. Dillard's first marriage to Peggy Armour. Note naming patterns.
- Search for connections between Cynthia (Dillard) Royston and the family of her possible mother, Peggy Armour, of Greene County, Georgia.
- Identify other possible candidates for the father of Cynthia (Dillard) Royston from the 1820 and 1830 census records of Georgia.
- Systematically research each candidate and possibly eliminate as a father for Cynthia.
- DNA testing and analysis of the descendants of Cynthia (Dillard) Royston and the known descendants of George W. Dillard could reveal a connection.

Is George W. Dillard the Father of Cynthia (Dillard) Royston?

RESEARCH REPORT

The objective of this research project was to determine if George W. Dillard born 1781 in Virginia and died 1854 in Lee County, Alabama was the father of Cynthia (Dillard) Royston. Cynthia was born about 1815 in Georgia. She married Thomas Beverly Royston about 1833 in Georgia or Alabama and died 2 August 1882 in Collin County, Texas.

BACKGROUND INFORMATION

The descendants of Cynthia (Dillard) Royston have long wondered which of the many Dillard men present in Georgia and Alabama in the early 1800s was her father. Several original records contain circumstantial evidence that points to George W. Dillard as a plausible candidate for her father. Among these are the following:

- George W. Dillard's 1820 household in Georgia included a female under 10.[1]
- Cynthia (Dillard) Royston's estimated birth year from the 1850 census is 1815.[2]

---

[1] 1820 U.S. Census, Greene County, Georgia, Capt E Woodhams District, population schedule, p. 202, line 2, George W. Dillard household; digital image, *Ancestry* (http://www.ancestry.com : accessed 7 June 2017); citing NARA microfilm publication M33, roll 8.

[2] 1850 U.S. Census, Chambers County, Alabama, population schedule, 19th District, p. 318 (stamped), dwelling 749, family 749, Thomas B. Royston household; digital image, *Ancestry* (http://www.ancestry.com : accessed 17 August 2016); citing NARA microfilm publication M432, roll 2.

- George W. Dillard was granted several land patents in Chambers County, Alabama, in 1837[3]
- Thomas and Cynthia (Dillard) Royston moved to Chambers County, Alabama by 1850.[4]

Research began by comparing the life events of Cynthia (Dillard) Royston and George W. Dillard, in hopes of making enough connections to indirectly prove a relationship.

CYNTHIA (DILLARD) ROYSTON LIFE EVENTS

Cynthia (Dillard) Royston was born between 1815-1818 in Georgia according to the 1850 - 1880 census records. Table 1 details her age in each census and her estimated birth year. Although it appears that Cynthia grows younger with time, it is not unusual for ages to vary in the census records. The informant was often the head of household who didn't necessarily know the exact ages of each family member. Generally the earlier listings of age are more accurate making 1815 the best estimate. The census records do agree on Georgia as her place of birth. The table reflects the spelling variations of her name in the records.

TABLE 1. CYNTHIA (DILLARD) ROYSTON'S AGE IN CENSUS RECORDS FROM 1850-1880

NAME	CENSUS YEAR	RESIDENCE	AGE	ESTIMATED BIRTH YEAR	BIRTH PLACE
Synthia Royston	1850[a]	Chambers Co., Alabama	35	1815	Georgia
Cynthia Royston	1860[b]	Chambers Co., Alabama	44	1816	Georgia
Cynthia Royston	1870[c]	Chambers Co., Alabama	53	1817	Georgia
Syntha Royston	1880[d]	Collin Co., Texas	62	1818	Georgia
a.	1850 U.S. Census, Chambers County, Alabama, pop. sch., p. 318 (stamped), dwell. 749, fam. 749, Thomas B. Royston.				
b.	1860 U.S. Census, Chambers County, Alabama, population schedule, Northern Division, Milltown Post Office, page 130 (penned), dwelling 915, family 895, Thomas B. Royston household; digital image, *FamilySearch*				

---

[3] George W. Dillard, (Chambers County, Alabama), 1837, cash entry patents no. 3733, 3768, 3770, 3771, "Land Patent Search," images, *General Land Office Records* (www.glorecords.blm.gov : accessed 17 March 2018).

[4] 1850 U.S. Census, Chambers County, Alabama, pop. sch., p. 318 (stamped), dwell. 749, fam. 749, Thomas B. Royston.

(https://familysearch.org: accessed 29 April 2016); citing NARA microfilm publication M653 roll 4.

c. 1870 U.S. Census, Chambers County, Alabama, population schedule, Beat No 2, p. 4 (penned), p.22 (stamped), dwelling 24, family 24, Cynthia Royston household; digital image, *Ancestry* (http://www.ancestry.com : accessed 26 April 2016); citing NARA microfilm publication M593, roll 6.

d. 1880 U.S. Census, Collin County, Texas, population schedule, Precinct 5, enumeration district (ED) 26, p.11 (penned), dwelling 93, family 95, Cynthia in Thomas L Royston household; digital image, *Ancestry* (http://www.ancestry.com : accessed 17 November 2016); citing NARA microfilm publication T9, roll 1296.

Marriage of Thomas Beverly Royston and Cynthia Dillard

A marriage record can state the names of parents and provide clues to the place of residence of the couple. No marriage record has been located for Thomas and Cynthia giving that information. Thomas was living in Morgan County, Georgia in 1831[5] and had moved to DeKalb County, Alabama by 1837[6] so marriage indexes were searched in both states.[7] The oldest daughter, Mary E. Royston, was born 4 May 1834, giving an estimated marriage year of 1833 for Thomas and Cynthia.[8] If born in 1815, Cynthia would have been about 18 years old at her marriage.

Alabama Residence and Family of Thomas Beverly Royston and Cynthia Dillard

Thomas and Cynthia appear to have never resided in Georgia as a married couple. The 1850 census names Alabama as the birth place for the nine children in the household, beginning

---

[5] Morgan County, Georgia, Superior Court, 1831 Tax Digest, page 2, entry for Thomas B. Royston, Morgan County, Archives, Madison, Georgia.

[6] Thomas B. Royston (DeKalb County) cash entry file, 1842, state volume patent no. 5969, Lebanon, Alabama, Land Office; Land Entry Papers 1800-1908, Record Group 49: Records of the Bureau of Land Management; National Archives, Washington, D.C.

[7] Negative searches for Royston-Dillard marriage: Pauline Myra Jones Gandrud and Lucille Smith Craddock, *Marriage, Death and Legal Notices from Early Alabama Newspapers, 1819-1893*, (Easley, South Carolina: Southern Historical Press, 1981). See also "Georgia, County marriages, 1785-1950," *FamilySearch* (https://www.familysearch.org : accessed 15 March 2018).

[8] *Find A Grave*, database with images (http://www.findagrave.com : accessed 12 November 2016), memorial 43662594, Mary Elizabeth Royston Slagle (1834-1915), gravestone photographed by Bennie Gross, member 47013847.

with oldest daughter, Mary, born 1834.[9] Thomas' 1842 application for a land patent in DeKalb County, Alabama, contains a witness statement that the "said Royston settled on said quarter prior to January 1837, that he erected a dwelling house in which he has lived and made his home from that time to the year 1840 . . . having a wife and children."[10] No mention is made of the exact date Thomas and Cynthia moved to DeKalb County, Alabama, but the household is enumerated there on the 1840 census; the three children denoted by tick marks: two males under five and one female 5-10. [11]

The Royston family moved to Chambers County, Alabama by 1850 and began operating a large cotton plantation with the conditions ideal for growing this lucrative crop.[12] The 1850 census shows Thomas B. Royston's real estate valued at $1800, much higher than the neighbors.[13]

Thomas owned three to four times more land than any individual in the vicinity. Slave labor ran the plantation and the 1860 slave schedule lists 16 slaves owned by Thomas B. Royston.[14]

Cynthia and Thomas had fourteen children between the years 1834 and 1863.[15] The Civil War greatly affected the Royston family, with five of their sons enlisting for the Confederacy, and three of them dying as a result of that conflict.[16]

---

[9] 1850 U.S. Census, Chambers County, Alabama, pop. sch., p. 318 (stamped), dwell. 749, fam. 749, Thomas B. Royston.

[10] Thomas B. Royston (DeKalb County), witness statement of Wm C Smith and Isaac DeWall, cash entry file, 1842, state volume patent no. 5969, Lebanon, Alabama, Land Office.

[11] 1840 U.S. Census, DeKalb County, Alabama, population schedule, Northern District, S.C. Newnan, p. 7 (penned), line 31, F.B. Royston household; digital image, *Ancestry* (http://www.ancestry.com : accessed 27 September 2016); citing NARA microfilm publication M704, roll 4.

[12] 1850 U.S. Census, Chambers County, Alabama, pop. sch., p. 318 (stamped), dwell. 749, fam. 749, Thomas B. Royston.

[13] Ibid.

[14] 1860 U.S. Census, Chambers County, Alabama, slave schedule, Northern Division, page 48 (penned), Thomas B. Royston owner; digital image, *Ancestry* (http://ancestry.com : accessed 13 November 2016); citing NARA microfilm publication M653 roll 4.

[15] See 1850, 1860, 1870, and 1880 census listings for the names of children, also the probate of Thomas Beverly Royston names 11 of the 14 children.

[16] For Benjamin and Charles Baldwin Royston see Compiled service record, Benjamin Royston, 61st Regiment Alabama Infantry, and C.B. Royston, Alabama 14th Infantry, Civil War; Carded Records Showing Military Service of Soldiers Who Served in Organizations from the State

Death of Thomas Beverly Royston and Cynthia (Dillard) Royston

Cynthia became a widow on 21 September 1868 with the death of her husband, Thomas Beverly Royston.[17] Cynthia appeared in court eight days later to begin the probate process. Cynthia's testimony under oath provides direct evidence of Thomas's death date.[18]

> Cynthia Royston widow and relict of Thomas B. Royston decd respectfully represents unto your Honor that the late Thomas B. Royston, who was an inhabitant of this county at the time of his death, departed this life on the 21st day of September AD. 1868 in said county & state. . .

She then lists as heirs, the eleven living children. Not mentioned are their three sons who died in the Civil War: Ulysses Franklin, Charles Baldwin, and Benjamin.[19]

> Your petitioner further states, that she is the widow of said deceased and that the next of kin of said decedent are his children [bullets inserted for ease of reading]

> - Sarah Parker who has intermarried with Franklin M. Parker, who reside in Coosa County
> - Adeline Royston over fourteen years of age & resides with your petitioner in said county
> - Joseph Royston over twenty-one years & resides in said county
> - Robert C Royston a minor over fourteen who resides with the petitioner in said county

---

of Alabama, compiled 1903-1927, documenting the period 1861-1865; *fold3* (https://www.fold3.com : accessed 15 November 2016); citing NARA publication M311, Record Group 109, Roll 39. For Ulysses Royston see Chambers County, Alabama Estates, box 26 folder 25, Ulysses Franklin Royston Sr, for petition papers of 1866; "Alabama, Wills and Probate Records, 1753-1999," case file for Ulysses Franklin Royston Sr, 1866-1872; *Ancestry* (http://www.ancestry.com : accessed 13 November 2016), digital image 220.

[17] *Find A Grave*, database with images (http://www.findagrave.com : accessed 8 September 2016), memorial 60407551, Thomas Beverly Royston (1806-1868), gravestone photographed by Churchwell, member 46607715.

[18] Chambers Co. Al. Estates, box 26 folder 24, case file for Thos B Royston, 1867-1883; "Alabama, Wills and Probate Records, 1753-1999," *Ancestry* (http://www.ancestry.com : accessed 19 August 2016) petition papers 29 September 1868, images 145-146.

[19] See the listings of the three boys on the 1850 U.S. Census, Chambers County, Alabama, pop. sch., p. 318 (stamped), dwell. 749, fam. 749, Thomas B. Royston. For Benjamin and Charles Baldwin see Compiled military service record, Benjamin Royston, 61st Reg. Al. Inf., and C B Royston, Al. 14th Inf. Civil War; RG 109, NA-Washington. For Ulysses Royston see Chambers County, Alabama Estates, box 26 folder 25, Ulysses Franklin Royston Sr, for petition papers of 1866.

- Thomas Royston a minor over fourteen
- Margarette Royston a minor over fourteen
- Richard Royston under fourteen years age
- Leonidas Royston under fourteen years
- Mariah Royston under fourteen years
- Martha Royston under fourteen who all reside with petition in said county
- Mary Slaggle wife Joseph Slaggle who reside in Chambers County of full age

Seven years after Cynthia first appeared in court to begin the probate process of Thomas B. Royston's estate, several administration papers dated from 6 February to 27 March 1875 show that Cynthia has "removed to the State of Texas"[20] and an account paper of 1 November 1882 indicates that "Cynthia Royston departed this life in the state of Texas on or about the 2nd day of August 1882."[21]

A death certificate might reveal a father for Cynthia, but the state of Texas did not require death registration until 1903, twenty years after Cynthia's death.[22]

Identifying the Maiden Name of Cynthia (Dillard) Royston
Without a death certificate or marriage record, Cynthia's maiden name was determined by searching her children's death certificates. Of her fourteen children, only three lived to have a state registered death certificate that provided her maiden name.

- Martha Ann (Royston) Hogge's death certificate of 1932 gives her mother's name as "Cynthia Dilliard" born in Alabama: informant Charles Hogge, Martha's son and Cynthia's grandson.[23]
- Richard A Royston's death certificate of 1928 states: mother "Miss Cinthia Dillard," born in Alabama: informant Mrs. Luther Lockey, relationship not determined.[24]

---

20   Chambers Co. Al. Estates, box 26 folder 24, Thomas Beverly Royston, administration papers of 1875, images 143, 148, 172, and 173.

21   Chambers Co. Al. Estates, box 26 folder 24, Thomas Beverly Royston, account paper of 1882, image 165.

22   *The Handybook for Genealogists,* (Draper, Utah: Everton Publishers, 2002), 647.

23   Texas State Board of Health, death certificate, Mrs. Mattie Ann Hogge, No. 18070 (stamped), Ennis,1935; digital image, "Texas, Death Certificates, 1903–1982," database, *Ancestry*, Ellis 1935, April-June image 28 (http://search.ancestry.com : accessed 29 November 2016).

24   Texas State Board of Health, death certificate, R. Royston, No. 50544 (stamped), Decatur 1928; digital image, "Texas, Death Certificates, 1903–1982", database, *Ancestry*, Wise, 1928, Oct-Dec image 14 (http://search.ancestry.com : accessed 25 November 2016).

- Adeline (Royston) Spears' death certificate of 1920 gives her mother's name as "Dillard" born in Florida: informant M.C. [Mariah Catherine] Lovelady, Adeline's sister and Cynthia's daughter.[25]

Two of the death certificates give Alabama as Cynthia's place of birth, understandable since Cynthia and Thomas Royston resided in Alabama for nearly forty years. The other death certificate states Florida as the birth place, the informant, Mariah Catherine (Royston) Lovelady, was Cynthia's daughter. She would generally be the most reliable informant. However, she was 70 years old at the death of her sister Adeline and her mother, Cynthia had been dead for 40 years. She likely cited the birth place incorrectly. All the census records taken during Cynthia's lifetime agree on a birthplace of Georgia. This information was likely given by either Cynthia herself or her husband, Thomas Royston, and is more reliable evidence for her place of birth. A Florida connection to the Dillard's seems possible given Mariah's listing of that birthplace and could be explored in future research. Perhaps Mariah knew or had heard of a Dillard family member with ties to Florida.

What clues can be garnered from examining the life of Cynthia (Dillard) Royston? With an estimated birth date of 1815 in Georgia, candidates for her father would have been born before 1805 and been living in Georgia during the early 1800's. A candidate would probably be listed on the 1820 and 1830 census records residing in Georgia with a female of appropriate age in the household. Families often moved together into new lands, so when Native American land opened up in Alabama during the 1830's it is likely that Cynthia's Dillard relatives also moved to Alabama. Additionally some of Cynthia's 14 children could be named for Dillard relatives.

GEORGE W. DILLARD

The life events of Cynthia (Dillard) Royston laid a strong foundation for a possible father candidate: born before 1805 and resident of Georgia in the early 1800s. Research turned to George W. Dillard, who met these criteria.

1820 and 1830 Census Records

George W. Dillard first appears on the census records of Georgia in 1820, residing in Greene County.[26] Table 2 details his household of two young females; one under 10, the appropriate

---

[25]   Texas State Board of Health, death certificate, Mrs. Adline Spears, No 27410 (stamped), Registered No. 105 (penned). Bowie, 1920; digital image, "Texas, Death Certificates, 1903–1982," database, *Ancestry*, Montague 1920, Jul-Sep image 10 (http://search.ancestry.com : accessed 18 November 2016).

[26]   1820 U.S. Census, Greene County, Georgia, Capt E Woodhams District, population schedule, p. 202, line 2, George W. Dillard household; digital image, *Ancestry*

age category for Cynthia (Dillard) Royston born about 1815, the other young female age 10-16. George's age of 26-45 places his birth date between 1775 and 1796, well in the range for Cynthia's father. The males under 16 in the household are likely Cynthia's brothers if George is her father. Identifying and tracing them could provide valuable connections to Cynthia. The household included 21 slaves, among them were six adult males and 9 adult females. Eleven total individuals were engaged in agriculture suggesting that George W. Dillard was growing cotton, the primary crop in Georgia in 1820.[27]

Table 2. George W. Dillard household in 1820

Locality			1820, Greene County, Georgia												
			Free White Males						Free White Females						
Page	Line	Head-of-Family	0 to 10	10 to 16	16 to 18	16 to 26	26 to 45	45 +	0 to 10	10 to 16	16 to 26	26 to 45	45 +	All Others	Slaves
202	2	George W. Dillard	2	1		1	1		1	1		1			21

The 1830 census reveals the move of G.W. Dillard's household to Muscogee County, on the western border of Georgia, next to Alabama.[28] Muscogee County was created from Creek Indian lands in 1826. As new lands opened up in the west, many settlers migrated because of the fertile land. Table 3 illustrates the George W. Dillard household in 1830 with several males age 20 to 40 as well as 10 slaves. The slave listing shows only one adult male and two adult females, with seven children. The makeup of this household is much different than that of 1820, suggesting a different situation for George W. Dillard in the new location. If Cynthia was born about 1815, she would be 15 years of age in 1830 and would fit into the household as the female age 15-20.

(http://www.ancestry.com : accessed 7 June 2017); citing NARA microfilm publication M33, roll 8.

[27] John C. Inscoe, "Georgia in 1860," *New Georgia Encyclopedia* (https://www.georgiaencyclpedia.org/artiles/history-archaeology/georgia-1860 : accessed 29 march 2018).

[28] 1830 U.S. Census, Muscogee County, Georgia, population schedule, p. 277 (penned), line 2, G.W. Dillard household; digital image, *Ancestry* (http://www.ancestry.com : accessed 7 June 2017); citing NARA microfilm publication M19, roll 19.

Table 3. George W. Dillard household in 1830

Pg. Ln.	Head of Family		0 to 5	5 to 10	10 to 15	15 to 20	20 to 30	30 to 40	40 to 50	50 to 60	60 to 70	70 to 80	80 +	Slaves
Locality			1830, Muscogee County, Georgia											
277	George W. Dillard	M	3				5	7	1					4
2		F	1			1	1							6

Marriage Records for George W. Dillard

Comparing the oldest females of the 1820 and 1830 census enumerations reveals a discrepancy. The oldest female in the 1820 census household is listed as age 26-45 and would be between 36-55 years of age on the 1830 census. Instead the oldest female is only 20-30 years old and the presence of four children under the age of five suggests a second marriage. A search of Georgia marriage records revealed two marriages for George W. Dillard.

- George W. Dallard to Peggy Armour, Greene County Georgia, 9 November 1801[29]
- George W. Dillard to Martha F Wells, Greene County, Georgia, 29 July 1822[30]

With the discovery of the 1801 marriage record, a possible mother for Cynthia (Dillard) Royston was identified: Peggy Armour of Greene County, Georgia. Peggy Armour likely died about 1821, soon after the 1820 census enumeration and before the 1822 marriage of George W. Dillard and Martha F Wells. Researching the Armour family of Greene County, Georgia, could provide connections to Cynthia (Dillard) Royston. Of interest is Cynthia's naming of two daughters, Margaret and Martha, perhaps after her possible mother and step-mother.

---

[29] Greene County, Georgia, "Marriage Licenses 1786 To 1810," p. 9, Dallard-Armour marriage, 9 November 1801; "Georgia, County Marriages, 1785-1950," image 21 of 659, *FamilySearch* (https://familysearch.org : accessed 7 June 2017); citing "Marriage Records 1786-1849," FHL microfilm # 159,052.

[30] Greene County, Georgia Marriages 1829-1849, Dillard - Wells, 29 July 1822, p. 186; "Georgia, Marriage Records from Select Counties, 1828-1978," image 201, *Ancestry,* (http://www.ancestry.com : accessed 10 March 2017).

George W. Dillard in Newspaper Articles

Newspapers can reveal important information about an individual and his involvement in the community. George W. Dillard had moved to Muscogee County, Georgia by 1828 where he placed an advertisement in the *Athenian*.[31]

> The Subscriber begs leave to inform his friends and the Public in general, that he is prepared to accommodate from fifty to a hundred Gentlemen, who may wish to visit this place at the sales; his Table shall be furnished with the best the country affords, attentive Ostlers, and an ample supply of provinder has been procured, this Establishment is retired, it being situated on the main road leading to Alabama, near the Ferry. GEORGE W. DILLARD.

> A Stage-Coach runs regularly from this place to Fort Mitchell three times a week for the accommodation of passengers. G.W.D.

With the newly formed county attracting settlers, George had opened an inn on the main road leading to Alabama. He provided food, and ostlers, men employed to look after the horses of people staying at an inn. This could account for the 12 males present in the household in 1830, (see Table 2).[32]

In October of 1832, the *Columbus Enquirer* ran an advertisement for three consecutive weeks providing evidence of George W. Dillard's continued residence in the city of Columbus, located in Muscogee County, Georgia: "FOR SALE. A comfortable two-story Dwelling, with convenient out-houses and garden, at the upper end of Oglethorpe street now in the occupancy of Capt. Geo. W. Dillard, in a healthy and beautiful part of Columbus."[33]

---

[31] *Athenian*, 27 May, 1828, p. 3 col. 3, para. 4, George W. Dillard advertisement for inn; *Georgia Historic Newspapers: Athens* (http://dlg.galileo.usg.edu/athnewspapers/id:ath1828-0083 : accessed 8 November 2017).

[32] 1830 U.S. Census, Muscogee County, Georgia, pop. sch., p. 277 (penned), line 2, G.W. Dillard household.

[33] *Columbus Enquirer*, 13 October 1832, p. 4, col. 5, para. 1, Capt. Geo. W. Dillard occupancy of dwelling; *Georgia Historic Newspapers: Columbus Enquirer* (enquirer.galileo.usg.edu : accessed 19 June 2017). See also the same source for identical listings on 20 October 1832 and 27 October 1832.

Subsequent news articles from the *Columbus Enquirer* show George W. Dillard's involvement in the community during the 1830s.

- George W. Dillard, elected commissioner, 9 January 1835[34]
- George W. Dillard, advertisement for a stray horse, 9 January 1835 and October 1835[35]
- G.W. Dillard, elected Alderman, 8 January 1836[36]
- George W. Dillard, part of the grand jury, April 1837[37]
- Geo. W. Dillard, included in a list of an accounting of city funds, 19 April 1838
- George W. Dillard, notice to pay a debt to Daniel Walling, several issues of 1839

In 1840, George W. Dillard ran two advertisements in the *Columbus Enquirer* indicating his move across the Alabama/Georgia state line into Russell County, Alabama.[38] Although the wording doesn't clearly state that the "Pleasant Hill House" was another inn, it is possible since he had operated that type of establishment in 1828. George also advertised a piece of property for sale and included his place of residence as Russell County, Alabama.

PLEASANT HILL HOUSE.

> The subscriber has located himself four miles from Columbus, on the road leading to LaFayette, Chambers county, and Auburn, Macon County Ala. -- It will give him great pleasure in entertaining all persons that may feel disposed to favor him with a call. GEORGE W. DILLARD

> The subscriber has a lot of land in Summerville, Ala. containing 12 acres, two miles and a half from Columbus. There is in the above named place good schools and good society. His lot is well improved with a comfortable dwelling house and all necessary

---

[34] *Columbus Enquirer*, 9 January 1835, p. 3, col. 2, para. 3, Geo. W. Dillard elected commissioner.

[35] Elizabeth Evans Kilbourne, *Columbus, Georgia, Newspaper Clippings (Columbus Enquirer Volume II, 1835-1837)*, (Savannah, Georgia : E. Evans Kilbourne, 1997-2009), no page number on photocopy from book.

[36] *Columbus Enquirer*, 8 January 1836, p. 2, col. 4, para. 4, G.W. Dillard elected Alderman.

[37] Kilbourne, *Columbus, Georgia, Newspaper Clippings (Columbus Enquirer Volume II, 1835-1837)*, no page number on photocopy from book.

[38] *Columbus Enquirer*, 14 October 1840, p. 3, col. 3, para. 6, George W. Dillard advertisements; *Georgia Historic Newspapers: Columbus Enquirer* (enquirer.galileo.usg.edu : accessed 19 June 2017).

out buildings with a good spring and well water, which he offers for sale at a reduced price. Possession given the first of January next. G.W. DILLARD Russell co. Ala. Oct 14

If Cynthia was George's daughter, she was probably also living in Columbus, Muscogee County, Georgia, from at least 1828 when he ran his first advertisement in the *Athenian*.[39] In 1833, she would have been about 18 and approaching marriage. The county clerk generally recorded the marriages during this time period, but a fire in 1838 destroyed the courthouse and all records were lost.[40] This record loss could explain the missing marriage record of Cynthia (Dillard) Royston and Thomas Beverly Royston.

THOMAS BEVERLY ROYSTON

The Georgia/Alabama Frontier

If Cynthia had moved with her proposed father, George W. Dillard to the newly organized Muscogee County, Georgia, was Thomas B. Royston in proximity to have met and married her? The 1830 census shows no listing for Thomas B. Royston[41] but tax records reveal his residence in Morgan County, Georgia, with his payment of a poll tax in 1831.[42] Morgan County, in the north-central portion of the state, borders Greene County, George W. Dillard's residence in 1820.

Thomas possibly knew the Dillard family during the 1820s, but a land record dated 21 December 1831 in Lees County, Georgia, puts him much closer to Muscogee County, and the Dillard family's new residence on the border of Georgia and Alabama.

Georgia is a state-land state, meaning that the state government distributed its land, not the federal government. Georgia used a lottery system from 1805-1832 to distribute land that had been formerly occupied by the Creek and Cherokee Indians. Each lottery had unique requirements for applicants. Persons entitled to a draw in the 1827 land lottery included the wife or child (with a three year residence in Georgia) of a husband or father who had been

---

[39]   *Athenian*, 27 May, 1828, p. 3 col. 3, para. 4, George W. Dillard advertisement for inn.

[40]   *The Handybook for Genealogists*, (Draper, Utah: Everton Publishers, 2002), 158.

[41]   1830 U.S. Census, negative search for Thomas Royston and name variants, Georgia, population schedules; database with images, *Ancestry* (http://www.ancestry.com : accessed 10 October 2016.)

[42]   Morgan County, Georgia, Superior Court, 1831 Tax Digest, page 2, entry for Thomas B. Royston, Morgan County, Archives, Madison, Georgia.

absent from the state for three years.[43] Thomas B. Royston won this lottery and is listed on the land grant as "John Royston's orphan of Gaines District, Morgan County."[44] No Royston is found on the 1830 census for Morgan County, Georgia and Thomas B. Royston is the only Royston on the tax lists of 1831, making him the sole candidate for "the orphan of John Royston." Additional evidence identifies John Royston as the father of Thomas Beverly Royston.[45]

The grant dated 21 December 1831 was for 202 ½ acres in Lees County. In 1831, Lees County and Muscogee County were much larger than present day and nearly bordered one another. Thomas Beverly Royston would have had to visit Lees County to either live on his newly granted land or sell the land. Deed records in the Lees County courthouse could lend clarity to his actions, but the courthouse burned in 1858 and all records were lost.[46]

Would Thomas B. Royston have traveled from Lees County to Columbus, Muscogee County? A history published in 1854 describes the area: "No country is more highly favoured with extensive water facilities than Muscogee County. The principal stream is the Chattahoochee, affording to the inhabitants a steamboat navigation to the Gulf of Mexico. . . Columbus is the seat of justice . . . it was laid out in 1828 and is the third city in the State. "[47] As the main city of the area, Columbus would have drawn visitors from the surrounding counties. The newspaper evidence presented earlier clearly shows the visibility of George W. Dillard in the community of Columbus, Muscogee County. If Cynthia was his daughter, Thomas B. Royston could have met her while in the area, possibly staying at the Dillard inn.

Two entries in the *Columbus Enquirer* for 1841 show "Thomas Royston" in a list of letters remaining at the Post Office at Columbus, Muscogee County, Georgia. The newspaper

---

[43] *Georgia Archives*, "1827 Land Lottery, (http://www.georgiaarchives.org/research/1827_land_lottery : accessed 12 Nov 2016).

[44] Georgia, Surveyor General, *Land Lottery Grants, 1827-1848*, (Atlanta, Georgia : State Dept. of Archives and History, 1967), 20th District, p. 101, FHL microfilm 519,043.

[45] Diana Elder, "Research Report: Thomas Beverly Royston 1806-1868," 2017, person details for Thomas Beverly Royston KFR2-8KY, *FamilySearch* (https://www.familysearch.org : accessed 18 March 2018).

[46] The Handybook for Genealogists, (Draper, Utah: Everton Publishers, 2002), 157.

[47] George White, *Historical Collections of Georgia : Containing the Most Interesting Facts, Traditions, Biographical Sketches, Anecdotes, etc., Relating to its History and Antiquities, from its First Settlement to the Present Tie, Compiled from Original Records and Official Documents, Illustrated by Nearly One Hundred Engravings,* (New York : Pudney & Russell, 1854), 568-9.

notices provide direct evidence of Thomas Royston's presence in the area.[48] Thomas B. Royston was living in DeKalb County, Alabama in 1840,[49] which might explain why the letters were still at the post office in Columbus. That had evidently once been his postal address.

ALABAMA CONNECTIONS – 1840 CENSUS

George W. Dillard and the 1840 census

As mentioned in the newspaper advertisements, by 1840, George W. Dillard had moved across the Georgia/Alabama border to Russell County, Alabama.[50] Table 4 shows his household containing only two females: an older female, probably George's wife, Martha, and a female age 15-20, probably the same female age 5-10 on the 1830 census. The female age 15-20 on the 1830 census would be 25-30 in 1840 and is not present in the Dillard household, indicating a death or marriage. If this female was Cynthia (Dillard) Royston, her absence is additional evidence that she had married by 1840 and was living in her husband's household. The younger males in the household are probably sons of George and Martha; the oldest a possible son of George and first wife, Peggy.

Table 4. George W. Dillard household in 1840

Locality			1840, Russell County, Alabama											
Pg. Ln.	Head of Family		0 to 5	5 to 10	10 to 15	15 to 20	20 to 30	30 to 40	40 to 50	50 to 60	60 to 70	70 to 80	80 +	Slaves
Pg. 35 Ln .25	George W. Dillard	M	2			2	1				1			6
		F				1		1						5

---

[48] *Columbus Enquirer*, 8 December 1841, p. 3, col. 6, para. 7, Thomas Royston, letters remaining at Post Office; "Georgia Historic Newspapers," *Digital Library of Georgia*, (https://gahistoricnewspapers.galileo.usg.edu :: accessed 11 April 2018).

[49] 1840 U.S. Census, DeKalb County, Alabama, population schedule, Northern District, S.C. Newnan, p. 7 (penned), line 31, F.B. Royston household; digital image, *Ancestry* (http://www.ancestry.com : accessed 27 September 2016); citing NARA microfilm publication M704, roll 4.

[50] 1840 U.S. Census, Russell County, Alabama, population schedule, p. 35 (penned), line 25, G.W. Dillard household; digital image, *Ancestry* (http://www.ancestry.com : accessed 7 June 2017); citing NARA microfilm publication M704, roll 15.

Thomas B. Royston and the 1840 census

Where are Thomas and Cynthia Royston living in 1840? That census enumeration reveals their residence in DeKalb County, Alabama,[51] to the north of Russell County, Alabama, residence of George W. Dillard in 1840.[52] Table 5 illustrates Cynthia as the only older female in the house. Her age of 20-30 is appropriate to her estimated birth year of 1815. The household also includes several older males. With five individuals involved in agriculture, these could be relatives, or farm hands. Confusion might come in Thomas being listed as "F.B. Royston" on the census. Names on the census record are often miswritten and need to be used with other records to confirm identity.

Table 5. Thomas B. Royston household in 1840

Locality			1840, DeKalb County, Alabama											
Pg. Ln.	Head of Family		0 to 5	5 to 10	10 to 15	15 to 20	20 to 30	30 to 40	40 to 50	50 to 60	60 to 70	70 to 80	80 +	Slaves
Pg. 7	F. B.	M	2					5						5
Ln.31	Royston	F		1			1							4

Land records can provide evidence of residence and help to fill in details the census only hints at. As previously discussed, the 1842 land case file for Thomas B. Royston in DeKalb County, Alabama, helps to determine that the F.B. Royston on the census is Thomas B. Royston. On 1 May 1845 after having lived on and improved the land for several years, Thomas was granted a land patent from the United States government.[53] To receive the patent, Thomas had to pay fees, and provide witnesses that he had lived on the land. These documents make

---

51 1840 U.S. Census, DeKalb Co., Alabama, pop. sch., p. 7 (penned), line 31, F.B. Royston household.

52 1840 U.S. Census, Russell County, Alabama, pop. sch., p. 35 (penned), line 25, G.W. Dillard household.

53 Thomas B. Royston, (DeKalb County, Alabama), cash entry patent no. 5969, "Land Patent Search," images, *General Land Office Records* (www.glorecords.blm.gov : accessed 13 September 2016).

up his land case file for the DeKalb County land. The witness statement dated 23 May 1842 gives the following information:[54]

- Royston settled on the land prior to January 1837
- He erected a dwelling house in which he lived and made his home from then until 1840
- He was the head of a family having a wife and children

Thomas received his DeKalb County land under the Preemption Act of 1838, which entitled a settler over the age of twenty-one or the head of a family to purchase up to 160 acres for $1.25 an acre. He had to have lived on the land for four months preceding the act. He qualified for the land, paid $200.85 and then assigned the land to John Graves. No mention is made in the case file or the land tract book of any payment between Graves and Royston for the land, but it is possible that a large sum of money changed hands and that is how Thomas purchased the land for his plantation in Chambers County.[55] The deed index for DeKalb County, Alabama, 1835-1897 has no listing for a Royston, so the federal land patent is the sole land record for Thomas in that county.[56]

ALABAMA CONNECTIONS - CHAMBERS COUNTY

Land Records for George W. Dillard – Chambers County

Following the American Revolution, the state of Georgia pressured the Native American Creek tribe to cede their land. Beginning in 1790, their land was gradually given over to Georgia and then to Alabama. The Creeks signed a treaty in 1832 that agreed to the removal of the 20,000 tribe members still in Alabama; sending them to land allocated as Indian

---

[54] Thomas B. Royston (DeKalb County), witness statement, cash entry file, state volume patent No. 5969, Lebanon, Alabama, Land Office; Land Entry Papers 1800-1908, Record Group 49: Records of the Bureau of Land Management; National Archives, Washington, D.C

[55] DeKalb County, Alabama, Tract Books, p. 62, entries arranged by legal land description; see Township 9 South, Range 7 East, Section 20, SE 1/4, Thomas B. Royston, 1842; "United States Bureau of Land Management Tract Books, 1800-1955," Alabama, Vol. 6B (Lebanon), image 72 of 208, *FamilySearch* (https://www.familysearch.org : accessed 27 March 2018).

[56] Negative searches in DeKalb County Alabama, "Index to deeds and mortgages 1835-1897" FHL microfilm 103174. DeKalb County Alabama, "Deed records, v. A 1835-1845," FHL microfilm 1035174. DeKalb County, Alabama, "Deed records, v. B-D 1842-1855," FHL microfilm 1034175.

Territory, now Oklahoma.[57] With the Creek Cession of 1832, Native American lands opened up in Alabama. The state of Alabama distributed the new land under the federal land patent system. George W. Dillard received multiple land patents between 1837 and 1841 in Crenshaw, Tallapoosa, and Chambers Counties.[58] Of particular interest are the land patents in Chambers County, where Thomas and Cynthia Royston had settled by 1850. George W. Dillard received five land patents in Chambers County, four in 1837 and one in 1840.[59]

Following the transfer of land from the state to an individual, the county deed books listed the transfer of land from individual to individual. The Chambers County deed books reveal only one land transaction for George W. Dillard, selling the land he originally patented in 1840 to Robert Mitchell of Chambers County.[60] In that deed, George and his wife, Martha F. Dillard, are named as residents of Russell County, Alabama.

By 1850 George and Martha Dillard had moved from Russell County, Alabama to Macon County, Alabama, its neighbor to the west. The 1850 federal census shows George and Martha residing in Macon County, Alabama with four children: Columbus, Alonzo, Leonidas, and Zenora.[61] Although relationships are not stated, the ages of household members do correlate with earlier census records.

---

[57]   Claudio Saunt, "Creek Indians," (University of Georgia, 2002); *New Georgia Encyclopedia* (https://www.georgiaencyclopedia.org/articles/history-archaeology/creek-indians : accessed 26 March 2018).

[58]   Bureau of Land Management, George W. Dillard, "Land Patent Search," images, *General Land Office Records* (www.glorecords.blm.gov : accessed 17 March 2018).

[59]   Bureau of Land Management, George W. Dillard, (Chambers County, Alabama), 1837, cash entry patents no. 3733, 3768, 3770, 3771; also 1840 Indian Allotment, state volume patent no. 2, "Land Patent Search," images, *General Land Office Records* (www.glorecords.blm.gov : accessed 17 March 2018).

[60] Chambers County, Alabama Probate Court, Deed Records 1840-42, Vol. 4, page 282, Dillard to Mitchell, 10 June 1844, the land granted by Chief Emarthal as the Indian Allotment in 1840, FHL microfilm 1,854,661.

[61]   1850 U.S. Census, Macon County, Alabama, population schedule, 21st District, p. 272 (stamped), dwelling 1088, family 1096, George W. Dillard household; digital image, *Ancestry* (http://www.ancestry.com : accessed 10 March 2017); citing NARA microfilm publication M432, roll 9.

George died in 1854 and is buried in current day Lee County, Alabama.[62] Lee County was created in 1866 from Chambers, Russell, Macon, and Tallapoosa counties.[63] It appears that George never lived in Chambers County. What happened to the 480 acres of land patented in 1832? Studying the deed index for Chambers County between the years 1834-1876, few deeds up to 1850 were recorded and no other land transactions for George W. Dillard are listed.[64] Could the land have been gifted to Cynthia (Dillard) Royston? Could it appear in Royston land records of Chambers County, Alabama?

Land Records for Thomas Beverly Royston - Chambers County

Studying the deeds for Thomas B. Royston of Chambers County revealed that he owned two separate plantations located just a few miles apart.[65] As a federal land state, Alabama land was divided into a grid pattern of townships and sections. A township was a six mile square of land divided into 36 sections, each section one mile square.[66] The land was first distributed by the federal government with an individual eventually receiving a land patent after fulfilling the various requirements. Further land sales were recorded in the county deed books. Thomas B. Royston did not patent any land in Chambers County, Alabama but the county deed books reveal him both buying and selling land. Figure 2 depicts the location of the two distinct Royston plantations, both located in Township 24 North, Range 26 East.

---

[62] *Find A Grave*, database with images (http://www.findagrave.com: accessed 6 June 2017), memorial 8971146, George Wellington Dillard, (1781-1854), gravestone photographed by JC, member 46615432.

[63] *The Handybook for Genealogists*, (Draper, Utah: Everton Publishers, 2002), 38.

[64] Chambers County, Alabama Probate Court, "Direct index v. 1 1834-1876," FHL microfilm 1,862,630, negative search for additional deeds for George W. Dillard.

[65] See Table 5 for specific land descriptions and transaction details. Also Figure 2 for the approximate location of the Royston land.

[66] See Table 5 for specific land descriptions and transaction details.

Figure 2. Township 24 North Range 26 East, St. Stephens Meridian, Alabama

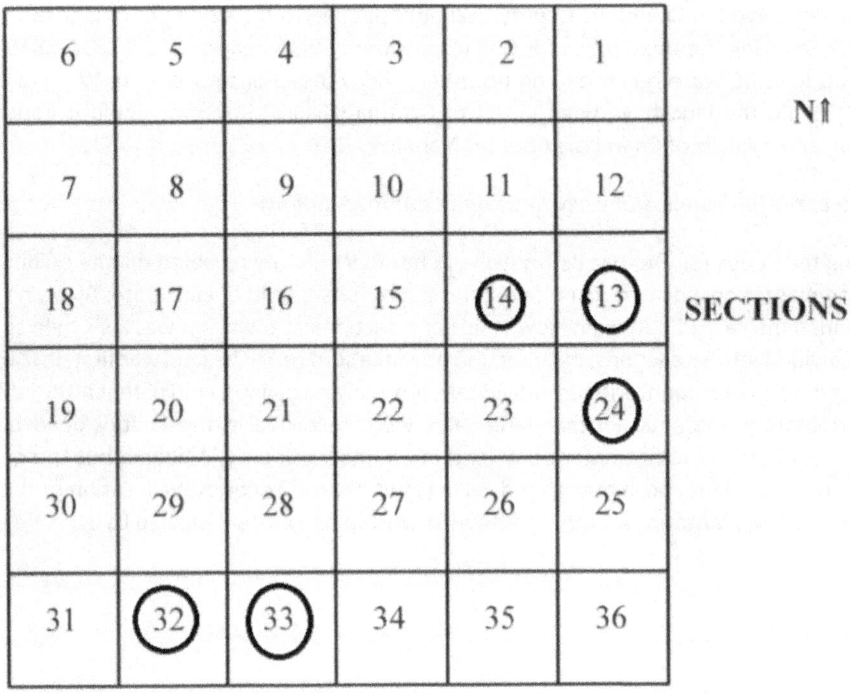
6 5 4 3 2 1
N↑
7 8 9 10 11 12
18 17 16 15 14 13
SECTIONS
19 20 21 22 23 24
30 29 28 27 26 25
31 32 33 34 35 36

The original land patents for Sections 32 and 33 are dated 1837 and 1841.[67] Those for sections 14, 13, and 24 are dated 1840, 1843, and 1857.[68] Thomas B. Royston in 1840 was patenting land in DeKalb County, Alabama. What brought him to Chambers County? Possibly the lure of better land invited the move. Sometime before 1850, he purchased the land in Sections 32 and 33. No deed exists to show this purchase[69] but the 1850 census clearly

---

67 Bureau of Land Management, "Land Patent Search," St. Stephens Meridian, Township 24 North Range 26 East Sections 32 and 33, entries for Smith, Yarborough, Stroud, Dougherty, and McLemore, Chambers County, Alabama, *General Land Office Records* (www.glorecords.blm.gov : accessed 17 March 2018).

68 Bureau of Land Management, "Land Patent Search," St. Stephens Meridian, Township 24 North Range 26 East Sections 13, 14, and 24, entries for Yarborough, Stroud, Dougherty, McLemore, and Merritt Chambers County, Alabama, *General Land Office Records* (www.glorecords.blm.gov : accessed 17 March 2018).

69 Chambers County, Alabama Probate Court, "Direct index v. 1 1834-1876," FHL microfilm 1,862,630, negative search for additional deeds for Thomas B. Royston.

provides evidence of land ownership with his real estate valued at $1800.[70] In 1853, Thomas B. Royston sold 420 acres of his land in Sections 32 and 33 to John Daniel for $2200.[71]

A few months earlier, on 6 October 1852, Thomas B. Royston had purchased 450 acres from William Ingram in sections 13 and 24.[72] In 1853 he completed his plantation with a purchase of land in section 14 from James H. Meritt for $1000, no acreage listed.[73] Of note is the unusual fact that James H. Merritt didn't receive his final land patent until 1857, four years after selling the same land to Thomas B. Royston. In 1854, Thomas B. Royston sold the portion of his plantation in Section 14 to son-in-law, Joseph Slagle. The last land transaction recorded for Thomas B. Royston was the sale of four acres to the Deacons of the Baptist Church at Mount Hickory on 19 February 1857.[74]

---

[70] 1850 U.S. Census, Chambers County, Alabama, pop. sch., p. 318 (stamped), dwell. 749, fam. 749, Thomas B. Royston.

[71] Chambers County, Alabama, "Deeds v. 11 1852-1854," page 639, Royston to Daniels, 19 July 1853; FHL microfilm 1,854,664.

[72] Chambers County, Alabama, "Deeds v. 11 1852-1856," page 256, Ingram to Royston, 6 October 1852; FHL microfilm 1,854,664.

[73] Chambers County, Alabama, "Deeds v. 11 1852-1856," page 326, Meritt to Royston, 30 June 1853; FHL microfilm 1,854,664.

[74] Chambers County, Alabama, "Deeds v. 12 1852-1854," page 46, Royston to Deacons, Baptist Church at Mount Hickory, 19 February 1857; FHL microfilm 1,854,664.

Table 6. Select Chambers County, Alabama Land Transactions involving Royston land

Land Description	Original Patentee	Date of patent	Grantor (Seller)	Grantee (Purchaser)	Date of Land Transaction	Purchase Price
SECTIONS 13, 14, AND 24						
E ½ Sect. 24	William Dougherty	1840	William Ingram	Thomas Beverly Royston	6 October 1852[a]	$1500 450 acres in all
E ½ Sect. 13	William Dougherty	1840				
W ½ Sect. 13	Stroud, Dougherty, and McLemore	1843				
W½ of the SE ¼ Sect. 13 NE ½ of the NE ¼ of Sect. 13			William Ingram	Thomas Beverly Royston	6 October 1852	$1500 450 acres in all
S ½ Sect. 14	James H. Merritt	1857	James H. Meritt	Thomas B. Royston	30 June 1853[b]	$1000 320 acres
NE ¼ of the SE ¼ ; SW ¼ of Sect. 14			Thomas B. Royston	Joseph Slagle	23 December 1854[c]	$300 280 acres
SECTIONS 32 AND 33						
SW ¼ Sect. 33	Joseph Yarborough[d]	1837	Thomas B. Royston	John Daniel	19 July 1853[e]	Total: $2200 420 acres
E ½ SE ¼ Sect.32	Joseph Yarborough	1837	Thomas B. Royston	John Daniel	19 July 1853	
NW ¼ SE ¼ Sect. 32	Robert W Smith	1837	Thomas B. Royston	John Daniel	19 July 1853	
S ½ NW ¼ Sect. 32			Thomas B. Royston	John Daniel	19 July 1853	
N ½ Sect. 32	Stroud, Dougherty, and McLemore	1841				

a. Chambers County, Alabama, "Deeds v. 11 1852-1856," page 256, Ingram to Royston, 6 October 1852; FHL microfilm 1,854,664.

b. Chambers County, Alabama, "Deeds v. 11 1852-1856," page 326, Meritt to Royston, 30 June 1853; FHL microfilm 1,854,664.

c. Chambers County, Alabama, "Deeds v. 12 1852-1854," page 46, Royston to Slagle, 23 December 1854; FHL microfilm 1,854,664.

d. Bureau of Land Management, "Land Patent Search," St. Stephens Meridian, Twp. 24 N Rng. 26E Sections 32 and 33, Chambers County, Alabama, *General Land Office Records* (www.glorecords.blm.gov : accessed 17 March 2018).

e. Chambers County, Alabama, "Deeds v. 11 1852-1854," page 639, Royston to Daniels, 19 July 1853; FHL microfilm 1,854,664.

Table 6 makes sense of the various land transactions. If the row is complete, the original land patent description matches the land description in the deed. For instance, William Dougherty patented the East ½ of Section 24 in 1840; then William Ingram sold land of the same description to Thomas B. Royston in 1852.

Incomplete rows indicate a division of the original land patent. For example, William Dougherty also patented the East ½ of Section 13 in 1840. Only part of that land was sold to Thomas B. Royston in 1852: the West ½ of the South East ¼ of Section 13. Missing in the table and the deed index are the deeds showing the land transfers from the original patentees to the grantors, probably before 1850.

The land study was done in hopes of finding a connection between George W. Dillard and Thomas and Cynthia (Dillard) Royston. Studying the land descriptions for both the land patented to George W. Dillard and the land Thomas B. Royston sold revealed that these were separate tracts of land. The Dillard land was located in Township 21 North, Section Range 25 East. The Royston land was located in Township 24, Range 25 and 26 East. Although the Chambers County deed books are not complete for the years 1836-1850, studying the original land patents showed that Thomas B. Royston likely purchased his land from the original patentees. He did not receive the land from George W. Dillard.

From the existing deed records, no connection could be made between George W. Dillard and Thomas and Cynthia Royston.

PROBATE RECORDS FOR GEORGE W. DILLARD

The headstone for George W. Dillard states his death date as 21 May 1854.[75] The full inscription reads: "1856. Erected by his children in memory of George W. Dillard who was born August 26, 1781; and died May 21st 1854. An honest man is the noblest work of God. Requiescat in peace." George was buried in the Pine Hill Cemetery, Auburn, Lee County, Alabama. Future research could seek more information on the children mentioned on the inscription and other cemetery records. Cynthia (Dillard) Royston lived in Chambers County, Alabama, just to the north of Lee County, and could have been one of those children.

A will or other probate records could name Cynthia Royston as a daughter of George W. Dillard. Alabama probate records have been indexed and a search discovered no records for George.[76] Because the last residence of George W. Dillard was the 1850 census in Macon

---

[75] *Find A Grave*, database with images (http://www.findagrave.com : accessed 6 June 2017), memorial 8971146, George Wellington Dillard, (1781-1854), gravestone photographed by JC, member 46615432.

[76] Negative search for George Dillard, "Alabama, Wills and Probate Records, 1753-1999," database with images, *Ancestry* (http://www.ancestry.com : accessed 17 August 2016). 1,617,060 item 1. Also "Macon County, Alabama, probate records, 1834-1930", probate minutes

County, probate records of that location were also searched.[77] No mention of George W. Dillard was found. Future research could extend to Lee County, Alabama, the place of the burial.

NAMING PATTERNS

The repetition of a name in families can be strong evidence of kinship. The 1850 census household of George W. Dillard in Macon County, Alabama includes Leonidas Dillard, age 9.[78] The Chambers County 1860 census of Thomas B. and Cynthia Royston lists Leonidas Royston, age 3.[79] If Cynthia was the daughter of George W. Dillard and his first wife, Peggy [Margaret] Armour, Leonidas Dillard, son of George W. Dillard and second wife, Martha, would be her half-brother. Macon County and Chambers County share a border and it is possible that the two families were in contact. Future research could discover other naming connections between the two families.

CONCLUSION

This research project sought to establish connections between George W. Dillard and Cynthia (Dillard) Royston. Without a marriage record for Thomas B. Royston and Cynthia, Cynthia's maiden name of "Dillard" appears only in three of her children's death certificates. The census records from 1850-1880 provide evidence of her birth about 1815 in Georgia.

Because of the proximity of George W. Dillard to Cynthia (Dillard) Royston in Chambers County, Alabama, his life was studied as a candidate for her father. The 1820 and 1830 census households for George W. Dillard show a female of appropriate age to be Cynthia. His presence in Muscogee County, Georgia, from 1828 to 1840 is well documented in newspaper

---

1854-1856, *FamilySearch* (https://www.familysearch.org : accessed 8 November 2017); FHL microfilm 1,617,060 item 2.

[77] "Macon County, Alabama, probate records, 1834-1930", Orphan's book v. 1-2 1834-1841, *FamilySearch* (https://www.familysearch.org : accessed 8 November 2017); FHL microfilm 1,293,633 Item 2-4. Also "Macon County, Alabama, probate records, 1834-1930", probate minutes 1852-1854, *FamilySearch* (https://www.familysearch.org : accessed 8 November 2017); FHL microfilm 1,617,060 item 1.

[78] 1850 U.S. Census, Macon County, Alabama, population schedule, 21st District, p. 272 (stamped), dwelling 1088, family 1096, George W. Dillard household; digital image, Ancestry (http://www.ancestry.com : accessed 10 March 2017); citing NARA microfilm publication M432, roll 9.

[79] 1860 U.S. Census, Chambers County, Alabama, population schedule, Northern Division, Milltown Post Office, page 130 (penned), dwelling 915, family 895, Thomas B. Royston household; digital image, *FamilySearch* (https://familysearch.org: accessed 29 April 2016); citing NARA microfilm publication M653 roll 4.

articles. A land record puts Thomas B. Royston in Lee County, Georgia, near Muscogee in 1831, making a meeting between him and Cynthia Dillard possible. A newspaper notice of Thomas Royston in a list of letters remaining at the post office at Columbus, Muscogee County, Georgia provides direct evidence of his presence in the same area as the Dillard family. The Muscogee County courthouse fire in 1838 could explain the lack of a marriage record for Cynthia and Thomas B. Royston.

The move of both George W. Dillard and Thomas B. and Cynthia Royston into Alabama by 1840 also points to a possible connection, with families often migrating together. George W. Dillard patented land in three different Alabama counties, including Chambers County, where Thomas and Cynthia settled by 1850. Studying the land transactions of Thomas B. Royston revealed no connections to the land George W. Dillard patented.

The presence of a "Leonidas" in both the Dillard and Royston households also points to a possible connection. Future research could examine the descendants of George W. Dillard for other similar naming patterns.

Although evidence continues to point to George W. Dillard as the possible father for Cynthia (Dillard) Royston, further research should be done to eliminate other candidates.

FUTURE RESEARCH SUGGESTIONS

- Search the probate records for Lee County, Alabama for George W. Dillard.

- Order the land case entry files from the National Archives for George W. Dillard's land patents in Alabama between 1834 and 1841. The case entry files might have further clues that could uncover a relationship between Cynthia (Dillard) Royston and George W. Dillard.

- Build up the FAN club (friends, associates, and neighbors) for George W. Dillard and Thomas and Cynthia (Dillard) Royston looking for connections.

- Research the possible children of George W. Dillard from the 1850 census: Columbus, Alonzo Leonidas, and Zenora. Note naming patterns among their descendants.

- Research Lorenzo and Nathaniel Dillard. They also patented land in Chambers County, Alabama, and could be related to George W. Dillard and/or Cynthia (Dillard) Royston.

- Research other Dillard men in Alabama from 1830-1860 to discover possible brothers to Cynthia from George W. Dillard's first marriage to Peggy Armour. Note naming patterns.

- Search for connections between Cynthia (Dillard) Royston and the family of her possible mother, Peggy Armour, of Greene County, Georgia.

- Identify other possible candidates for the father of Cynthia (Dillard) Royston from the 1820 and 1830 census records of Georgia.

- Systematically research each candidate and possibly eliminate as a father for Cynthia.

- DNA testing and analysis of the descendants of Cynthia (Dillard) Royston and the known descendants of George W. Dillard could reveal a connection.

Work Sample 2: Research Project

Moses W. Isenhour Confederate Service

Nicole Dyer

Introduction

The first time I joined a Research Like a Pro Study Group, I was in the middle of gathering data about my relatives who were Confederate Soldiers. I decided to practice the *Research Like a Pro* method with the brothers of my ancestor, Barnet Isenhour. Barnet died before the Civil War, but three of his brothers were alive and could have enlisted in the Confederate States Army. I created the following objective:

Discover the actions of three brothers, sons of John D. Isenhour and Sarah Bailey prior to and during the Civil War.

- Valentine Isenhour, born 1820 in North Carolina, died after 1870, probably in Texas, married Margaret Ann Hendricks on 3 September 1854
- Moses W. Isenhour born 1823 in Cape Girardeau, Missouri, died 16 February 1862 in Fort Thompson, married Amanda Martha McKinney on 1 October 1846 in Montgomery, Arkansas
- Josiah Edmond Isenhour, born 1825 in Missouri, died 13 December 1868 in New Orleans, Louisiana

As I started creating a chronology and evidence analysis for these three men, I realized that my objective was large. I completed a locality guide with a few details about several of the locations the Isenhour brothers lived, a research plan, and began researching. My research log became long and difficult to navigate. I wrote the research report but neglected to include everything I found in my research log. I learned a narrow objective is key to being successful in this process. Looking back, I would do things differently. Here are two ways to tackle a multi-person objective:

1. Divide your objective into separate research questions for each person. Complete all the steps for one person at a time. It's likely that you'll need different locality guides for each person in your project if they didn't all stay in the same location.

2. Keep the multi-person objective but create separate chronologies/timelines for each person. Create a locality guide for the main places of residence for each person. In the research phase, keep a separate sheet in the research log for each person. When you write the report, create separate sections for each person.

In preparing for this book, I revisited my Isenhour Brothers research. I wanted to share it as a work sample, but as my first project, I knew it would need some polish. At first, I decided to keep the multi-person objective I had started with. I refined my chronology, reviewed my research plan, and reorganized the report to include transitions from one brother to the next. I noticed several parts of my research plan hadn't been completed. I finished the research, added several sections to the report, and then noticed how long it had become! It was a little too unwieldy to share as a work sample in this appendix.

At this point, I decided to redo my project and divide my objective into three separate research questions. I chose Moses W. Isenhour as the brother to focus on for this work sample. I copied and pasted all his entries in the chronology into a new document. I created a locality guide for Montgomery County, Arkansas, where Moses resided just prior to the Civil War. I created a new report, focusing only on Moses and his service in the Confederate States Army. It was much simpler and I made many more connections about Moses when I was focused just on him.

Although researching the brothers together helped me gain a picture of their shared experiences, it was easier to learn the Research Like a Pro process when I researched about just one person.

So, as you embark on this experience to learn to Research Like a Pro, consider creating a narrow objective. It will save you a headache!

Chronology & Evidence Analysis - Moses W. Isenhour

Objective

The objective of this research project is to discover the actions of Moses W. Isenhour prior to and during the Civil War. He was born in 1823 in Cape Girardeau, Missouri, and died 16 February 1862 in Fort Thompson, [state unknown], United States. Moses was the son of John D. Isenhour and Sarah Bailey and married Amanda McKinney 1 October 1846 in Montgomery, Arkansas.

The purpose of this chronology is to review what is already known about Moses W. Isenhour. The following sources will be reviewed:

1. 1840 Census of John Ishower
2. 1844 Probate of John Isenhower
3. 1845 Deed of M. Isenhour to J.E. Isenhour
4. 1846 Marriage of Moses W. Isenhower to Manda Mckinney
5. 1850 U.S. Federal Census of Moses W. Isenhour Household
6. 1861 Compiled Military Service Record (CMSR) for Moses Isenhower
7. *Find A Grave* Memorial for Amanda Martha McKinney Isenhour

1. 1840 Census of John Ishower[1]

U.S. Federal Census, Torance, Cape Girardeau County, Missouri
"John Ishower"

- 1 male 10-15 - possibly Josiah (about age 15)
- 1 male 15-20 - possibly Moses (about age 17)

---

[1] 1840 U.S. Census, Cape Girardeau, Missouri, population schedule, Torance, p. 268 (stamped), line 21, John Ishower household; digital image, *Ancestry* (http://www.ancestry.com : accessed 27 September 2016); citing NARA microfilm publication M704, roll 221.

- 2 males 20-30 - possibly Valentine (about age 19-20) and Barnet (about age 19-20)
- 1 male 50-60 - probably John
- 1 female 10-15 - possibly Sarah Emmeline (age 11)
- 1 female 15-20 - possibly Patty (age 19)
- 1 female 40-50 - Sallie

Moses is likely living at home with his parents in 1840. The only child who is probably not living at home is the oldest daughter, Mahala, who married Enos M. Johnson on 27 February 1831.

Analysis
- **Source**: Image of an *original.* George H. Shell, marshal, recorded the information on the page in legible handwriting. The image is a little blurry and has some bleeding from the page behind it.
- **Information**: *Undetermined.* The household information was likely given by John Isenhower. The residence information was recorded by George H. Shell, marshal, and that information is likely primary, as the marshals were instructed to visit each home and find out who lived there.
- **Evidence**: This provides *indirect* evidence of Moses' residence in Cape Girardeau County, Missouri, in 1840 prior to the Civil War.

2. 1844 Probate of John Isenhower[2]

- Will found in Missouri Wills and Probate Records, Register Book B Cape Girardeau County Court
- Will was probated 17 Feb 1844, Cape Girardeau County, Missouri
- John lists his wife Sallie and many people who are assumed to be his children: Mahaly Johnson, Valentine Isenhour, Patty Blalock, Barnet Isenhour, Moses Isenhour, Josiah E. Isenhour, and Sarah Emmeline Isenhour.

Analysis
- **Source**: Image of an *original.* Image appears unaltered and is legible.
- **Information**: *Primary.* The will of John Isenhower gives primary information about his heirs, and the recording of the will is primary information about his death date and place.

---

[2] Cape Girardeau County, Missouri, Wills and Letters, Vol B 1829-1847, John Isenhower, probate 17 February 1844, p. 354; "Missouri, Wills and Probate Records, 1766-1988," case file for John Isenhower, *Ancestry* (http://www.ancestry.com : accessed 10 November 2017).

- **Evidence**: This provides *direct* evidence that Moses is an heir of John and received an inheritance in Cape Girardeau, Missouri, prior to the Civil War.

3. 1845 Deed of M. Isenhour to J.E. Isenhour[3]

- Record Book M, County of Cape Girardeau, Deed Records
- M. Isenhour sold land to J.E. Isenhour, 11 October 1845.

Analysis
- **Source**: Image of an *original*. This is a high-quality image of the original deed book, legible, and unaltered.
- **Information**: *Primary*. The informant was a justice of the peace, Casper Shell, who witnessed the two parties signing the deed.
- **Evidence**: This provides *direct* evidence that Moses and his brother Josiah owned land in Cape Girardeau, Missouri, and that Moses sold the land to Josiah. This is indirect evidence that Moses moved away from Missouri about 1845, before the Civil War.

4. 1846 Marriage of Moses W. Isenhower to Manda Mckinney[4]

- Arkansas, County Marriages, 1837-1957
- 1 October 1846 - Moses W. Isenhower, age 23, married Manda Mckinney, age 16 in Montgomery County, Arkansas.
- Moses' calculated birth year: 1823

Analysis
- **Source**: Image of an *original*. The image is legible and appears unaltered.
- **Information**: *Primary*. Beverly Allen, The Justice of the Peace of Montgomery County in Sulphur Springs, is the informant. He certified that they were married by consent.

---

[3] Cape Girardeau County, Missouri, Deed Book, vol. M, p. 53, M. Isenhour to J.E. Isenhour, 11 Oct 1845, digital image 379, "Deed records, 1805-1910; indexes 1805-1904," *FamilySearch* (http://familysearch.org : accessed 21 March 2018); citing FHL microfilm 925635.

[4] "Arkansas, County Marriages, 1837-1957," database with images, image 394, *FamilySearch* (https://familysearch.org : 4 November 2017), Moses W. Isenhour and Manda Mckinney, 1 October 1846; citing Montgomery, Arkansas, United States, county offices, Arkansas; FHL microfilm 1,011,071.

- **Evidence**: This provides *direct* evidence of the marriage and spouse of Moses Isenhour. It also provides direct evidence of Moses' residence prior to Civil War.

5. 1850 U.S. Federal Census of Moses W. Isenhour household[5]

Sulphur Springs, Montgomery, Arkansas
- Moses W. Isenhour, age 27, male, farmer, born in Missouri
- Amanda M. Isenhour, age 20, female, born in Arkansas
- Martha E. Isenhour, age 2, female, born in Arkansas
- Wm. Martin Isenhour, age 10/12, male, born in Arkansas

Analysis
- **Source**: Image of *original* census record - legible, does not appear to be altered.
- **Information**: *Undetermined.* Informant is unknown, but it is likely the head of household, because the instructions to the assistant marshals were for them to "inquire at every dwelling house, or by personal inquiry of the head of every family, and not otherwise." Names, dates, and places of birth are given for each child and seem consistent with other sources. The assistant marshal, G.W. Wellington, most likely visited the home and his information about the Isenhour family's residence in Montgomery, Arkansas, is primary.
- **Evidence**: This provides *direct* evidence for residence and household of Moses prior to the Civil War.

6. 1861 Compiled Military Service Record (CMSR) for Moses Isenhower[6]

- 19 October 1861 - Moses enlisted
  - Moses Isenhower joined for duty and enrolled with the 11th Regiment Arkansas Infantry, Company I in Little Rock, Arkansas, for 1 year, age 35

---

[5] 1850 U.S. Census, Montgomery County, Arkansas, population schedule, Sulphur Springs, p. 394 (stamped), dwelling 9, family 9, Moses W. Isenhour household; digital image, *FamilySearch* (http://familysearch.org : accessed 10 November 2017); citing NARA microfilm publication M432, roll 28.

[6] Compiled service record, Moses Isonhower, Pvt., Co. I, 11 Arkansas Infantry (Confederate); "Compiled Service Records of Confederate Soldiers Who Served in Organizations from the State of Arkansas," database with images, *Fold3* (https://www.fold3.com/image/271/221329313 : accessed 10 October 2017); citing Carded Records Showing Military Service of Soldiers Who Fought in Confederate Organizations, compiled 1903 - 1927, documenting the period 1861 - 1865, Record Group 109, The National Archives.

years old. If Moses was 35 years old when he enlisted on 29 October 1861, his calculated birth year would be about 1826. Other records show that his birth year was about 1823.

    ○   Moses travelled 50 miles to the rendezvous point. If he travelled from Montgomery County to Little Rock, where he enlisted, the mileage would be about 100 miles. Perhaps he had changed residences.

- 29 Oct 1861 - 23 Sept 1862: Moses present on muster rolls
  ○ Moses Isenhower appears on the company muster roll of the 11th Regiment Arkansas Infantry, Company I.
  ○ Received no pay.
- 16 February 1862: Moses died at Fort Thompson

Analysis

- **Source**: *Derivative.* An abstract of a company muster roll created by the federal government in an effort to consolidate information about each individual soldier. O. T. Taylor was the copyist.
- **Information**: *Undetermined.* The informant was likely a member of the regiment and thus the information is probably primary. Moses was enlisted for duty by Anderson Cunningham and Thos Rector, who may have been the informants for his enlistment.
- **Evidence**: This provides *direct* evidence of the Civil War service and death of Moses Isenhour.

7. *Find A Grave* Memorial for Amanda Martha McKinney Isenhour[7]

BIRTH - 1830 Montgomery County, Arkansas, USA
DEATH - 1892 (aged 61–62) Fort Worth, Tarrant County, Texas, USA
BURIAL - Oakwood Cemetery, Fort Worth, Tarrant County, Texas, USA
MEMORIAL ID - 135262666

Analysis

- **Source:** *Authored.* The memorial at Findagrave.com was created by Charlotte Hardamon Coble. A headstone photo is not included, and Charlotte does not list a source of the information.

---

[7] *Find A Grave,* (https://www.findagrave.com : accessed 4 April 2018), memorial 135262666, Amanda Martha McKinney Isenhour (1830–1892), citing Oakwood Cemetery, Fort Worth, Tarrant County, Texas, USA; memorial maintained by Charlotte Hardamon Coble (contributor 46886606).

- **Information**: *Undetermined*. The creator of the memorial does not cite a record. It could be from a gravestone that has not been photographed or from a cemetery record.
- **Evidence:** This provides *indirect* evidence about Moses' actions prior to and during the Civil War. Amanda's residence in Texas and death date may provide clues leading to a widow's pension containing information about Moses' Civil War service.

Montgomery County, Arkansas Locality Guide

BACKGROUND

Quick Facts

- County Seat: Mount Ida
- Formed 9 December 1842 from Hot Spring County
- Arkansas received statehood 15 June 1836
    - State birth and death records began in 1914, full compliance 1920s
    - Arkansas is a Federal Land State

Online Research Guides

- Montgomery County, Arkansas FamilySearch Wiki Article
  https://www.familysearch.org/wiki/en/Montgomery_County,_Arkansas_Genealog
  y
- Montgomery County, Arkansas Genealogy Guide (Random Acts of Genealogical
  Kindness)
  https://www.raogk.org/arkansas-genealogy/montgomery-county/
- Montgomery County, Arkansas: Family History & Genealogy, Census, Birth,
  Marriage, Death Vital Records & More (Linkpendium)
  http://www.linkpendium.com/montgomery-ar-genealogy/
- Montgomery County ARGenWeb Project (ARGenWeb, part of USGenWeb)
  http://www.argenweb.net/montgomery/index.htm
- Arkansas USGenWebArchives Project (USGenWeb Archives)
  http://www.usgwarchives.net/ar/montgomery/montgome.html

Geography and Maps

Neighboring counties:
- Clark
- Garland

- Hot Spring
- Howard
- Pike
- Polk
- Scott
- Yell

Maps and Gazetteers:
- Adams, Louis A. *Adam's Directory of Points and Landings on Rivers and Bayous in the States of Alabama, Arkansas, Florida, Georgia, Indiana, Illinois, Kentucky, Iowa, Louisiana, Minnesota, Mississippi, Missouri, Nebraska, Ohio, Tennessee, Texas and Wisconsin. (includes Tennessee)* (New Orleans: W.L. Murray, 1877). Book digitized at https://archive.org/details/cu31924095607135
- Interactive Map of Arkansas County Formation History - Map of US http://www.mapofus.org/arkansas/
- 1860 Arkansas Slave Map - ArkansawTraveler.comhttp://www.arkansawtraveler.com/2012/01/1860-arkansas-slave-map/
- Map resources for Montgomery County, Arkansas - ARgenweb.net http://www.argenweb.net/montgomery/map_info.htm

Timeline of County Formation

- 1803 - U.S. purchased French Louisiana from Napoleon Bonaparte (including all of Arkansas)
- 1813 - Arkansas County created in Missouri Territory
- 1818 - Clark County created from Arkansas County
- 1819 - "Territory of Arkansaw" created from Missouri Territory
- 1829 - Hot Spring County created from Clark County
- 1836 - Arkansas received statehood
- 1842 - Montgomery County formed from Hot Spring County
- 1850 - Salem became the county seat of Montgomery County. Later in the year the county seat changed to Mount Ida, where the post office was located.
- 1854 - Mount Ida incorporated 1854

History

In 1891, historians wrote of Montgomery County that it was only one county away from Indian Territory and the crops grown there included cotton, tobacco, all the cereals, esculent roots, and vegetables.[8]

---

[8] Southern Publishing Company, *Biographical and historical memoirs of western Arkansas: comprising a condensed history of the state, a number of biographies of distinguished*

Timeline
1812 - First white settlers arrived when Martin and Mary Collier settled Caddo Gap[9]
1835 - Granville Whittington built a road from Hot Springs, Arkansas to his farm a mile north of the settlement of Montgomery[10]
1836 - Arkansas received statehood
1842 - Whittington opened Mount Ida Post Office
1861 - Arkansas seceded from the United States; most of Montgomery County favored the Confederacy[11]

Articles about the History of Montgomery County, Arkansas
- Montgomery County at the Encyclopedia of Arkansas History & Culture
  http://www.encyclopediaofarkansas.net/encyclopedia/entry-detail.aspx?entryID=793
- Montgomery County at Arkansas Municipal League
  http://local.arkansas.gov/local.php?agency=Montgomery%20County
- Montgomery County, Arkansas at Wikipedia
  https://en.wikipedia.org/wiki/Montgomery_County,_Arkansas

Law and Government

About the county court, from the 1898 *Biographical and historical memoirs of western Arkansas:* "The county was not fully and actually organized until sometime in 1844. No record of the county court has been preserved prior to July, 1845, and only a part of the record of the July term of that year is preserved."[12]

---

citizens of the same, a brief descriptive history of each of the counties mentioned, and numerous biographical sketches of the citizens of such counties (Chicago: Southern Publishing Company, 1891) p. 466-467; digitized book, *Internet Archive* (https://archive.org : accessed 2 April 2018).

[9] *Wikipedia* (https://en.wikipedia.org) "Montgomery County, Arkansas," reviewed 2 April 2018, 12:40pm.

[10] Ibid.

[11] Ibid.

[12] Southern Publishing Company, *Biographical and historical memoirs of western Arkansas: comprising a condensed history of the state, a number of biographies of distinguished citizens of the same, a brief descriptive history of each of the counties mentioned, and numerous biographical sketches of the citizens of such counties* (Chicago: Southern Publishing Company, 1891) p. 470; digitized book, *Internet Archive* (https://archive.org : accessed 2 April 2018).

Libraries and Archives

Montgomery County Courthouse
1 George Street
Mount Ida, AR 71957
Phone: 870.887.3521
http://local.arkansas.gov/local.php?agency=Montgomery%20County

Montgomery County Public Library
145A Whittington Street
Mount Ida, AR 71957
http://montgomerycountyarlibrary.org/

Heritage House Museum of Montgomery County
819 Luzerne Street
Mount Ida, Arkansas 71957
www.hhmmc.org

Southwest Arkansas Regional Archives
201 Highway 195 South
P.O. Box 134
Washington, Arkansas 71862
870-983-2633
http://archives.arkansas.gov/sara/sara-about-us.aspx

Genealogical Societies and Publications

Montgomery County Historical Society
P.O. Box 578
Mount Ida, AR 71957
www.rootsweb.com/~armontgo/

The publication of the Montgomery County Historical Society is called *The Crystal:*
- Montgomery County Historical Society (Arkansas), *The Crystal,* (Mount Ida, Arkansas: Montgomery County Historical Society (Arkansas), 1989 - 1996).
- Vol 1-8 available at the Family History Library https://www.familysearch.org/search/catalog/521298

Record Loss

No known record loss.

Local History

- Sesquicentennial Committee of Montgomery County, Arkansas. *Montgomery County, our heritage: quartz crystal capital of the world* (Dallas, Texas: Taylor Pub. Co., c. 1986-1990). https://www.familysearch.org/search/catalog/627771
- Montgomery County, AR Bibliography - local history book listing at http://www.argenweb.net/montgomery/bibliography.htm

Reference Books

- Herndon, Dallas T., *Centennial History of Arkansas Vol II* (Chicago-Little Rock: The S. J. Clarke Publishing Company, 1922). Contains biographies of prominent men. Digital version available at https://archive.org/details/centennialhistor00hern
- Herndon, Dallas T., *The high lights of Arkansas history* (Little Rock: The Arkansas History commission, 1922). Digital Version at https://archive.org/details/highlightsofarka00hern
- Southern Publishing Company, "Montgomery County," *Biographical and historical memoirs of western Arkansas: comprising a condensed history of the state, a number of biographies of distinguished citizens of the same, a brief descriptive history of each of the counties mentioned, and numerous biographical sketches of the citizens of such counties* (Chicago: Southern Publishing Company, 1891), 466. Digital version available at https://archive.org/details/biographicalhist00sout
- Charlie Daniels, *Historical Report of the Arkansas Secretary of State 2008* (University of Arkansas press, 2009). Digital version available at https://books.google.com/books?isbn=0615232140

RECORD COLLECTIONS

These are only collections that are specific to Montgomery County, Arkansas. This list does not include general Arkansas record collections. For general Arkansas records, see Arkansas, United States Genealogy *at the FamilySearch wiki:*
>   *https://www.familysearch.org/wiki/en/Arkansas,_United_States_Genealogy*

General Collections

FamilySearch Catalog Listings for Montgomery County, Arkansas
>   https://www.familysearch.org/search/catalog/ > place > United States, Arkansas, Montgomery

County Clerk - listing of records maintained by the Montgomery County Clerk at montgomerycounty.arkansas.gov
>   http://montgomerycounty.arkansas.gov/departments/detail/county-clerk

Cemetery Records

Cemeteries in Montgomery County, Arkansas - Listings at:
    http://www.argenweb.net/montgomery/cem.htm

Montgomery County Historical Society, *Montgomery County, Arkansas cemeteries* (Mount Ida, Arkansas: Montgomery county Historical Society (Arkansas), c. 1997). FamilySearch Catalog listing:
    https://www.familysearch.org/search/catalog/718725

Cemeteries in Montgomery County, Arkansas - ArkansasGravestones.org - some burials listed:
    https://arkansasgravestones.org/cemeteries.php?selected_cid=37

Cemeteries in Montgomery County, Arkansas - FindAGrave.com - many burials listed:
    https://www.findagrave.com/cemetery/search?locationId=county_141&page=1#cem-54458

Church Records

Records of Religion and Spirituality at the Arkansas State Archives finding aid
http://ahc.digital-ar.org/cdm/singleitem/collection/p16790coll13/id/297
- Montgomery County Mt. Gilead Baptist Church records, 1828-1925 [MG08164] 25
- Mt. Ida Baptist Church records, 1914-1956 [MG08166]

Caddo River Baptist Association Minutes, 1867-1900 - USGenWeb Archives
    http://www.usgwarchives.net/ar/montgomery/montgome.html

Court Records

Chancery court record, v. A, 1858-1893 - Family History Library, digitized microfilm
    https://www.familysearch.org/search/catalog/787292

Circuit court records, 1845-1883 - Family History Library, digitized microfilm
    https://www.familysearch.org/search/catalog/402210

County court records, 1845-1880 - Family History Library, digitized microfilm
    https://www.familysearch.org/search/catalog/400944
- Land sold for taxes 1868-1877; delinquent taxes; township officers, school warrants.
- County Court record, v. 1& B 1845-1880

Land Records

Deed Index 1850-1914 - Family History Library, digitized microfilm
    https://www.familysearch.org/search/catalog/400951

Montgomery County, Arkansas, Federal Land Recrods; list of BLM land records before 1908
in Montgomery County - USGenWeb
    http://files.usgwarchives.net/ar/montgomery/land/montgome.txt

Military Records

4th Regiment, Arkansas Infantry (Confederate) - Civil War Regiment formed with men from
Montgomery County, FamilySearch Wiki
    https://www.familysearch.org/wiki/en/4th_Regiment,_Arkansas_Infantry_(Confederate)

33rd Regiment, Arkansas Infantry (Confederate), Company I - Civil War Regiment formed
with men from Montgomery County, FamilySearch Wiki
    https://www.familysearch.org/wiki/en/33rd_Regiment,_Arkansas_Infantry_(Confederate)

Newspapers

Montgomery County, Arkansas newspaper listings from the US Newspaper Directory, at
Chronicling America (https://chroniclingamerica.loc.gov/search/titles/). These newspapers
are not digitized but are available as microfilm copies at various libraries.

1. The Herald. (Mt. Ida, Ark.) 18??-1???

2. The Bear Mountain miner. (Bear City, Ark.) 188?-1???

3. The Montgomery County herald. (Mt. Ida, Ark.) 1890-1930s - A few transcriptions
   from this newspaper is available here -
   http://www.argenweb.net/montgomery/herald.htm

4. The Womble news. (Womble [Norman], Ark.) 19??-19??

5. The Caddo Gap eagle. (Caddo Gap, Ark.) 1909-19??

6. Montgomery County review. (Womble [Norman], Montgomery County, Ark.)
   1913-192?

7. Montgomery County Democrat. (Mt. Ida, Ark.) 1914-192?

8. The County seat broadcaster. (Mount Ida, Ark.) 192?-19??

9. The Review-Democrat. (Womble [Norman], Ark.) 1924-192?

10. The Montgomery County herald. (Mount Ida, Ark.) 1926-1928

11. The Norman visitor. (Norman, Ark.) 1927-1929

12. The Herald. (Mount Ida, Ark.) 1928-1940

13. The Norman sentinel. (Norman, Ark.) 1929-1938

14. Crystal. (Crystal Springs, Ark.) 193?-194?

15. The Montgomery County herald. (Mount Ida, Ark.) 1940-1953

16. Montgomery County news. (Mount Ida, Montgomery County, Ark.) 1951-current

Montgomery County, Arkansas newspaper listings from the University of Arkansas, available on microfilm - https://library.uark.edu/

Books about Arkansas Newspapers
- Allsopp, Fred W., *History of the Arkansas Press for a Hundred Years and More*, 1922, reprint (Easley, South Carolina: Southern Historical Press, 1978).
  - https://books.google.com/books?id=gdA3u6qwl3QC
  - FHL book 976.7 B3a: https://www.familysearch.org/search/catalog/177553
- Union List of Arkansas Newspapers, 1819-1942. Little Rock, Arkansas: Historical Records Survey, 1942. Digitized versions available:
  - FHL book 976.7 B3h, https://www.familysearch.org/search/catalog/179902
  - FHL film 897366 item 2, https://www.familysearch.org/search/catalog/179902
  - FHL fiche 6051358, https://www.familysearch.org/search/catalog/179902

Probate Records

Montgomery County, Arkansas, loose probate records, 1842-1930 - Family History Library, digitized microfilm
  https://www.familysearch.org/search/catalog/622509

Probate records, 1845-1954 Family History Library, digitized microfilm
  https://www.familysearch.org/search/catalog/400940

Index to "Montgomery County, Arkansas, Loose Probate Records, 1842-1930" by Marion Stark Craig - at usgwarchives.net
  http://files.usgwarchives.net/ar/montgomery/history/pub/prob1842.txt

Vital Records (Birth, Marriage, Death)

Birth and Death

Statewide birth and death records in Arkansas began 1 February 1914. Full compliance wasn't reached until the 1930s.

Marriage

James M. and Lillian Hart, editors, Marriage records Montgomery County, Arkansas: book A & B, vol. 1 & 2 - Family History Library, digitized book
> https://www.familysearch.org/search/catalog/2343060

Montgomery County (Arkansas) County Clerk, Marriage records, 1851-1958: index, ca. 1846-1972 - Family History Library, digitized microfilm
> https://www.familysearch.org/search/catalog/400933

Research Plan - Moses W. Isenhour

Objective

The objective of this research project is to discover the actions of Moses W. Isenhour prior to and during the Civil War. He was born in 1823 in Cape Girardeau, Missouri, and died 16 February 1862 in Fort Thompson, [state unknown], United States. Moses was the son of John D. Isenhour and Sarah Bailey and married Amanda McKinney 1 October 1846 in Montgomery, Arkansas.

Known Facts

1. In 1840, Moses W. Isenhour was living with his parents in Cape Girardeau County, Missouri.

2. In 1844 John Isenhower, father of Moses, died. In his will, John lists his wife Sallie and heirs who are assumed to be his children: Mahaly Johnson, Valentine Isenhour, Patty Blalock, Barnet Isenhour, Moses Isenhour, Josiah E. Isenhour, and Sarah Emmeline Isenhour.

3. In 1845 (11 October) Moses sold land to his brother, Josiah E. Isenhour

4. In 1846 (1 October) Moses Isenhour married Amanda Martha McKinney in Montgomery, Arkansas.

5. In 1848, Moses' daughter Martha E. Isenhour was born.

6. In 1849, Moses' son William Martin Isenhour was born.

7. In 1850, Moses resided in Montgomery, Arkansas.

8. In 1852, Moses' son George Washington Isenhour was born in Arkansas.

9. In 1854, Moses' son James M. Isenhour was born in Texas.

10. In 1857, Moses' son John Marshall Isenhour was born in Texas.

11. In 1861, (29 October) Moses enlisted in the CSA in Company I, 11th Regiment Arkansas Infantry.

12. In 1862 (February 16) Moses died at "Fort Thompson."

13. In 1892, Moses' widow, Amanda Martha McKinney Isenhour died in Fort Worth, Tarrant, Texas.

Questions

- When did Moses' family migrate to Texas? If they all moved there together, why did Moses serve in an Arkansas regiment? Did he also serve in a Texas regiment?

- What battles was Moses' regiment engaged in from October 1861 - February 1862?

- How did Moses die? Where is "Fort Thompson?"

- Did Amanda apply for a pension in Texas before she died?

Working Hypothesis

When John Isenhour died in 1844 in Cape Girardeau, his children, including Moses, moved away. This could have been because of antebellum unrest in Missouri. Moses moved to Montgomery County, Arkansas, where he married "Manda McKinney." Moses enlisted in the Confederate States Army in Arkansas and died after 4 months of service, leaving Amanda widowed with five children. Amanda moved to Texas and may have applied for a Confederate widow's pension.

Identify Sources to Search

- 1860 census in Arkansas and Texas
- Wikipedia articles containing references to "Fort Thompson" during the Civil War
- Muster Rolls from Arkansas, Company I, 11th Regiment Arkansas Infantry
- Regimental history for the 11th Arkansas Infantry
- Texas Confederate Pension records for widow Amanda

Research Strategy

1. Identify Moses and Family

    a. The 1860 census should be searched in Arkansas and Texas for Moses and his wife Amanda and children. They could be in either state. The time of their migration is unknown. Online family trees estimate their son John M. Isenhour was born in Texas in the 1850s.

    b. The 1870 census should be searched for Amanda Isenhour in Texas.

    c. The 1880 census should be searched for Amanda Isenhour in Texas.

    d. Court Records in Montgomery County, Arkansas 1845-1880 could show more about Moses' community involvement and migration timeline. The FamilySearch Library has digitized the county court books. https://www.familysearch.org/search/catalog/400944

    e. Tax records in Cass County, Texas: Texas county tax rolls, 1846-1910 could give clues about when Moses migrated to Texas. https://www.familysearch.org/search/catalog/986276

2. Civil War Service

    a. Texas Civil War service records

        i. "Compiled Service Records of Confederate Soldiers Who Served in Organizations from the State of Texas" at Fold3 may contain a record for Moses W. Isenhour. https://www.fold3.com/browse/271/h6o8f1tVq

        ii. Library of Texas Civil War and Texas State Troops muster rolls online - Muster rolls, payrolls, rosters, etc. from 1,500 companies of Texas State Troops and Confederate States Army stationed in Texas during the civil War. May contain the soldier's name and rank, commanding officer, designation of organization, etc. https://tsl.access.preservica.com/archive/sdb%3Acollection%7C798a5331-558c-458d-8b90-5962965c378b/

        iii. "Texas Muster Roll Index Cards" at Ancestry.com - 170,000 index cards with information extracted from original muster rolls relating to Texas units for both Confederate, Union, and Texas State Troops. http://search.ancestry.com/search/db.aspx?dbid=2059

    b. "Texas Confederate Pension records 1899-1975" at the Texas State Library will not likely include an application from Moses' widow Amanda - These began in 1899 after Amanda's death. She died in 1892. https://www.tsl.texas.gov/apps/arc/pensions/

      c. Contact descendants of Moses for stories that were passed down about his service. Find descendants using online family trees at Ancestry.com and FamilySearch.org.

3. Civil War Context

      a. Search Wikipedia for articles that mention "Fort Thompson"

      b. Regimental History of 11th Regiment Arkansas Infantry by Anthony Rushing, *Ranks of honor: a regimental history of the 11th Arkansas Infantry Regiment and Poe's Cavalry Battalion, C.S.A., 1861-1865.* Find out what battles the regiment was involved in from October 29, 1861 - February 16, 1862.

Research Log Sample

Moses W. Isenhour

Research Objective:	Discover the actions of Moses W. Isenhour, son of John D. Isenhour and Sarah Bailey, in the antebellum period and during the Civil War. Moses was born 1823 in Cape Girardeau, Missouri, died 16 February 1862 in Fort Thompson, Missouri, and was married to Amanda McKinney in 1846.
Name Variants:	Isenhour Isonhour Isenhower Isenhour Isonhour Isonhouer Eisenhower Eisenhour Icenhower Icenhour Isenhauer Isenhowr Isebour
Localities:	Arkansas, Texas

Date	Website or Repository	URL / Call # / Microfilm #	Searching For	Locality	Source	Results/Comments
10/19/17	Ancestry	Moses Isenhower Texas Muster Roll	Isenhours in Confederate service from Texas		Moses Isenhower, Pvt. Co K, 1st Regt., Bosque and Coryell Counties, 2nd Brig., TST, enlisted August 1863, "Texas, Muster Roll Index Cards, 1838-1900" database with images of index cards, *Ancestry* (www.ancestry.com : accessed 11 Nov 2017); citing Civil War Muster Rolls index Cards (both Confederate and Union). Also Texas State Rangers. Austin, Texas: Texas State Library and Archives Commission.	Found another Moses Isenhower. This one enlisted in the Texas State Troops in 1863, later TST were turned into CSA. This man was born in 1823 and the troops were from Bosque and Coryell Counties in Texas.
10/19/17	Texas State Library and Archives Commission Website	https://tsl.access.preservica.com/file/sdb%3Adigital File%7C7C560f9bbd-e280-48d7-8d6c-b63b4cec242c/	Moses Isenhour on muster roll	Texas	Moses Isenhower, Private, Muster roll of Company K, Bosque and Coryell Counties, 1st Regiment, 2nd Brigade, Texas State Troops under Captain W.S. Gouldy, March 18, 1864, Texas State Library and Archives Division, "Texas Adjutant General's Department Civil War military rolls," database with images, *Texas Digital Archive*, (https://tsl.access.preservica.com/ : 11 Nov 2017) MR 262, Record 0262.	Isenhower, Mos. Rank: private, age 40, Enlisted March 18, 1864 in Camp McCullough
10/19/17	Fold3	https://www.fold3.com/image/7751861 4	Moses Isenhour in Civil War collection at Fold3 - is this a different Moses?	Texas	1860 U.S. census, Bosque County, Texas, population schedule p. 27 (penned), dwelling 184, family 190, Moses Isenhower household; image, *Fold3* (http://www.fold3.com : accessed 11 Nov 2017); citing NARA microfilm publication M653, roll 1289.	Moses Isenhower, age 36, born Tennessee. (est. birth year 1823). Wife Catherine, children Simeon, Elizabeth, Manda E, David F, Ellena, Rosetta, Martha E. (This is a different family). Will call him Moses Isenhower 2.

Date	Website or Repository	URL / Call # / Microfilm #	Searching For	Locality	Source	Results/Comments
10/19/17	*Find A Grave*	https://www.findagrave.com/memorial/41628818	Death of Moses Isenhower 2 - show that this is a different Moses	Texas	*Find A Grave*, database and images (http://www.findagrave.com : accessed 11 Nov 2017), memorial 41628818, Moses Isenhower (1823-1906), citing Saint James Cemetery, Milford, Barton County, Missouri; gravestone photograph by Sandy [--?--].	Died 27 Oct 1906 Gravelton, Wayne, Missouri, parents Martin David Eisenhower and Anna Catherine Knull Eisenhower, spouse Catherine Bird Isenhower.
10/19/17	Ancestry		Moses Isenhour residence 1860	Montgomery, Arkansas	1860 U.S. Census, Montgomery County, Arkansas, population schedule, negative search for Moses Isenhower; *Ancestry.com*. (http://www.ancestry.com : accessed 11 Nov 2017); citing NARA microfilm publication 653.	none found
10/19/17	*FamilySearch*	https://www.familysearch.org/ark:/619 03/3:1:939F-4V96-R8?i=15&cc=1827575	Isenhours in Cass, Texas Tax lists	Cass, Texas	Moses Isenhower, 1855, Cass County, "Texas, County Tax Rolls, 1837-1910," database with images, *FamilySearch* (https://familysearch.org : accessed 11 Nov 2017), image 16; citing State Archives, Austin.	Moses W. Isenhower, Cass County, 1855, no property listed; 50 cents poll tax, 50 cents state tax, 25 cents county tax
11/21/17	Pima County Library Interlibrary Loan - obtained from Little Rock, Arkansas	OCLC Number on WorldCat.org : 712628944	11th Arkansas Infantry Regiment	Arkansas	Anthony C. Rushing, *Ranks of Honor: A Regimental History of the eleventh Arkansas Infantry Regiment & Poe's Cavalry Battalion C.S.A., 1861-1865* (Little Rock: Eagle Press, 1990), 172, 175.	Moses Isenhower, Pvt, Died at Fort Thompson Feb. 16, 1862. Many details about the Battle of Island No. 10 and what occupied the regiment prior to that battle.
4/10/18	*FamilySearch*	https://www.familysearch.org/ark:/619 03/3:1:3Q9M-C9BW-XQBY-5?i=115&cat=400944	Moses W. Isenhour	Montgomery, Arkansas	Montgomery County, Arkansas, Circuit Court Record Book 1, p. 165, Court order book Moses W Isenhower, July 1849; images, *FamilySearch*, (https://www.familysearch.org : accessed 13 Nov 2017); citing Montgomery County, Arkansas Court Record, v. 1; FHL microfilm 1011079, item 1, image 116.	Ordered by the court that Moses W Isenhower overseer of the road district No. 17 Be allowed the sum of six dollars as per bill filed at this court.

Moses W. Isenhour Confederate Service Research Report

Nicole Dyer

Research Objective

Discover the actions of Moses W. Isenhour prior to and during the Civil War. He was born in 1823 in Cape Girardeau, Missouri, and died 16 February 1862 in Fort Thompson, Missouri, United States. Moses was the son of John D. Isenhour and Sarah Bailey and married Amanda McKinney 1 October 1846 in Montgomery, Arkansas.

Background Information

Moses W. Isenhour, born 1823 in Cape Girardeau, Missouri, was the son of John D. Isenhour, grandson of a German immigrant and resident of North Carolina, who migrated with his family to Missouri about 1821-1822.[1] They likely migrated there after Missouri received statehood in 1821. The conditions of Missouri's statehood were hotly contested, with congressional leaders striving to keep the number of slave and free states equal. Congress finally agreed to admit Missouri to the Union with the Missouri Compromise of 1820. The compromise allowed Missouri to enter the Union as a slave state, Maine to enter as a free state, and made slavery illegal in all territory north of 36°30' latitude, except Missouri.

In 1840, John D. Isenhour resided in Cape Girardeau County, Missouri with seven others, likely his wife Sarah/Sallie Bailey and six of their seven known children. They owned no slaves.[2] In 1844, John's will was recorded in Cape Girardeau County. His wife Sallie and seven

---

[1] John D. Isenhour 24YK-X5N, "Family Tree," *FamilySearch* (https://www.familysearch.org : accessed 26 March 2018).

[2] 1840 U.S. Census, Cape Girardeau County, Missouri, population schedule, Torance, p. 268 (stamped), line 21, John Ishower household; digital image, *Ancestry* (http://www.ancestry.com : accessed 27 September 2016); citing NARA microfilm publication M704, roll 221.

other heirs are named: Mahaly Johnson, Valentine Isenhour, Patty Blalock, Barnet Isenhour, Moses W. Isenhour, Josiah E. Isenhour, and Sarah Emmeline Isenhour.[3]

The heirs of John D. Isenhour did not stay in Cape Girardeau County. In 1845, Moses sold land to brother, Josiah.[4] He then moved to Montgomery County, Arkansas, where he married "Manda McKinney" in 1846.[5] By 1850, most of Moses' siblings were also residing in Montgomery County, Arkansas:

- Mahala [Isenhour] and Enos M. Johnson were listed with five children - Francis, Juliet, William, Josiah, and Amanda.[6]

- Valentine Isenhour was listed with two young girls - Margaret and Sarah. It is presumed his first wife died.[7] He married again in 1854 to "Margrett Ann Hendrix" and the marriage was performed by his brother-in-law Enos M. Johnson, justice of the peace, in Montgomery County, Arkansas.[8]

---

[3] Cape Girardeau County, Missouri, Wills and Letters, Vol B 1829-1847, John Isenhower, probate 17 February 1844, p. 354; "Missouri, Wills and Probate Records, 1766-1988," case file for John Isenhower, *Ancestry* (http://www.ancestry.com : accessed 10 November 2017).

[4] Cape Girardeau County, Missouri, Deed Book, vol. M, p. 53, M. Isenhour to J.E. Isenhour, 11 Oct 1845, digital image 379, "Deed records, 1805-1910; indexes 1805-1904," *FamilySearch* (http://familysearch.org : accessed 21 March 2018); citing FHL microfilm 925635.

[5] "Arkansas, County Marriages, 1837-1957," database with images, image 394, *FamilySearch* (https://familysearch.org : 4 November 2017), Moses W. Isenhour and Manda Mckinney, 1 October 1846; citing Montgomery, Arkansas, United States, county offices, Arkansas; FHL microfilm 1,011,071.

[6] 1850 U.S. Census, Montgomery County, Arkansas, population schedule, Sulphur Springs, p. 27 (penned), household 24, family 24, Enos M. Johnson household; digital image, *FamilySearch* (http://familysearch.org : accessed 21 March 2018); citing NARA microfilm publication M432, roll 28).

[7] 1850 U.S. Census, Montgomery County, Arkansas, population schedule, Polk, p. 815 (penned), sheet 406 (stamped), dwelling 16, family 16, Valentine Isenhour household; digital image, *FamilySearch* (http://familysearch.org : accessed 10 November 2017); citing NARA microfilm publication M432, roll 28.

[8] "Arkansas, County Marriages, 1837-1957," database with images, image 332, *FamilySearch* (https://familysearch.org : 4 November 2017),Valentine Isenhour and Margrett Ann Hendrix, 3 September 1854; citing Montgomery, Arkansas, United States, county offices, Arkansas; FHL microfilm 1,011,071.

- Barnet and Mary Ann Isenhour were listed with two girls - Sarah and Eliza.[9]

- Moses and Amanda M. Isenhour were listed with two children - Martha and William.[10]

- Lewis and Sarah Emmeline [Isenhour] Trammell were listed with three children - one-year-old Thomas Trammell as well as Margaret and Sarah Isenhour, likely the same girls listed in Valentine's household.[11]

Moses' siblings Patty and Josiah moved elsewhere:

- William and Patty Martha [Isenhour] Blalock were residing in Graves County, Kentucky, in 1850 with several children.[12]

- Josiah E. Isenhour's residence in 1850 is unknown. In 1848, he was appointed postmaster in Cape Girardeau, Missouri.[13] Sometime soon after that, he moved with his business to New Orleans, Louisiana.[14]

---

[9] 1850 U.S. Census, Montgomery County, Arkansas, population schedule, Polk, p. 405 (stamped), household 6, family 6, Barnet Isenhour household; digital image, *FamilySearch* (http://familysearch.org : accessed 21 March 2018); citing NARA microfilm publication M432, roll 28.

[10] 1850 U.S. Census, Montgomery County, Arkansas, population schedule, Sulphur Springs, p. 394 (stamped), dwelling 9, family 9, Moses W. Isenhour household; digital image, *FamilySearch* (http://familysearch.org : accessed 10 November 2017); citing NARA microfilm publication M432, roll 28.

[11] 1850 U.S. Census, Montgomery County, Arkansas, population schedule, Polk, p. 802 (penned), household 9, family 9, Lewis Trammell household; digital image, *FamilySearch* (http://familysearch.org : accessed 21 March 2018); citing NARA microfilm publication M432, roll 28.

[12] 1850 U.S. Census, Graves County, Kentucky, population schedule, District 1, p. 434 (stamped), dwelling 140, family 140, W. Blaylock household; digital image, *FamilySearch* (http://familysearch.org : accessed 21 March 2018); citing NARA microfilm publication M432, roll 201.

[13] Record of Appointment of Postmasters, 1832-1971, Josiah E. Isenhour, 1848, Jackson Hole, Cape Girardeau, Missouri, "Appointments of U.S. Postmasters, 1832-1871," database with images, *Ancestry.com* (https://ancestry.com : accessed 11 April 2018); citing Record of Appointment of Postmasters, 1832-1971. NARA Microfilm Publication, M841, 145 rolls. Records of the Post Office Department, Record Group Number 28. Washington, D.C.: National Archives.

[14] Cape Girardeau County, Missouri, Will Record, Vol D 1867-1894, Succession of Josiah E. Isenhour, 30 December 1868, Testimony of B.M. Horrell, p. 61; "Missouri, Wills and

What was life like for Moses and his family in Montgomery Coutny, Arkansas? In 1850, Arkansas was the frontier of the United States. Residents in the north part of the state were subsistence farmers while landowners in the southeastern part of the state relied on slave labor to produce cotton.[15] The Isenhours lived in the towns of Sulphur Springs and Polk in Montgomery County, located in the western part of Arkansas near Indian Territory. There were only eight slave owners between the two towns in 1850, and none of them seem to be related to the Isenhours.[16] The crops grown in Montgomery County included "cotton, tobacco, all the cereals, esculent roots, and vegetables."[17]

In 1860, tension was rising between the North and the South as the nation prepared to vote in the November presidential election. Abraham Lincoln was running on the Republican platform which was opposed the spread of slavery into the territories. Lincoln was not even on the ballot in most the slaves states that would secede in 1861. Most southerners voted for John C. Breckinridge of the Southern Democratic Party.[18] Where did Moses W. Isenhour reside during this tumultuous time?

In 1854, "Moses W. Isonhour" appears on the tax list of Cass County, Texas.[19] His brother, Barnet, also migrated to Texas. In 1860, Barnet's wife Mary Ann and their children were

---

Probate Records, 1766-1988," *Ancestry* (http://www.ancestry.com : accessed 10 November 2017), digital images 36-40.

[15] Thomas A. DeBlack, "Civil War through Reconstruction, 1861 through 1874," *The Encyclopedia of Arkansas History & Culture* (www.encyclopediaofarkansas.net : accessed 21 March 2018).

[16] 1850 U.S. Census, Montgomery County, Arkansas, slave schedule, Sulphur Springs and Polk, p. 141 (penned); digital images 2-3, *FamilySearch* (http://familysearch.org : 21 March 2018); citing NARA microfilm publication M432.

[17] Southern Publishing Company, *Biographical and historical memoirs of western Arkansas: comprising a condensed history of the state, a number of biographies of distinguished citizens of the same, a brief descriptive history of each of the counties mentioned, and numerous biographical sketches of the citizens of such counties* (Chicago: Southern Publishing Company, 1891) p. 467; digitized book, *Internet Archive* (https://archive.org : accessed 2 April 2018).

[18] *Wikipedia* (https://en.wikipedia.org) "United States presidential election, 1860," reviewed 23 March 2018, 1:10pm.

[19] "Texas, County Tax Rolls, 1837-1910," Cass county, 1854, line 37, Moses W. Isonhour, image 14, database with images, *FamilySearch* (https://familysearch.org : 22 March 2018); citing State Archives, Austin.

enumerated in Johnson County, Texas with Esquire Blevins.[20] Barnet Isenhour likely died between 1850 and 1860 in either Arkansas or Texas, and Mary Ann remarried.

Moses' wife Amanda appears on the 1860 census of Cass, Texas in the household of J.T. Summerlin, but Moses is absent.[21] Where did Moses go? Previous research has already shown that Moses W. Isenhour enlisted with the 11th Arkansas Infantry regiment in 1861.[22] Why didn't he enlist in a company from Texas? The following research findings show what he was doing in Arkansas and Texas prior to the war and what his experience was like during the war.

Research Findings

Prior to the War

Court records in Montgomery County were searched and show that Moses served in various positions in the local government, including overseer of roads for District No. 17 in Montgomery County in 1849.[23] Road overseers were appointed for one year and were required to keep the roads in their district in good repair.[24]

----

[20] 1860 U.S. Census, Johnson County, Texas, population schedule, Comanche Peak Post Office, p. 24 (penned), household 167, family 168, Esquire Blevins household; digital image, *FamilySearch* (http://familysearch.org : accessed 21 March 2018); citing NARA microfilm publication 653, roll 1298.

[21] 1860 U.S. Census, Cass County, Texas, population schedule, Beat 1, p. 31 (penned), household 215, family 219, J.T. Summerlin household; digital image, *FamilySearch* (http://familysearch.org : accessed 20 March 2018); citing NARA microfilm publication M653, roll 1290.

[22] Compiled service record, Moses Isonhower, Pvt., Co. I, 11 Arkansas Infantry (Confederate); "Compiled Service Records of Confederate Soldiers Who Served in Organizations from the State of Arkansas," database with images, *Fold3* (https://www.fold3.com : accessed 10 October 2017); citing Carded Records Showing Military Service of Soldiers Who Fought in Confederate Organizations , compiled 1903 - 1927, documenting the period 1861 - 1865, Record Group 109, The National Archives.

[23] Montgomery County, Arkansas, Circuit Court Record Book 1, p. 173, Moses W Isenhower appointed Overseer of Road District No. 17, July 1849; images, *FamilySearch*, (https://www.familysearch.org : accessed 13 Nov 2017); citing Montgomery County, Arkansas Court Record, v. 1; FHL microfilm 1011079, item 1, image 120-121.

[24] E.H. English, *A Digest of the Statutes of Arkansas, Embracing All Laws of a General and Permanent Character in Force at the Close of the Session of the General Assembly of 1846: Together*

"V. Isenhour" and "M. Isenhour" served as Coroner for Montgomery County, Arkansas for the term of 1856-1858, and 1860-1862, respectively.[25] County coroners were elected in each county and held office for a term of two years. The duties of Coroner were to investigate the cause of death for persons who were killed or who died an unnatural death and bring to trial those responsible.[26] The County Sheriff, Coroner, Treasurer, and Surveyor were elected by the residents of the county and served a term of two years. During that time they were required to "reside in their respective counties during their continuance in office."[27]

This explains why Moses was missing from the 1860 census with his family in Cass, Texas, and why he didn't enlist in a Texas regiment. Moses had been elected Coroner in Montgomery County and still had ties there, including his older brother Valentine and his family, who lived there until about 1862. Moses may have even lived with his brother after he left his family in Cass County, Texas to serve as Coroner.

Civil War Service

Previous research found that Moses W. Isenhour enlisted in the 11th Arkansas Infantry in 1861 and died in 1862.[28] However, during this research session, another military record was found for "Mos Isenhower" during the Civil War. A company muster roll of the Texas State troops contains the following:

> Mos Isenhower, Pvt. Co K, 1st Regt., Bosque and Coryell Counties, 2nd Brigade, Texas State Troops, age 40 (born about 1823), enlisted August 1863.[29]

---

with Notes of the Decisions of the Supreme Court Upon the Statutes (Little Rock: Reardon & Garritt, 1848) 899-900; image copy, Google Books (https://books.google.com : accessed 3 April 2018).

[25]   Charlie Daniels, *Historical Report of the Arkansas Secretary of State 2008* (University of Arkansas press, 2009) p. 482; digitized book, Google Books (https://books.google.com : accessed 20 March 2018).

[26]   E.H. English, *A Digest of the Statutes of Arkansas,* 272-274.

[27]   English, *A Digest of the Statutes of Arkansas,* 64.

[28]   Compiled service record, Moses Isonhower, Pvt., Co. I, 11 AR Inf. "Compiled Service Records of Confederate Soldiers...from...Arkansas," database with images, *Fold3.*

[29]   Moses Isenhower, Private, Muster roll of Company K, Bosque and Coryell Counties, 1st Regiment, 2nd Brigade, Texas State Troops under Captain W.S. Gouldy, March 18, 1864, Texas State Library and Archives Division, "Texas Adjutant General's Department Civil War military rolls," database with images, *Texas Digital Archive,* (https://tsl.access.preservica.com/ : 11 Nov 2017) MR 262, Record 0262.

In contrast, the Compiled Military Service Record (CMSR) for "Moses Isonhower" of Arkansas lists the following information, with a different calculated birth year and death date:

> *Moses Isonhower, Pvt. Co. I, 11th Regt. Arkansas Infantry; Enlisted 29 October 1861, Age 35 (born about 1826), died 16 February 1862.*[30]

These two records cannot be for the same man. If "Moses Isonhower" of the 11th Arkansas Infantry died in 1862, he could not have enlisted in the Texas State Troops in 1863.

Which of these two military records belongs to Moses W. Isenhour, son of John D. and Sarah Isenhour? Moses W. Isenhour was born 1823 in Cape Girardeau, Missouri, married Amanda McKinney in 1846, and had the middle initial "W."[31] It is not known where he resided in 1860, only that his wife and children were residing in Cass County, Texas.

To further identify the man of the same name who was a private in the Texas State Troops, the 1860 Federal census records were searched in Bosque and Coryell Counties. A man named Moses Isenhower, residing in Bosque County, Texas, was found:

> *Moses Isenhower, head of household, age 36, born in Tennessee (estimated birth year 1823) with other household members including Catherine age 36, Simeon 14, Elizabeth 12, Manda E 10, David F 9, Ellena 7, Rosetta 3, Mary A 6/12.*[32]

Additionally, the image of a gravestone for Moses Isenhower in Milford, Barton County, Missouri, was found.[33] The inscription reads:

> *Moses Isenhower*
> *Born Oct 8, 1823*

---

[30] Compiled service record, Moses Isonhower, Pvt., Co. I, 11 AR Inf. "Compiled Service Records of Confederate Soldiers...from...Arkansas," database with images, *Fold3*.

[31] "Arkansas, County Marriages, 1837-1957," database with images, image 394, *FamilySearch* (https://familysearch.org : 4 November 2017), Moses W. Isenhour and Manda Mckinney, 1 October 1846. See also "Texas, County Tax Rolls, 1837-1910," Cass county, 1854, line 37, Moses W. Isonhour, image 14, database with images, *FamilySearch*.

[32] 1860 U.S. census, Bosque County, Texas, population schedule, p. 27 (penned), dwelling 184, family 190, Moses Isenhower household; database with images, *Fold3* (http://www.fold3.com : accessed 11 Nov 2017); citing NARA microfilm publication M653, roll 1289.

[33] *Find A Grave*, database and images (https://www.findagrave.com : accessed 11 Nov 2017), memorial 41628818, Moses Isenhower (1823-1906), citing Saint James Cemetery, Milford, Barton County, Missouri; gravestone photograph by Sandy [--?--] (contributor 47007984).

Died Oct 27, 1906
Catherine Bird, his wife
Born Oct 24, 1824
Died Mar 10, 1905

These census and gravestone records show that the Texas State Troops muster roll for Moses Isenhower almost certainly belongs to the Moses Isenhower who was born 8 October 1823, died 27 October 1906, and married Catherine Bird. He was not the son of John D. and Sarah Isenhour.

It follows then, that John D. Isenhour's son, Moses W. Isenhour, was the soldier who enlisted with the 11th Arkansas Infantry regiment. Although his CMSR has already been located, this research session sought to provide greater understanding of his experience in the Civil War, answering the following questions:

- What battles did he engage in?
- How did he die?
- Where is "Fort Thompson" located?
- Why did Moses report his age as 35 when other sources agree that in 1861, his calculated age should have been 38?

Living descendants of Civil War soldiers often possess family stories about their ancestors' military service. Beth Echols, a second-great-granddaughter of Moses Isenhour was contacted for this purpose. She did have additional family stories and information to share about Moses Isenhour. Beth sent a paragraph written by an unknown descendant of Moses W. Isenhour who postulated that Moses lied about his age when he enlisted in 1861 "because the army was not taking volunteers at age 38, especially those with a family."[34]

Moses' CMSR shows a reported age of 35 (calculated birth year 1826).[35] His reported age on the 1850 census and marriage record agree on a calculated birth year of 1823.[36] Many

---

[34] Beth Echols, Cass County, Texas [E-ADDRESS FOR PRIVATE USE] to Nicole Dyer, message communicated via Ancestry.com e-mail, 24 March 2018, "Echols and Isenhour tree," Personal Correspondence Folder, Isenhour Research Files; privately held by Nicole Dyer (nicole@familylocket.com, [STREET ADDRESS FOR PRIVATE USE], Tucson, Arizona, 2018.

[35] Compiled service record, Moses Isonhower, Pvt., Co. I, 11 AR Inf. "Compiled Service Records of Confederate Soldiers...from...Arkansas," database with images, *Fold3*.

[36] 1850 U.S. Census, Montgomery County, Arkansas, population schedule, Sulphur Springs, p. 394 (stamped), dwelling 9, family 9, Moses W. Isenhour household; digital image, *FamilySearch* (http://familysearch.org : accessed 10 November 2017); citing NARA microfilm publication M432, roll 28. See also "Arkansas, County Marriages, 1837-1957," database with images, image 394, *FamilySearch* (https://familysearch.org : 4 November 2017), Moses W.

circumstances could explain the difference in Moses' reported ages. A likely explanation for this difference is a misreading of the original muster roll as it was copied to the index card during the creation of Compiled Military Service Records in 1903.

Moses would not need to lie about his age to enlist, as the army was accepting volunteers of all ages. A conscription law was passed in April 1862 by The Confederate States of America requiring white males ages 18-35 who were citizens of the Confederacy to enroll.[37] In October of that year, the age parameters were broadened to 18-45.[38] It is known that Moses was not drafted, but enlisted in the 11th Arkansas Infantry, a regiment composed of volunteer companies.[39] Even if he hadn't volunteered, he would have still been within the ages eligible for conscription at age 38. The original muster rolls could be consulted at the National Archives to see if the age written for Moses is legible.

Beth Echols also shared a clipping of a biography of Moses' son, William Martin Isenhour, that mentioned "Moses Isenhower" and his military service.[40] An image copy of the book containing the biography was located and contains the following information:

- "Moses gained pioneer honors in Texas and prior to the Civil War he here gave service as overseer for a number of the largest slave-owners in the state, including Reese Hughes, Mark Sumner, Wilber Peacock, and a widow named Driver."
- "When the Civil War was precipitated he entered service as a loyal soldier of the Confederacy, and at the battle of New Madre, near Memphis, Tennessee, he received a severe wound in the head, he having been taken to a military hospital in Memphis and his death having there occurred, in 1864, as a result of his wound."
- "William M. Isenhower was a child at the time of the family removal from Arkansas to Texas, and his early education was acquired in the schools of Cass and Johnson counties."

Isenhour and Manda Mckinney, 1 October 1846; citing Montgomery, Arkansas, United States, county offices, Arkansas; FHL microfilm 1,011,071.

[37] Martin, "Civil War Conscription," para. 2.

[38] Ibid., para. 5.

[39] *Wikipedia (https://en.wikipedia.org)* "11th Arkansas Infantry Regiment," reviewed 28 March 2018, 10:00am.

[40] Clarence Ray Wharton, "William Martin Isenhower, *Texas Under Many Flags: Texas biography* (Chicago: American Historical Society, 1930), vol 3, 167-168; image copy, *FamilySearch* (https://familysearch.org : accessed 24 March 2018), digital image 660 of 1350; citing FHL microfilm 1000594.

This biography contains valuable information about Moses W. Isenhour, especially about his occupation as an overseer and cause of death. How reliable is the information about his death? It was published in 1930, three years after Moses' son, William Martin Isenhower, died. The author/informant is unknown, but that person was almost certainly not an eyewitness to Moses' death. At best, the information is second or third-hand, passed on from a comrade of Moses to his family, then from William Martin Isenhower to one of his children.

What do original records, created close to the time of Moses' military service, reveal about his cause of death? The CMSR for Moses Isenhour, compiled from original muster rolls, states that Moses enlisted in Captain Cunningham's Company on 29 October 1861 in Little Rock, Arkansas. This company later became became Company I in the 11th Arkansas Infantry.[41] In October 1861, Moses was near the end of his duty as elected coroner of Montgomery County, Arkansas.[42] He travelled 50 miles to Little Rock, Arkansas, to enlist.[43] The distance from the county seat, Mt. Ida, to Little Rock, Arkansas, is about 100 miles. Where was Moses traveling from, if not the county seat? Company I of the 11th Arkansas regiment was formed from men living in Saline County, Arkansas, which bordered Montgomery County to the east.[44] It seems likely that Moses was living in Montgomery County near the border with Saline county when he enlisted and travelled 50 miles to Little Rock. Perhaps when his duties as Coroner were coming to a close, he found the nearest company to join.

The CMSR does not contain detailed information about the movements of a soldier's regiment. To learn which battles Moses' regiment was involved in, a regimental history was located about the 11th Arkansas Infantry Regiment.[45]

Most of the 11th Arkansas enlisted in July 1861 in Little Rock. They proceeded to Pine Bluff, then Oakland, then Memphis Tennessee. They lacked proper rifles so the colonel of the regiment, Jabez M. Smith, went to New Orleans repeatedly to procure weapons. In September 1861, the regiment moved to Fort Pillow, Tennessee. Moses, with Company I,

---

[41] Compiled service record, Moses Isonhower, Pvt., Co. I, 11 AR Inf. "Compiled Service Records of Confederate Soldiers...from...Arkansas," database with images, *Fold3*.

[42] Daniels, *Historical Report of the Arkansas Secretary of State 2008*, 482.

[43] Compiled service record, Moses Isonhower, Pvt., Co. I, 11 AR Inf. "Compiled Service Records of Confederate Soldiers...from...Arkansas," database with images, *Fold3*.

[44] *Wikipedia* "11th Arkansas Infantry Regiment," reviewed 24 November 2017, 2:30pm.

[45] Anthony C. Rushing, *Ranks of Honor: A Regimental History of the eleventh Arkansas Infantry Regiment & Poe's Cavalry Battalion C.S.A., 1861-1865* (Little Rock: Eagle Press, 1990).

joined the regiment in November, when they moved up the Mississippi River to Island Number Ten.[46]

The Confederate Army of the Mississippi chose Island Number 10 to defend the Mississippi River from Union forces. Nearby town, New Madrid, Missouri was a weak point. The Confederate Army fortified it with Fort Thompson and Fort Bankhead.[47]

New Madrid, Missouri and Island Number 10 were the Confederate Army's last stronghold in the State of Missouri.[48] The 11th Arkansas was ordered to New Madrid on 26 December 1861 where they performed picket duty in mud and bad weather until February, when they were ordered to garrison Fort Thompson on the 26th in preparation for a battle with Union forces which were closing in. In the ensuing battle of Island Number 10, Union forces commanded by General John Pope overtook the Confederate Army of the Mississippi, surrounding them with Ironclad ships on the river as well as land troops. Most of the 11th Arkansas Infantry were captured on 8 April 1861 and sent to Fort Douglas.[49]

According to his CMSR, Moses died on 16 February 1862 at Fort Thompson.[50] The CMSR lists the Company I muster roll for 29 October 1861 - 23 September 1862 as the source of this death information. If this is correct, his death occurred before the battle of Island Number 10, and before the 11th Arkansas participated in any skirmishes. Anthony C. Rushing states that many members of the regiment succumbed to illness during the winter months leading up to the battle of Island Number 10.[51] See Table 1 for a timeline of events for the 11th Arkansas Infantry regiment.

---

[46] Ibid., 4-10.

[47] City of New Madrid, "Civil War in New Madrid," *New Madrid, Missouri* (http://www.new-madrid.mo.us/index.aspx?NID=152 : accessed 21 November 2017), para. 2.

[48] City of New Madrid, "Driving Tour of Civil War Sites of New Madrid," front brochure page, image online, *New Madrid, Missouri* (http://www.new-madrid.mo.us/DocumentCenter/Home/View/422 : accessed 21 November 2017), col. 3, bullet point 3.

[49] Rushing, *Ranks of Honor*, 10.

[50] Compiled service record, Moses Isonhower, Pvt., Co. I, 11 AR Inf. "Compiled Service Records of Confederate Soldiers...from...Arkansas," database with images, *Fold3*.

[51] Rushing, *Ranks of Honor*, 14.

Table 1: Timeline of the 11th Arkansas Infantry July 1861 - April 1862

Main entries are from the regimental history of the 11th Arkansas Infantry.[52] Entries in bold are from the CMSR of Moses W. Isenhour.[53]

July 1861	After enlisting in Little Rock, AR, the regiment trekked to Pine Bluff, Arkansas, then headed downstream for Memphis, TN
19 September 1861	Moved to Union City, TN; Col. Smith went to New Orleans seeking better guns
26 September 1861	Embarked for Fort Pillow
October 1861	90% of men still unarmed, yet started drilling at Fort Pillow. Men uneasy, wanted guns
29 October 1861	**"Moses Isenhower" enlisted in Captain Cunningham's Company at Little Rock, Arkansas**
November 1861	Captain Cunningham's Company joined the regiment and became Company I; Col. Smith left again to get weapons
20 November 1861	Regiment moved to Island Number Ten, made camp near Reelfoot Lake and hunted wild game
27 November 1861	Bivouacked on Island Number Ten, built works and batteries with picks and shovels. Col. Smith returned with no rifles
December 1861	Col. Smith sent 1 Lieutenant Selvidge to New Orleans to stay until he got the weapons. He returned with them in a few weeks
26 December 1861	Regiment moved to New, Madrid, Missouri, west side of river
December - March 1862	Regiment did picket duty around New Madrid; bad weather and mud. Much disease and men sent to hospitals; many men died and some never returned to the ranks until later that fall.
16 February 1862	**"Moses Isenhower" died at Fort Thompson**
26 February 1862	Regiment ordered to garrison Fort Thompson along with the 12th Arkansas infantry
28 February - 8 April 1862	Battle of Island Number 10 / New Madrid. Federals captured the entire regiment. All were taken prisoner and sent to Camp Douglas

---

[52] Rushing, *Ranks of Honor*, 14.

[53] Compiled service record, Moses Isonhower, Pvt., Co. I, 11 AR Inf. "Compiled Service Records of Confederate Soldiers...from...Arkansas," database with images, *Fold3*.

The reliability of the muster roll containing Moses' death information is in question. Muster rolls are usually for the period of two or three months, but this roll is for an entire year. An explanation is given in the record of events for the muster roll.[54] The creator of the muster roll (unnamed), wrote:

> Company I was captured by the federals at Island Ten, Tenn. on the 8th day of April 1862 and such patron as was captured remained in prison at Johnson's Island and Camp Douglass until the 16 and 17th days of Sept 1862 at which time they was released. Previous to the capture all company books and papers was sent off for safekeeping which I have not received as yet and this muster is made on to the best of my ability under the circumstances.

When the unnamed officer of Company I reconstructed the muster roll for the entire year previous, he may not have remembered the date of Moses' death correctly.

The evidence for Moses' death on the Company I muster roll conflicts with the biography of William Martin Isenhower, which states that Moses received a head wound in the battle of New Madre [sic] and died in a Memphis, Tennessee hospital in 1864.[55] The third-hand information from the biography is less reliable than the muster roll. Although the muster roll was recreated later to the best of the unnamed officer's abilities, he still likely had firsthand knowledge of Moses' death. It is possible that Moses died in a hospital in Memphis, but it was probably in 1862, not 1864.

No burial site was located for Moses Isenhower in Missouri, but the City of New Madrid tourist pamphlet points out several cemeteries containing Civil War soldiers who are in unmarked graves, including the East Side Cemetery and the Sand Hill Cemetery. [56]

---

54 Co. I, 11 Reg't Arkansas Infty, Captions and Record of Events, Company Muster Roll, 29 October 1861 - 23 September 1862, "Compiled Service Records of Confederate Soldiers Who Served in Organizations from the State of Arkansas," index card, *Fold3* (https://www.fold3.com/ : accessed 21 November 2017); citing Carded Records Showing Military Service of Soldiers Who Fought in Confederate Organizations , compiled 1903 - 1927, documenting the period 1861 - 1865, Record Group 109, National Archives.

55 Wharton, "William Martin Isenhower, *Texas Under Many Flags: Texas biography*, vol 3, 167-168.

56 City of New Madrid, "Driving Tour of Civil War Sites of New Madrid," front brochure page, image online, *New Madrid, Missouri*, No. 13. East Side Cemetery. See also City of New Madrid, "Driving Tour of Civil War Sites of New Madrid," back brochure image online, *New Madrid, Missouri* (http://www.new-madrid.mo.us/DocumentCenter/Home/View/423 : accessed 21 November 2017), No. 7, Sand Hill Cemetery.

Moses left a 32-year-old widow and five children when he died in 1862. Amanda did not remarry. In 1870, she lived in Hopkins County, Texas, with her three youngest sons, George, James, and John. George was engaged in farming and Amanda was keeping house. The value of real estate she owned was $600 and personal estate, $358.[57] In 1880, Amanda was still in Hopkins County with her two youngest sons, James and John.[58] Most Southern states offered pensions to indigent soldiers and their widows who resided in their state after the Civil War. Texas did not offer pensions to disabled Confederate veterans or their widows until 1899.[59] Amanda died in 1892, so no pension application exists for her.[60]

Conclusion

The objective of this research project was to discover the actions of Moses W. Isenhour prior to and during the Civil War. As road overseer, county coroner, and plantation overseer, Moses was deeply connected to the local government and the slave-labor economy of the South. Although he did not own slaves, his civil service, occupation, and willingness to join the Confederate cause indicate that he was loyal to Southern ideals. He died soon after joining the Confederate States Army while his regiment was stationed at Fort Thompson, Missouri, before they were captured at the Battle of Island Number Ten. More research is needed to understand the story passed down in his family about his death at a hospital in Memphis, Tennessee, which conflicts with evidence that he died at Fort Thompson, Missouri.

---

[57] 1870 U.S. Census, Hopkins County, Texas, population schedule, Precinct 2, p. 54 (penned), dwelling 381, family 379, Amanda Isenhower household; digital image, *FamilySearch* (https://www.familysearch : accessed 26 October 2017); citing NARA microfilm publication M593, roll 1592.

[58] 1880 U.S. Census, Hopkins County, Texas, population schedule, Precinct 2, p. 18 (penned), dwelling 161, family 165, Amanda Isenhower household; digital image, *FamilySearch* (https://www.familysearch.org : accessed 4 April 2018); citing NARA microfilm publication T9, roll 1311.

[59] Edmund Thornton Miller, "A Financial History of Texas" *Bulletin of the University of Texas* 37 (July 1916): 250; image copy, *Google Books* (https://books.google.com : accessed 4 April 2018).

[60] *Find A Grave,* (https://www.findagrave.com : accessed 4 April 2018), memorial 135262666, Amanda Martha McKinney Isenhour (1830–1892), citing Oakwood Cemetery, Fort Worth, Tarrant County, Texas, USA; memorial maintained by Charlotte Hardamon Coble (contributor 46886606). See also "Alabama, Texas and Virginia, Confederate Pensions, 1884-1958" [database on-line], negative search for Amanda Martha Isenhower; *Ancestry* (https://search.ancestry.com : accessed 20 November 2017); citing Texas, Confederate Pension Applications, 1899-1975. Vol. 1–646 & 1–283, Austin, Texas: Texas State Library and Archives Commission.

Summary of Results

- Found court records showing Moses' appointment as road overseer in Montgomery County, Arkansas in 1849.
- Found the *Historical Report of the Arkansas Secretary of State* which showed M. Isenhour was elected as Montgomery County Coroner and served from 1860-1862.
- Located *A Digest of the Statutes of Arkansas, 1846,* which detailed the duties of road overseers and Coroners.
- Analyzed the compiled military service record (CMSR) of Moses W. Isenhour of the 11th Arkansas Infantry Regiment.
- Found another Civil War era service record for "Moses Isenhower" In Bosque and Coryell Counties, Texas. Identified this second Moses as the husband of Catherine Bird, born 8 October 1823 and died 27 October 1906, not the subject of this report.
- Contacted a descendant of Moses W. Isenhour and received additional information about Moses, including a paragraph about him written by one of his descendants.
- Located the biography of Moses W. Isenhour's son, William Martin Isenhower, which contained details about Moses' career as an overseer and cause of death.
- Located a regimental history for Moses W. Isenhour's regiment and extracted information pertaining to Moses' service.
- Located a battle map of Island No. Ten in the Mississippi River during the Civil War.
- Created a timeline of the 11th Arkansas Infantry including events from Moses W. Isenhour's CMSR.
- Hypothesized that Moses died due to exposure and illness prior to the battle of New Madrid/Battle of Island No. Ten.
- Found cemeteries in the City of New Madrid containing Civil War soldiers in unmarked graves; possible locations of Moses W. Isenhour's burial.
- Evaluated the conflicting evidence about Moses W. Isenhour's death.

Future Research Suggestions

- Search for the plantation owners that Moses worked for in Texas in the 1860 census: Reese Hughes, Mark Sumner, Wilber Peacock, and a widow named Driver.
- Search for descriptions of Civil War era hospitals in Memphis, Tennessee which may have housed Confederate soldiers from Fort Thompson.
- Search for Moses W. Isenhour in Memphis, Tennessee Civil War era hospital rolls.
- Search for Moses W. Isenhour in Memphis, Tennessee Civil War era cemeteries.
- Search for Civil War era cemeteries in Memphis, Tennessee that contain burials of unmarked Confederate soldiers.

Work Sample 3: Proof Argument

Determining the Father of Mary Ann (French) Bryan Atwood

Diana Elder, AG

Introduction

What is the difference between a research report and a proof argument? A research report is the final step of a research project. It's where you detail the searches you performed, where you looked, and what you found. If you've proved your identity, relationship, or ancestor's action, it can stand alone as a proof summary. You've found enough evidence for proof and using source citations have written your findings clearly. A proof summary doesn't involve complicated problems that involve indirect evidence. It simply states all of the facts clearly and succinctly. An example would be a report detailing all of the children of a couple where vital records clearly show relationships and dates.

What about those trickier genealogical problems that need a great deal of indirect evidence to prove identity, a relationship, or an action? A written proof argument gives you the opportunity to put together all of the evidence you've discovered in your research. It may be the culmination of years of work and several research reports. A proof argument uses source citations to lend credibility to the research findings. It is organized in a manner that helps the reader understand the logic.

For example, my husband had researched his ancestor, Mary (French) Atwood Bryan, but never written anything proving that her father was James French. He asked if I would do a research project for him and write up his research. After reviewing his findings I created a research plan to discover additional information. I put it all together in a report with source citations and tables and charts detailing the records. Writing out each facet of the research, I realized that everything had come together to prove Mary's father was James French.

I wrote a formal proof argument, taking essential pieces from the report that proved James French as the father of Mary. I eliminated some of the tables from the report and simply stated the necessary items. My proof argument is a more compact version of the research report.

Determining the Father of Mary Ann (French) Bryan Atwood: Proof Argument

A Case of Indirect Evidence
Diana Elder, AG

Determining the maiden name and parents of a woman born in the late 1700s is one of the most difficult genealogical undertakings. Because women were not mentioned in many of the records of the era, few sources exist to prove their parentage. Combine that with record loss and the task becomes even more difficult. Descendants of Ignatius Bryan, born about 1775 in Maryland and died 1803 in Hardin County, Kentucky have long wondered about the origins of his wife Mary.

Who was Mary's father? No marriage record has yet been located for the couple and without a maiden name, it might seem impossible to prove a relationship between a woman and her parents.

Fortunately, enough records have survived that when carefully analyzed; prove that Mary Ann, wife of Ignatius Bryan, is the daughter of James French of Hardin County, Kentucky. The surname, Bryan, lends itself to numerous spelling variations which will be used when quoting the original record.[1]

---

[1] Name variations in the records include Brian, Brien, Brayant, Briant, Brient, and Bryant.

Land Records of Hardin County

A deed dated 15 August 1826 names "Mary Bryan Widow of Ignatius Bryant deceased." [2] The record further reveals three children and their spouses, who along with Mary Bryan and second husband, George Atwood, are the heirs of Ignatius Bryan who "departed this life intestate." Without a will to formally name the wife and children of Ignatius Bryan, the deed directly states kinship.

> *Indenture made 15 August 1826*
> *Hardin County, Kentucky [Bullet points inserted for clarity; children of Ignatius and Mary bolded]*
>
> - *George Atwood & Mary his wife late Mary Bryan Widow of Ignatius Bryant deceased*
> - *William Norris & Elizabeth his wife late **Elizabeth Bryant***
> - *John Atwood Medly and Elen his wife late **Elen Bryant***
> - ***Benjamin Bryant** and Treacy his wife*

The deed describes the sale of "the tract of land situated on the waters of the Rolling Fork near the mouth of Clear Creek containing 85 acres. Being the same land conveyed by James Murdough to Ignatius Bryan, 6 November 1800, recorded in Deed Book B, page 191." With the death of Ignatius Bryan, the land had "ascended to his heirs the parties of the first part to this indenture."

The original 1800 deed for the 85 acres on the Rolling Fork provides evidence of Ignatius Bryan's residence prior to his move to Hardin County, Kentucky; being noted "of Nelson County." [3] Ignatius and Mary Bryan moved onto the Hardin County land by 1802 where he was taxed as a male above 21 years of age and owning 3 horses. [4] The land description in the tax record is the same as in the 1800 deed and the 1826 deed: 85 acres on the Rolling Fork

---

[2] Hardin County, Kentucky, Deeds Book K, 1825-1828, p. 148, Heirs of Ignatius Bryan to James Crawford, 15 August 1826, FHL microfilm 388,595, item 2.

[3] Hardin County, Kentucky, Deed Book B, 1795-1804, p. 191, William Murdough to Ignatius Brien, 26 November 1800, FHL microfilm 388,591, item 2.

[4] Hardin County, Kentucky, Tax Books 1799-1817, Ignatius Briant, 1802 entry, image 200 of 1380, *FamilySearch* (https://familysearch.org : accessed 25 March 2017); FHL microfilm 7,834,447.

water course. After Ignatius' death in 1803, "Mary Brian" is listed on the 1804 tax records for this same land.[5]

Marriage Record for Ignatius and Mary Bryan

A marriage for Ignatius and Mary Bryan could reveal Mary's maiden name and possibly list her father. The 1800 deed provides a residence of Nelson County, Kentucky for her husband, Ignatius. Cemetery records for the three children of Mary and Ignatius reveal birth dates from 1797-1800, suggesting a marriage date of 1796 or earlier in Nelson County.[6] No marriage record has been located for Mary and Ignatius in that location, the marriage possibly taking place before their migration to the newly formed state of Kentucky.[7]

Probate of the Estate of Ignatius Bryan

The 1826 deed states that Ignatius Bryan died intestate, meaning that he left no will. In this circumstance, if there was property involved, the probate proceedings were set in motion. At a county court for Hardin County, Kentucky on Monday, the 19th of September 1803, "Mary Brian & Barton Rheuby" applied for and were granted the right of administration of the estate of "Ignatius Brian, deceased."[8] Together with James French and Isaac Irwin, they gave bond of £200 with securities for the faithful performance of administration.

---

[5] Hardin County, Kentucky, Tax Books 1799-1817, Mary Brian, 1804 entry, image 290 of 1380, *FamilySearch* (https://familysearch.org : accessed 25 March 2017); FHL microfilm 7,834,447.

[6] *Find A Grave*, database with images (http://www.findagrave.com: accessed 24 March 2018), memorial 5700279, Elizabeth Norris, (1797-1863), no gravestone photograph. Also *Find A Grave*, memorial 59577205, Elenor Bryan Medley, (1799-1891), gravestone photograph added by Jason Snyder, member 47187221. Also *Find A Grave*, memorial 173002587, Benjamin Bryan, (1800-1842), no gravestone photograph.

[7] "Kentucky, County Marriages, 1783-1965," database with images, *Ancestry* (http://ancestry.com : accessed 4 April 2017). Also Annie Walker Burns, *Nelson County, Kentucky, Marriages, 1784-1851,* (1934); Also Charles M. Franklin, *Nelson County, Kentucky Marriages,* (Indianapolis, Indiana : Ye Olde Genealogie Shoppe, 1985). Also Mary Harrel Stancliff, *Marriage Bonds of Nelson County, Kentucky, 1785-1832,* (Houston, Texas: M.H. Stancliff, 1963). Also Lillian Ockerman, *Nelson County Kentucky Marriages, Bonds, Consents and Minister's Returns* (Bardstown, Kentucky: Nelson County Genealogical Society, 198?-2006).

[8] Hardin County, Kentucky, Order Book A, Ignatious Brian estate administration, 19 September 1803, p. 416; "Kentucky Probate Records, 1727-1990," images 234-5 of 296, *FamilySearch* (https://familysearch.org : accessed 5 April 2014); FHL microfilm 390,776.

Generally, those applying for administration of an intestate estate were the surviving spouse and next of kin, so what was Mary Bryan's relationship to Barton Rheuby, (generally named in the records as Roby), James French, and Isaac Irwin?

Additional probate records showed that Barton Roby acted as administrator for all further actions for the estate of Ignatius Bryan and also for the estate of James French.[9] He received payment for his service and appears throughout the local court records administering various estates. He seems to have been the family attorney.

Records show that Isaac Irwin was born in 1774 and would have been about age 30 when he gave security for the estate bond, too young to be Mary's father.[10] Isaac was also named in another court order with Ignatius in 1802 as a potential appraiser of an estate.[11] There is no indication that he was related to Mary Bryan. Of the three men listed with Mary in the administration of Ignatius Bryan's estate, only James French remains a possible candidate for Mary's father.

Probate administration for the estate of Ignatius Bryan lasted from 1803 until 1821. The estate was duly appraised and inventoried on 22 November 1803.[12] The allotment of widow's dower to Mary Bryan of 32 ½ acres was recorded on 28 September 1807.[13] The final settlement of the estate occurred 8 January 1821 with Barton Roby, administrator to the

---

[9] Hardin County, Kentucky, Will book B, Will of James French, 1815, p. 241; "Kentucky Probate Records, 1727-1990," images 132-33 of 183, *FamilySearch* (https:/familysearch.org : accessed 10 April 2017); FHL microfilm 390,773.

[10] "Isaac Irwin 1774-1858," FamilySearch ID LP97-3BB, *FamilySearch* (https://familysearch.org/tree/person/L9P7-3BB/details : accessed 12 April 2017). Multiple original sources such as Hardin County, Kentucky bonds, census records, tax lists, and court records establish his residence in the county as well as an estimated birth year of 1774.

[11] "Kentucky Probate Records, 1727-1990," database with images, image 204 of 296; *FamilySearch* (https://familysearch.org : accessed 3 April 2017), Hardin County, Kentucky, Order books, Vol. A 1793-1804, p. 355.

[12] Hardin County, Kentucky, Will Book A, p. 175, Estate Inventory, Ignatius Bryan, 21 September 1803; "Kentucky Probate Records, 1727-1990," images 106-7 of 625, *FamilySearch* (https://familysearch.org : accessed 5 April 2017); FHL microfilm 390,777, item 1.

[13] Hardin County, Kentucky, 1805-09, Will Book A, p. 288, Allotment of dower of Mary Bryan, 20 August 1804; "Kentucky Probate Records, 1727-1990," image 168 of 625, *FamilySearch* (https://familysearch.org : accessed 5 April 2017); FHL microfilm 390,776.

estate of "Ignateous Brayant" listing an accounting of fees and payments.[14] James French does not appear in the probate administration after his initial posting security for the bond in 1803.

County Histories and Church Records

Who was the James French mentioned in the probate of Ignatius Bryan? County histories became popular in the late 1800's and can be valuable sources of information about early settlers in an area. In the 1887 publication of *The Centenary of Catholicity in Kentucky,* author Benedict Joseph Webb discussed early Catholic settlers in the area of Hardin County, Kentucky.[15] Beginning his study in 1872, Webb's preface to the book describes his thorough efforts in "securing the names, both family and baptismal, of the original Catholic colonists in the eight leading Catholic settlements of Kentucky." [16]

In the section discussing the missions of Hardin and Meade Counties, Webb names James French: "The first church station at this point was the house of one James French where mass was said by Father Badin as early as the years 1804-5."[17] Webb goes on to name several of the "old Catholic settlers of the locality." In addition to James French, Raphael French and "William, known as "Bee," Bryan are also listed.[18]

More insight into the state of the Catholic settlers in Kentucky comes from a life sketch written about Reverend Stephen Theodore Badin, a French cleric sent to the backwoods of Kentucky in 1793. "When M. Badin first came to Kentucky, he estimated the number of Catholic families in the State at three hundred. These were much scattered; and the number was constantly on the increase."[19]

---

14 Hardin County, Kentucky, Will Book C, p. 414-416, Ignateous Brayant estate final settlement, 8 January 1821; "Kentucky Probate Records, 1727-1990," images 607-608 of 625, *FamilySearch* (https://familysearch.org : accessed 5 April 2017); FHL microfilm 390,773, item 3.

15 Benedict Joseph Webb, *The Centenary of Catholicity in Kentucky,* (---------- : *Charles Rodgers, 1884), reproduction* (Evansville, Indiana : Unigraphics, 1977); Google Books.

16 Webb, *The Centenary of Catholicity in Kentucky,* 4.

17 Webb, *The Centenary of Catholicity in Kentucky,* 412.

18 Ibid.

19 M.J. Spalding, and Stephen T. Badin, *Sketches of the Early Catholic Missions of Kentucky*, (Bardstown, Kentucky: Feast of Corpus Christi, 1844), 55.

It is highly probable that Ignatius and Mary Bryan were among the Catholic settlers in the Rolling Fork congregation in Hardin County, Kentucky given that James and Raphael French as well as William "Bee" Bryan were all mentioned as settling in that area.

Mary Ann (French) Bryan Atwood and George Atwood

Following the death of her husband, Ignatius Bryan in 1803, Mary Bryan continued to reside as a widow for several years in Hardin County, Kentucky, and appears on the tax lists intermittently from 1804 to 1812, generally taxed for the same 85 acres on the Rolling Fork purchased by Ignatius in 1800.[20] A marriage for "Mary Bryan" and "George Atwood" is recorded in Hardin County on 26 October 1813, performed by C. Nemrock, no witnesses listed.[21] The George Atwood household is next enumerated in 1820 in Hardin County, Kentucky, with Mary almost certainly noted as the female age 45 and over.[22]

Mary and George Atwood, as well as the grown children of Mary and Ignatius Bryan, named on the 1826 deed had moved to Meade County, Kentucky, by 1830.[23] All are listed on the same census page. The names are not alphabetically arranged, so the proximity of the listings suggests the family moved together and were living near one another in the new location. The household of George Atwood is made up of a male and female both age 60-69, appropriate ages for George and Mary. The other heads of household are Mary's son Benjamin Bryan, and sons-in-law William Norris and John B. Medley.

---

[20] Hardin County, Kentucky, Tax Books 1799-1817, Mary Bryan, entries for 1804, 1809, 1810, 1811, 1812, *FamilySearch* (https://familysearch.org : accessed 24 March 2018); FHL microfilm 7,834,447.

[21] Hardin County, Kentucky Marriage Register Book A, Atwood-Bryan, 26 October 1813, p. 10; "Kentucky, County Marriages, 1797-1954," image 12 of 527, *FamilySearch* (https://familysearch.org : accessed 10 April 2017); FHL microfilm 390,788.

[22] 1820 U.S. Census, Hardin County, Kentucky, population schedule, Little York, p. 36 (penned), line 15, George Atwood; digital image, *Ancestry* (http://www.ancestry.com : accessed 18 February 2018); citing NARA microfilm publication M33, roll 23.

[23] 1830 U.S. Census, Meade County, Kentucky, population schedule, Brandenburg, p.274 (penned), line 22, George Atwood; digital image, *Ancestry* (http://www.ancestry.com : accessed 18 February 2018); citing NARA microfilm publication M19, roll 39. For other family members on the same page see Benjamin Brian line 20, William Norris line 21, and John B Medley line 29.

The 1840 census index does not reveal a George Atwood.[24] Where is Mary living by 1840? If George had died, Mary could be living alone or with one of her children. By 1840, Benjamin Bryan had moved back to Hardin County.[25] His household includes a female age 70-80 that could be Mary. The William Norris household is listed on the 1840 census of Nelson County, Kentucky, no female over 50 listed.[26] Only the John B. Medley household remained in Meade County, Kentucky in 1840. The census shows no female over age 50. [27]

Although Mary could be the female age 70-80 living in the household of her son, Benjamin Bryan, this female could also be the mother of Benjamin's wife or another relative. A church record in Perry County, Missouri, about 200 miles west of Meade County, Kentucky, reveals a "Mary Ann French," and provides an important connection to James French of Hardin County, Kentucky.

1835 Barrens Parish Census, Perry County, Missouri

As noted previously, the Bryans and Frenchs were among the early Catholic settlers of Kentucky. Catholic Church records often give important genealogical information listing members. After the 1826 deed naming Mary as the wife of George Atwood and "widow of Ignatius Bryant deceased," Mary next appears in a census of the Barrens Parish of the Church of the Assumption of the Blessed Virgin located in Perry County, Missouri; listed in the household of John Layton, her brother-in-law.[28]

> John Layton, Sr., son of John, 56 years
> **Monica French, wife, daughter of James, 50 years**
> Layton, Louis, son, 24 years

---

[24] 1840 U.S. Census, population schedule, *Ancestry* (http://www.ancestry.com : accessed 21 March 2018), negative search for George Atwood.

[25] 1840 U.S. Census, Hardin County, Kentucky, population schedule, p. 48 (penned), line 19, Benj Bryan household; digital image, *Ancestry* (http://www.ancestry.com : accessed 18 February 2018); citing NARA microfilm publication M704, roll 113.

[26] 1840 U.S. Census, Nelson County, Kentucky, population schedule, p. 20 (penned), line 19, William Norris household; digital image, *Ancestry* (http://www.ancestry.com : accessed 18 February 2018); citing NARA microfilm publication M704, roll 113.

[27] 1840 U.S. Census, Meade County, Kentucky, population schedule, p. 20 (penned), line 26, John B Medley household; digital image, *Ancestry* (http://www.ancestry.com : accessed 18 February 2018); citing NARA microfilm publication M704, roll 113.

[28] 1835 Barrens Parish Census, Church of the Assumption of the Blessed Mary, John Layton, Sr household, Perry County, Historical Society, image of typewritten record; originally shared 15 November 2009 on *Ancestry.com* by mikeELBB.

Augustine, son, 20 years
Mary, daughter, 18 years
Amatus Alexander, 13 years
Mary Ann French, sister of Monica, 52 years

If Mary Ann French is the sister of Monica, her father would also be James French. Why are the women listed by their maiden names? It appears from the rest of the listings on the page that this was careful record keeping on the part of the parish. All women on the page are listed by their maiden name and their father is identified. Mary Ann French, age 52 years in 1835 would have been born about 1782-3. A marriage to Ignatius Bryan about 1796-7 would be plausible, although Mary would have been young. Census listings of age in the records can be off by a few years. Without knowing the source of the census information, the age can be used at best as an estimate.

John Layton and household are listed on the 1830 census in Perry County, Missouri.[29] John and Monica are the male and female age 50-59 noted by the tick marks. The 1840 census for the household shows a male and female age 60-69 with another female age 50-59. The additional woman is almost certainly John's sister-in-law, Mary Ann (French) Bryan Atwood.[30]

1799 Layton - French Marriage

A marriage record for Monica French and James Layton confirms the connection of James French of Hardin County to the sisters, Monica and Mary Ann French. The order book of Washington County, Kentucky, reveals the marriage listing of 14 September 1799, showing the couple and their parents.[31]

John Layton [groom]   John Layton, Jane Layton [parents]
Monarca French [bride]   James French, Susanna [parents]

---

[29] 1830 U.S. Census, Perry County, Missouri, population schedule, p.395 (penned), line 1, John Layton; digital image, *Ancestry* (http://www.ancestry.com : accessed 18 February 2018); citing NARA microfilm publication M19, roll 72.

[30] 1840 U.S. Census, Perry County, Missouri, population schedule, p. 28 (penned), line 6, John Layton household; digital image, *Ancestry* (http://www.ancestry.com : accessed 18 February 2018); citing NARA microfilm publication M704, roll 228.

[31] Washington County, Kentucky Marriage Register Index, Minister Returns, Layton-French, 14 September 1799, p. 30; "Kentucky, County Marriages, 1797-1954," image 223 of 1218, *FamilySearch* (https://familysearch.org : accessed 10 April 2017); FHL microfilm 241,382, item 2.

Washington County neighbors Hardin County, Kentucky so it is highly probable that this James French is the same James French as appears with Mary Bryan on the 1803 administration of Ignatius Bryan's estate in Hardin County. The name "Monarca" might be the original spelling of the name with "Monica" the shortened form. "Monarca" in the marriage record could also be an error in transcription by the clerk in compiling the order book.

Another key record connecting James French of Hardin County to Mary Ann (French) Bryan Atwood is his will of 1815.

1815 Will of James French

The will of James French of Hardin County, Kentucky provides evidence that he had a daughter, Mary, a son Ignatius, and a wife, Susanna.[32] His will leaves to his "beloved daughter Mary French, one feather bed and furniture and one foot wheel." Susanna is named as his dearly beloved wife and along with his son, Ignatius [French], given executorship of the estate.

The 1815 will was produced in court and proven on the oath of the witnesses, Barton Robey and Lewis Bright, on 19 July 1815 at the courthouse of Elizabethtown in Hardin County, Kentucky. Barton Robey is probably the same individual who was the administrator of the will of Ignatius Bryan. The use of Mary's maiden name "French" in the will is similar to the use of maiden names for Mary Ann and Monica French in the 1835 Barren Parish census. Perhaps with her second marriage to George Atwood in 1813, James wanted it clear that she was born Mary French.

Why the omission of Monica (French) Layton, daughter of James and Susanna in her father's will? In many cases, not all of the children are named in the will if they had received their inheritance previously. The will alludes to other children with the phrase, "after the death of my wife . . . all the Estate then belonging to her to be equally divided among all my children." Further administration of the will could name all of the heirs, but none has been located for James French, died 1815.[33]

The Mary French mentioned in the will of James French is almost certainly the same Mary who was the wife of Ignatius Bryan and George Atwood. Because the marriage record of

---

[32] Hardin County, Kentucky, Will book B, Will of James French, 1815, p. 241; "Kentucky Probate Records, 1727-1990," images 132-33 of 183, *FamilySearch* (https:/familysearch.org : accessed 10 April 2017); FHL microfilm 390,773.

[33] *FamilySearch*, "Kentucky Probate Records, 1727-1990," Hardin County order books, 1812-1819, vol. C. Negative search for additional will administration for James French.

"Monarca French" lists parents as James and Susanna and the parish census of 1835 lists Mary Ann as Monica's sister, with father James, it can be proven that James French was the father of Mary Ann. The table summarizes the evidence.

Evidence Connecting Mary Ann with sister, Monica, and parents, James and Susanna

RECORD	DATE	PLACE	DETAILS
Marriage of Monarca French and John Layton[a]	1799	Washington County, Kentucky	Names parents James French and Susanna
Probate of Ignatius Bryan[b]	1803	Hardin County, Kentucky	James French provided security for bond with Mary Bryan, widow of Ignatius Bryan
Will of James French[c]	1815	Hardin County, Kentucky	Names daughter, Mary French, and wife, Susanna
Barrens Parish Census[d]	1835	Perry County, Missouri	Names James French, father of Monica French and Mary Ann French, sister of Monica French (women listed by maiden name in household of John Layton)

a. Washington Co., Kentucky Marriage Register Index, Layton-French, 14 September 1799, p. 30.
b. Hardin County, Kentucky, Order Book A, Ignatious Brian estate administration, 19 September 1803, p. 416.
c. Hardin County, Kentucky, Will book B, Will of James French, 1815, p. 241.
d. 1835 Barrens Parish Census, Church of the Assumption of the Blessed Mary, John Layton, Sr. household.

Conclusion

No record directly names the father of Mary, wife of Ignatius Bryan. Numerous original records provide information on the couple. Although records listing females are not frequent in the early 1800s, Mary appears in several of those records. Land, tax, probate, and a second marriage record establish her as a resident of Hardin County, Kentucky.

- **Land and tax records** for both Ignatius and Mary Bryan show the purchase, taxation, and sale of 85 acres on the Rolling Fork water course of Hardin County, Kentucky

- **Probate records** for the estate of Ignatius Bryan detail key actions in the administration of the estate. Importantly, the initial motion lists James French with Mary as putting up bond for the administration of the estate.

- **Marriage records** for Nelson County do not show a marriage for Ignatius Bryan and Mary, but the 1813 marriage of Mary Bryan and George Atwood in Hardin County provides evidence of a second marriage.

Several important sources provided indirect evidence for Mary, daughter of James French of Hardin County, Kentucky.

- The **1815 will of James French** of Hardin County names his wife Susanna and daughter, Mary French.

- The **1799 marriage record** of Mary's sister, Monica French names parents James and Susanna French.

- The **1835 Barren Parish census** of Perry County, Missouri shows Mary Ann French, the sister of Monica French in the household of John Layton, Monica's husband. Monica's father is listed as James French, and thus indirectly proves James French as the father of Mary.

Correlation and analysis of the records prove that Mary, wife of Ignatius Bryan of Hardin County, Kentucky, was the daughter of James French, also of Hardin County.

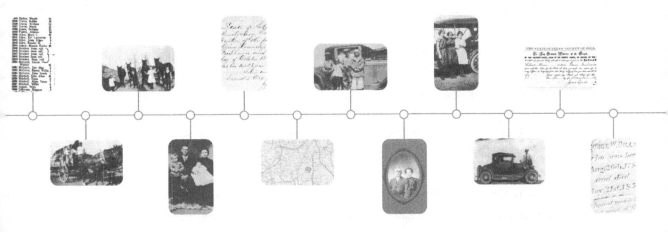

APPENDIX C
Source List

Board for Certification of Genealogists. *Genealogy Standards.* Nashville and New York: Turner Publishing, 2014.

Harris, Amy. "Documentation and Source Citation." Kory L. Meyerink, Tristan L. Tolman, Linda K. Gulbrandsen editors. *Becoming an Excellent Genealogist: Essays on Professional Research Skills.* [Salt Lake City, Utah]: ICAPGen, 2012. Chap. 18, pp. 173-178.

Jones, Thomas W. *Mastering Genealogical Proof.* Arlington, Virginia: National Genealogical Society, 2013.

Jones, Thomas W. *Mastering Genealogical Documentation.* Arlington, Virginia: National Genealogical Society, 2017.

Mills, Elizabeth Shown. *Evidence! Citation & Analysis for the Family Historian*. Baltimore: Genealogical Publishing Co., 2011.

Mills, Elizabeth Shown. *Evidence Explained: Citing History Sources from Artifacts to Cyberspace.* Third Edition. Baltimore: Genealogical Publishing Company, 2015.

Mills, Elizabeth Shown. "QuickLesson 1: Analysis & Citation." *Evidence Explained: Historical Analysis, Citation & Source Usage.* https://www.evidenceexplained.com/content/quicklesson-1-analysis-citation

Mills, Elizabeth Shown. "QuickLesson 19: Layered Citations Work Like Layered Clothing." *Evidence Explained: Historical Analysis, Citation & Source Usage.* https://www.evidenceexplained.com/content/quicklesson-19-layered-citations-work-layered-clothing

Mills, Elizabeth Shown. "Sample QuickCheck Models." *Evidence Explained: Historical Analysis, Citation & Source Usage.* https://www.evidenceexplained.com/content/sample-quickcheck-models

Mills, Elizabeth Shown. "Skillbuilding: Citing Your Sources." *Board for Certification of Genealogists.* http://www.bcgcertification.org/skillbuilding-citing-your-sources/.

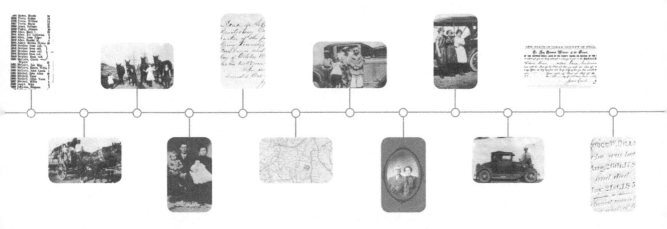

APPENDIX D

Supplemental Material

The following blog posts on my website, FamilyLocket.com, can give you ideas on organization, productivity, and education.

Organization

The Suitcase: Getting Started One Paper at a Time
http://familylocket.com/the-suitcase-getting-started-one-paper-at-a-time/

Creating a New Source on FamilySearch Family Tree
http://familylocket.com/creating-a-new-source-on-family-tree/

Productivity

Productivity Counts: Making the Best Use of Your Family History Time
http://familylocket.com/productivity-counts-making-the-best-use-of-your-family-history-time/

Daily Research Challenge 2016
http://familylocket.com/daily-research-challenge-2016/

Education

The Wonderful World of Webinars
http://familylocket.com/the-wonderful-world-of-webinars/

The FamilySearch Catalog: A Researcher's Best Friend
http://familylocket.com/the-familysearch-catalog-a-researchers-best-friend/

Index

Index

Made in the USA
Columbia, SC
06 February 2019